D0357166

Myth and Truth
about
Church,
Priesthood and Ordination

V. NORSKOV OLSEN

Loma Linda University Press
Riverside, California

This book was
Edited by Raymond F. Cottrell
Cover design by Joey Huerta

Printed in U.S.A.

Unless otherwise indicated, all Scripture quotations are from the *New
American Standard Bible,*© 1960, 1962, 1963, 1968, 1971, 1972, 1973,
1975, 1977 by the Lockman Foundation. Used by permission.

Bible texts credited to KJV are from *King James Version,* to LB are
from *Living Bible,* to RSV are from *Revised Standard Versions,* to NEB
are from *New English Bible,* to PME are from *Phillips Modern English,*
to JB are from *The Jerusalem Bible,* to NIV are from *New International Version.*

Cataloging in Publication Data
Olsen, V. Norskov (Viggo Norskov).
    Myth and truth about church, priesthood and ordination.
1. Church. 2. Ordination.
I. Title
BV600.2   262

Library of Congress Catalog Card Number: 90-062720
ISBN 0-944450-09-1

Other books by V. Norskov Olsen
    The New Testament Logia on Divorce.
        A Study of Their Interpretation from Erasmus to Milton.
    John Foxe and the Elizabethan Church
    Papal Supremacy and American Democrary
    Man, The Image of God: The Divine Design—The Human Distortion.

ACKNOWLEDGMENTS

I owe heartfelt thanks to Dr. B. B. Beach, Secretary of the Conference of Secretaries of Christian World Communions, and Dr. Arthur F. Glasser, Dean Emeritus, School of World Mission, Fuller Theological Seminary, for their willingness to write the Forwords. Both being known as churchmen who have their hand on the ecclesiastical pulse worldwide, their insights hold special value.

The unfailing encouragement of Dr. Barton W. Rippon and Dr. Niels-Erik Andreasen, respectively deans of the Graduate School and the School of Religion of Loma Linda University during the time devoted to the preparation of this book, has meant much to the writer.

As with previous publications it was a privilege to associate with Dr. Raymond Cottrell, the book editor. Dorene Sample assisted him in proofreading. In the overall planning for the publication of the book the cordial relationship with Dr. Bailey Gillespie, Director of the Loma Linda University Press, has been greatly appreciated.

The efficient services given by the Loma Linda University Library, especially the Department of Inter-Library Loan, has made my research easier.

To Antoinette Yakush, my secretary for many years, I am greatly indebted. Her patience, professional skill, and efficiency made it possible that the successive drafts of the manuscript could finally be presented as a book.

Last but not least, by my wife's unfailing support, expressed in so many ways, this book has been made possible.

V. Norskov Olsen
Loma Linda, California

CONTENTS

FOREWORD

Another helpful book has come from the pen of Dr. V. Norskov Olsen. This work should prove to be a landmark in Seventh-day Adventist ecclesiology. However, it should appeal to a wider ecumenical audience, for many, if not most, current theological problems boil down to issues in ecclesiology. The author deals gently, but ably, with some of these important questions.

The book quite rightly points in a comprehensive way to the functional correlation and theological interaction between ecclesiology and such other branches of theology as Christology, soteriology, and pneumatology.

After establishing a solid ecclesiological foundation, Dr. Olsen goes on to elaborate on the priesthood of believers and its organizational offspring, the pastoral ministry. Though the author does not avoid controversial issues, he deals considerately, albeit uncompromisingly, with several myths that have developed throughout church history connected with official ministerial priesthood, ordination to pastoral ministry, and threefold ministry to be allegedly found in the New Testament.

Not only does the writer come to grips with deep theological themes, but he also deals with questions of practical church life, such as the vital role of the laity in evangelism and the stifling nature of clericalism.

If I may be permitted a personal observation: Dr. Olsen has done some of his best and most creative theological writing since retirement. He is thus a living advertisement for the virtue of free time for cognitive thinking and for the fruitfulness of the "third age."

B. B. Beach, Secretary
Conference of Secretaries of
Christian World Communions

FOREWORD

I have been asked by one whom I esteem highly, Dr. Viggo Norskov Olsen, to write the foreword to this book. By chance he let me read some of the responses earlier received from his friends and colleagues. I found that after they studied this manuscript, their words were so expansive and respectful of his profound scholarship and wide reputation that to me his request was embarrassing: "I need to be baptized by you, and do you come to me?" But the persuasion of respect and friendship is such that I eventually capitulated—and now confess the pleasure that is mine in introducing this book to you and in giving you my reasons for endorsing it.

Church, priesthood, ordination—Dr. Olsen contends that a correct understanding of the biblical import of these themes is one of the most crucial issues facing the worldwide Christian movement in our day. Indeed, he contends that there is an urgency behind their significance. This follows because in many quarters, particularly among the older churches, membership is diminishing. All too often this is due to the clergy's everpresent temptation in their world-wise pursuit of "relevance" to reduce the "good news of the Kingdom" to social responsibility and political action—in short, to the humanization of society. Such reductionism of the gospel invariably accelerates membership decrease. And the reason is obvious: such themes do not satisfy the unprecedented argumentation, and sociological concerns have nothing to say to this hunger. Actually, the only means of satisfying it remains the bread of life which Jesus offers and which He accompanies with the promise that those who partake of it will never hunger again. His promise stills stands.

However, even among evangelicals with their professed acceptance of the authority and relevance of the whole Bible, significant church growth is not invariably what they are achieving. For instance, during the 1980s urban evangelism was widely promoted and acknowledged as the churches' top priority, to be matched only by a continuing concern for unreached people groups in rural areas throughout the two-thirds world. Never have there been so many publications, seminars, and case studies on the growing numbers of unsaved individuals in the cities of the world. But with what result? Despite the significant increase in knowledge of urban evangelism and much diligence in networking urban resources for evangelism, most city churches the world over are struggling to survive. Few report significant growth. More often than not those that are growing are led by people who have not been shaped by traditional theological education, nor are they within the older evangelical movement. There must be some basic flaw in the traditional understanding of ministry.

This is what makes Dr. Olsen's book so timely. He knows the Bible, is a top-notch historian, and has been burdened to produce this protest and to reinforce it with the appeal that Christians of all church traditions get back to the basic, by which he means the Word of God. He particularly encourages those preparing for or involved in a "career" ministry to face up to the full implications of the nature of church, her priesthood, and the abuse of ordination. He wants all Christians to sense the importance of discovering and implementing the implications of such questions as : What is the church? Who are called to its priesthood, it ministry? And what is the real significance of ordination?

Behind these questions is Dr. Olsen's conviction that the Head of the Church wills the growth of His Church. He is convinced—and rightly so—that a chief and irreplaceable element in her mission is the proclamation of the gospel to all peoples and the incorporation of those who respond into her communal life. Only through the deliberate multiplication of vast numbers of new congregations all over the world will the Church be able to evangelize this generation. But even church multiplication by itself is not enough. The ministry of the "good news of the Kingdom of God" involves not only all the members of the body of Christ, but also ministering to the whole person in all aspects of life. When the whole Church ceases to perform this comprehensive mission, something fundamental is lost in her very essence as the people of God in the midst of the nations. Dr. Olsen firmly believes that there is a sense in which he can say that his church, or any church that does not grow in membership and in mission, is to that degree out of the will of God.

Dr. Olsen is concerned for the renewal and growth of his church and of all other evangelical churches in these tumultuous days. His concern has prompted the writing of this book. He is convinced that unless solid answers are found to these basic questions, the people of God in our day will come short of realizing their full, God-intended potential of usefulness and will not fully reflect the motivation that comes through knowing themselves possessed by God for ministry within the fellowship of His Church.

Why am I happy to introduce you to the careful study of this book? My reasons are multiple. First and foremost, Dr. Olsen undergirds every dominant thesis in his understanding to the Church and its priesthood by affirming the reality of revelation. To him "the Bible is the supreme witness to the Voice from outside." Its underlying presupposition is that God speaks. He speaks through His "acts" in history, and by means of His prophets the authoritative meaning and significance of these acts is made patently clear. When He addresses Himself to His people,—invariably to individuals,—what He says is truth. As a result, when Dr. Olsen handles the Word of God, he conveys his quiet confidence that its revealed truth demands active obedience. Once one accepts the full implication of revelation, the only acceptable response is obedience. The God who speaks must be given personal response. Revelation should not be regarded as "teaching" or "truth" or "law" so much as divine action: God stepping into history to encounter His people in specific situations which can only be described as human encounters with the burning presence of the living God. Dr. Olsen has himself personally encountered God in the Scriptures. Hence, what he writes should not be regarded as good advice. It is much more!

Second, Dr. Olsen makes a clear distinction between the moments of revelation and the process we call history. The Bible presents history as the arena in which two wills clash—the divine and the human. Revelation takes place in this clash and confrontation. This means that the perspective of history must be carefully maintained when revelation is under consideration. Hence, I greatly appreciate the candor with which Dr. Olsen focuses on the distinction between truth and myth. He begins with Scriptures but moves beyond it into the realm of church history, and points out the tension between the full authority of Scripture—to which he gives unhesitating assent—and the reality of the empirical churches, which over the years have been at best only flawed responses to the gospel. All too often human fallenness and demonic activity have left their mark, and this despite the gracious patience and helpfulness of the Holy Spirit.

Third, this brings us to the complexity of any attempt to grasp the full import of the Church. As you read and reread Dr. Olsen's discussion of this theme, you will doubtless be impressed with a rather surprising fact. There is a sense in which it is impossible to speak with precision of the Church—what she claims to be and what she is. To the casual outsider the Church represents a religion not unlike all religions, in that she seeks to cope with the same problems and to suggest what appear to be similar remedies. Again, there is the Church of the biblical theologian—the one, holy, catholic, and apostolic Church—but few would confess that as such she actually exists. According to Scripture, only in her self-consciousness does she find her uniqueness. And the focal point of her self-consciousness is what she calls the gospel: a reality inseparable from an historic person called Jesus of Nazareth. Concerning Him she makes stupendous claims, which separate her from all the religions of the world. She knows Him as eminently rooted in history. He was not One who proclaimed human words about God. In contrast, in Him the very Word of God was spoken for all the peoples of the world. I rejoice that Dr. Olsen rightly regards Jesus Christ as the Church's greatest Treasure: the one Word of God which all peoples have a right to hear.

Dr. Olsen's understanding of the Church embodies neither an association in the typical, voluntary sense, nor a society of select members. The Church is a family. God is Father, Christ Jesus the Elder Brother, and all believing members are brothers and sisters. Hence, it cannot be "joined." As in a family, one is born into it through spiritual regeneration. All members are not only mutually interlinked, but all are equipped for full participation in the family ministry. This is the miracle of Pentecost: the fusion of all into one body and the baptism and infilling of the Holy Spirit so that all possessed gifts for ministry, men and women alike.

But to state this is to define the ideal, something hardly descriptive of the church in history. Dr. Olsen knows this. Hence, he confronts us with the typical church which is primarily an institution and not a family, wherein is little equality or unity, where religion, not Christ, is the object, and which lives more for herself than for the Kingdom of God.

Fourth, Dr. Olsen rightly accords "Christianity" a wider connotation than the primitive faith of the Apostolic Church. Initially, it meant faith, and nothing else than faith in Jesus the Christ who died for sinners and rose for their justification (Rom. 4:25). It did not include history, dogma, culture, and tradition—all the values, concepts, and ideas brought into the Church arising from her interaction with the Scriptures and with the nations. Not only has the Church to a greater or less extent modified every environment into which she has penetrated, but she has also in the course of her history taken on many of their cultural forms and organizational patterns in the process of seeking at-home-ness among each separate people. Hence, Dr. Olsen would have us hold tightly to Jesus Christ, to whom he accords preeminence, and hold every cultural loyalty loosely. He would have us understand and appreciate the ongoing of historic Christianity, its long process of development, as well as the wonder of its original faith in Jesus Christ. In this sense Dr. Olsen would have us regard Christendom as a complex mixture of truth and error. Christendom represents the totality of human response over the centuries to the gospel— a response in which people in their redeemed fallenness never fully apprehended the breadth and depth of its validities and in which the activity of "the powers" was never absent. But he would also have us recognize with grateful thanks the abiding presence and activity of the Spirit of God in the lives and thought of all who consciously came under the rule of Jesus Christ through repentance and faith.

Fifth, I rejoice that Dr. Olsen was not content to confine his study to the New Testament. The primitive church had its roots in the prophetic faith of the Old Testament. Indeed, the prophetic tradition constituted the spiritual milieu into which Jesus was born and brought up. We think of Elizabeth and Zechariah, their son John the Baptist, the saintly Simeon and Anna, as well as many, many more. These men and women—"the poor and humble in the land"—were waiting for the consolation of Israel. They put their hope not in the meticulous observance of the law (i.e., the Pharisees), but in the prophetic vision of the Messianic Age. By his extensive use of the Old Testament Dr. Olsen has made us realize that Christianity, to be correctly understood, must be regarded as bearing the indelible imprint of this Jewish eschatological faith in which it was cradled and with which it was so continuously in contact during its formative years. The tragedy is that this indebtedness has not always been either determined or acknowledged, and the resultant impoverishment has often made her prone to syncretism and to an unwarranted and shameful anti-Jewish hostility.

Finally, what shall I say of Dr. Olsen's extended discussion of "the priesthood of believers": its firm basis in the Sinaitic covenant and its preservation and expression in the early church during those centuries when the people of God had their backs to the wall, facing the hostility of pagan Rome? And what of the long centuries that followed when the Constantinian Era found a triumphal church linked arm-in-arm with the state and proudly swaggering through history? Dr. Olsen is at his best when he guides us through the tragic evolution of clericalism and hierarchical church structures, on to the present, to Vatican II and the Lima Consultation of the Faith and Order Commission of the World Council of Churches. His detailed exegetical study of the Apostolic Church's ministry in the New Testament provides us with normative data by which to evaluate the long history of this evolution. The growth of sacramentalism and priesthood, the centralization of clerical power and lay passivity, the Protestant revolt and the Anabaptist repudiation—all these movements are carefully explored.

We are all in Dr. Olsen's debt for his excellent and thorough study of the historical evolution of ordination in the practice of the post-Apostolic churches. Whereas we all recognize the need that Christians have felt for order in their congregational life, and endorse the patterns of leadership selection and elevation that are found in Scripture, with him we deplore the magical connotations that were gradually fused into the rites whereby God-appointed leaders were to be recognized by the communicants. This chapter is particularly noteworthy since it confronts us with the need to face the massive problem standing in the way of reinstating in our day the ministry to which all Christians have been called. In the end we find ourselves heartily resonating with his answers to the questions he initially posed: the Church—it is nothing more than the people of God seeking to worship and serve under the only true Vicar of Christ, the Holy Spirit. The priesthood—this embraces all who have experienced the new birth, all who have been called and equipped for ministry. None is called to passivity, to the role of spectators in the life, worship, and mission of the Church. And ordination—all those who serve the Church in a "career" fashion and have been dutifully and publicly so designated, should humbly confess they have no sacerdotal or ecclesiastical right to confine the ministry to what they seek to do. All Christians are called to ministry.

Dr. Olsen adds an extended epilogue in which he identifies the tradition to which he belongs and which has shaped his discipleship and ministry. I was pleased with this, for we need to be constantly reminded that the Adventist movement has its roots in Scripture and represents a forthright, evangelical response to the trinitarian faith that is so central to the biblical witness.

Arthur F. Glasser
Dean Emeritus, School of World Mission
Fuller Theological Seminary

INTRODUCTION

I pray that the eyes of your heart may be enlightened, so that you may know what is the hope of His calling, what are the riches of the glory of His inheritance in the saints, and what is the surpassing greatness of His power toward us who believe. These are in accordance with the working of the strength of His might which He brought about in Christ, when He raised Him from the dead, and seated Him at His right hand in the heavenly places, far above all rule and authority and power and dominion, and every name that is named, not only in this age, but also in the one to come. And He put all things in subjection under His feet, and gave Him as head over all things to the church, which is His body, the fulness of Him who fills all in all. —Apostle Paul

Many signs within Christendom indicate that the nature of the church, its ministry and ordination, will become a burning issue as we come to the close of the twentieth and enter the twenty-first century. This seems apparent not only in the dialogue between established churches, but also within the individual churches themselves. In the latter case it may be because of interaction with other churches and/or in seeking renewal of their own communion.

The decrees of the Second Vatican Council and the endeavors of the World Council of Churches have stimulated inquiry into the concept and nature of the church. In 1982 the Faith and Order Commission of the World Council of Churches, at a meeting in Lima, Peru, adopted the document, *Baptism, Eucharist and Ministry.* The document was the fruit of several worldwide conferences and study meetings over more than half a century. Since its adoption member churches of the World Council of Churches and nonmember churches have responded to the document. By 1987, 160 churches had given an official response to the document, and these have been published in several volumes.

When it comes to the responses regarding the structure of the church and its ministry we find differences depending upon the polity of the particular responding church (for example episcopalian or congregational). This was anticipated by the document, for the paragraph prior to the statements on "The Church and the Ordained Ministry" reads:

> Though the churches are agreed in their general understanding of the calling of the people of God, they differ in their understanding of how the life of the Church is to be ordered. In particular, there are differences concerning the place and forms of the ordained ministry. As they engage in the effort to overcome these differences, the churches need to work from the perspective of the calling of the whole people of God. A common answer needs to be found to the following question: How, according to the will of God and under the guidance of the Holy Spirit, is the life of the Church to be understood and ordered, so that the Gospel may be spread and the community built up in love?[1]

It should be noticed that in the Church of England's response it is stated that "the subject of the ministry divides the churches more strongly than baptism and eucharist."[2] Accordingly, the questions of church structure and the ministry of the church (the role of men and women, lay and clergy) and connected issues have come to the forefront. Attempts are made by most churches to meet the issues—which have to be met on all fronts—for no church can be neutral.

It must be acknowledged that no single book or person can deal adequately with all the ecclesiological viewpoints of the various churches. However, it is hoped that the present study may serve to help identify the most significant factors, as well as the undergirding theological and biblical rationale in any ecclesiological debate or inquiry. Accordingly, we have sought to bring together basic subjects which ought to be analyzed, questions which should be raised, answers which need to be sought; likewise, facts which should be noticed, and concepts or perspectives which must be observed. We will now briefly define our terminology.

The Christian concern for and the biblical study of the nature of the church, its essential characteristics, structure, ministry, and ordination, are expressed by the term ecclesiology ("the word about the church"). Every aspect of ecclesiology—and not least the defining of the ministry—is inseparable from theology ("the word about God"), Christology ("the word about Christ"), soteriology ("the word about salvation"), and pneumatology ("the word about the Holy Spirit"). This study will show a mutual interdependence and reciprocal influence between ecclesiology and these doctrines; the former serves as a pointer to the latter.

Further, the manifestation and practical applications of Christian doctrines are in and through the church, and this is the case for both the divine and human involvement. What we have sought to say is expressed in a different way in the following statement: "The Church is the clue to the Bible as history, and it is also the culmination of the Bible as theology." The same author continues by saying: "It might be said that the Church is both the theme of the Bible and its writer. Bible and Church explain each other, judge each other, need each other. Both are organs of the living God, and neither can function properly without the other. If the Church fails, it is because it is not Biblical enough, and if Bible study becomes pedantic and arid, it is because it is divorced from worship and service in the living fellowship of the Church."[3]

While ecclesiology should reflect true biblical theology, Christ-ology, pneumatology, and soteriology, we unfortunately find that church history reveals that non-biblical and non-Christian elements in various forms—sociological, political, economic, institutional, etc.—became deciding factors in one or several aspects of ecclesiology and thus in turn weakened, diluted and even changed biblical theology, Christology, and soteriology as well as the working of the Holy Spirit.

The understanding of the nature of the church and the formation of any structure of the church and its ministry become—for better or for worse—a test or expression of one's understanding of Christ and the biblical revelation. When an ecclesiology is in trouble or challeng-ed, it is, generally, because of distortions in theology, Christology, pneumatology, and soteriology, either on the theoretical or pragmatic level, or both. Whenever an issue regarding ecclesiology arises it should be solved in the light of theology, Christology, pneumatology, and soteriology, for the church is not an organization or institution of man, neither should it be administered as such, but a living organism—the body of Christ.

Since a study of the priesthood and ordination falls within ec-clesiology, it becomes necessary—in a preliminary way—to observe the basic doctrines and biblical truths making up the foundation of ecclesiology. These must serve as the framework for any inquiry into the meaning of priesthood, ministry, and ordination. Accordingly, Part

One deals with the biblical and theological foundation of the church, its nature, and characteristics.

Part Two deals with the subject of the priesthood of believers. This doctrine is constitutive for the concept and structure of the church and in turn has foundational consequences for the understanding of the ministry of the church, including the rite of ordination. In the New Testament the word "priest" is not used for any official minister, but only for the baptized believers. It is the total community of believers, which is "a royal priesthood." Professor Richard Hanson of the University of Manchester (in *Christian Priesthood Examined*) states: "Of offical Christian priests we must honestly admit there is in the New Testament not the faintest whisper." He also finds it "curious that neither those who favour a Christian priesthood nor those who reject it have been concerned to examine the evidence."[4] This present study will attempt to look at the New Testament evidence.

In the responses from about 160 churches to the World Council of Churches' document on the ministry, appreciation and agreement were expressed for its emphasis on the church as the people of God and the body of Christ. The document states: "The Holy Spirit unites in a single body those who follow Jesus Christ and sends them as witnesses into the world. Belonging to the Church means living in communion with God through Jesus Christ in the Holy Spirit. . . . All members are called to discover, with the help of the community, the gifts they have received and to use them for the building up of the Church and for the service of the world to which the Church is sent."[5]

The ecumenical movement, which has had significant influence on Christendom during the last half of the twentieth century, has rediscovered the importance of the laity. The same may also be said about the Second Vatican Council, which issued the "Decree on the Apostolate of the Laity."

The World Council of Churches' Department on the Laity has published a work, *The Layman in Christian History*. The closing chapter quotes Hendrik Kraemer (author of *A Theology of Laity*), who points out a new awareness of " 'the role and responsibility of the laity in Church.' " It is of significance to realize that this in turn " 'implies a new examination and general reshaping of all ecclesiologies which we have had for centuries' and it 'is the most important aspect of the longing for the renewal of the Church which arises in the Churches all over the world.' "[6] Theological and ecclesiological aspects of the priesthood of believers will be considered as well as their impact upon ecclesiology in general.

The church is a community or society and as such it must necessarily have a structure, but the nature of its structure is not comparable to any in the secular society. Neither should there be conflict between the concept of the priesthood of believers and an official appointed ministry; the latter should enhance the former. The terms "minister" and "ministry" are commonly used synonymously with "pastor" and "pastorate;" but, as will be observed, they have much broader meanings and manifold applications in the New Testament. Part Three will deal with the ministry in the New Testament; there we find charismatic and appointed ministries, and these will be analyzed.

How far was the ministry, described in the New Testament, implemented in the post-apostolic church and the centuries which followed? This question is considered in Part Four. The apparent two-fold pattern of presbyter-deacon of the New Testament was changed into a three-fold one of bishop, presbyter, and deacon.

As the centuries went by, churches developed within an episcopal system, although with variations as in the Roman Catholic, Orthodox, and Anglican churches. On the other hand, we have numerous Protestant churches with a presbyterian and congregational form of church structure. The question of the correct pattern of ministry is, to a large degree, the one which separates the churches. At the same time it must also be acknowledged that the very essence of the ministry reflects a church's theological and soteriological views, making the issue of the ministry not an administrative one, but a most important theological one. The changes in the pattern of ministry and church structure, which have taken place during the history of Christianity, have gone—for better or worse—hand in hand with theological developments.

In our historical survey we deal with the second century as a transition period with changes in the next two centuries leading to the Constantinian church and its sequel. The Protestant Reformation of the sixteenth century reacted against medieval ecclesiology and sought to restore New Testament church concepts. The ecclesiology of the Prostestant Fathers had not only theological and soteriological consequences, but also social ones. Luther's and Calvin's ecclesiology is examined as well as the one which gave birth to the Anabaptist movement. We close this part with the World Council of Churches' historical evaluation of the ministry.

Ordination is considered the legitimate rite and action admitting a person to the official ministry of the church. On this there is general agreement among churches, but when it comes to defining its theological meaning and ecclesiological usage and significance we find not only variations but fundamental differences. These will be examined in Part Five together with a biblical and historical inquiry into the subject of ordination.

In the course of history two concepts developed: the sacramental and the ritual. Likewise, there is disagreement about who should ordain, and who should be ordained. In the early stage of the Protestant Reformation the rite of ordination was not used, and Calvin, like many others, was never ordained.

When we turn to the New Testament we find that the word "ordain" is not found in the original Greek text. When translators use the word "ordain," pre-conceived ideas are often read into the text.

The sacrament or rite of ordination is performed by the laying on of hands. The rite of the laying on of hands is manifold, both in the Old and in the New Testament, and is also found within Judaism. When it comes to the laying on of hands for a specific ministry, there are in actuality only three instances in the New Testament. However, these were not for a local pastoral ministry.

The earliest historical record of an ordination service appears first in the third century. The points raised and other relevant aspects will be dealt with in our inquiry. In other words, the purpose is to deal with ordination as such, a necessary task before the issue of ordination of women is addressed. The question of male and female ministries, male-female oneness, equality, and functional relationship will require another volume.

The Epilogue contains a review of the material covered, together with some pertinent observations. This study is not intended as a final word on the subject of ecclesiology, but rather as a renewal of the subject—an attempted contribution to the ecclesiological quest.

Let us begin the present study with the prayer of the Apostle Paul for the church (Eph. 1:16-23). He speaks about "making mention of you in my prayers; that the God of our Lord Jesus Christ, the Father of glory, may give to you a spirit of wisdom and of revelation in the knowledge of Him." Then he offers the prayer as quoted on the title page of the Introduction.

1 THE CHURCH: ITS BIBLICAL FOUNDATION

No man can lay a foundation other than the one which is laid, which is Jesus Christ. —Apostle Paul

The church has one foundation,
'Tis Jesus Christ her Lord;
She is His new creation,
By water and the word;
From heaven He came and sought her
To be His holy bride;
With His own blood He bought her,
And for her life He died.

Elect from every nation,
Yet one o'er all the earth,
Her charter of salvation,
One Lord, one faith, one birth;
One holy name she blesses,
Partakes one holy food,
And to one hope she presses,
With every grace endued.
—Samuel J. Stone, 1866

THE GOD-MAN COVENANT RELATIONSHIP

The most common concept of the church—the people of God—binds together the meaning and oneness of *ekklesia* in all ages. In contemplating the meaning of "church" as the people of God, we must do so within a Christian worldview in order to have the proper theological undergirding. We therefore begin where the biblical revelation begins, "In the beginning God . . ." These opening words of Holy Scripture are most profound and of great significance. Divine reality preceded human reality. In all man's quest for, and evaluation of, the meaning, purpose, and condition of life, he must begin with God. This is the primeval and fundamental fact supporting everything else.

The Covenant of Life and a Moral Universe. God is the Originator of our moral obligations. The biblical Creation story clearly tells us that man as a moral being was placed in a covenant relationship with God. God not only "created" and "blessed" man, but in his first personal dealing with man "God said" and "the Lord commanded" (Gen. 1:27-28; 2:16). At the time of the first temptation it was acknowledged both by the serpent and by Eve that "God has said" (Gen. 3:1, 3). Life itself necessitated that decisions had to be made, and in order to be true to life these had to be made in accordance with the norms or laws established by the Creator. The prophet Isaiah exclaimed: "The Lord is our lawgiver" (Isa. 33:22).

The story of the tree of knowledge of good and evil (Gen. 2:16-17) illustrates the significance of the covenant relationship with God; we name this relationship the covenant of life. A covenant is an agreement between two partners, but since God is the Creator and everything is rooted in Him and His activities, it follows that the covenant is not negotiable but has to be a commanding covenant: obey and live, disobey and die. Accordingly, we speak about the covenant as a testament in which the testator makes his will known to heirs who will carry out his will, on his conditions. For this reason the books of the Bible are referred to as the Old and New Testaments.

The covenant of life was more than a mere mandate or order; it was a statement regarding the facts of the law-governed universe, which grew out of love, the very essence of God. This covenant embodied the very principles of life; we therefore call it the covenant of life. Life was based on conformity to, or oneness with, the principles that constituted the very life itself. Failure of conformity could only result in the loss of life—that is death. God's judgments are not capricious, they are natural consequences of the sin involved.

The Covenant of Redemption. A moral universe presupposes personal freedom or self-determination with the possibility of a wrong choice—something contrary to God's will. Choosing the latter is disobedience (sinning). This results in separation from God, with death as the final end.

By inference we are told that when God created the moral universe He also established the covenant of redemption. It made the provision that in Christ Jesus man could be redeemed from the consequences of disobedience. God planned to redeem man in Christ "before the foundation of the world" (Eph. 1:4; Heb. 4:3; 1 Peter 1:20), and "through the blood of the eternal covenant, even Jesus our Lord" (Heb. 13:20). Christ is "the Lamb slain from the foundation of the world" (Rev. 13:8, KJV). Like the two sides of a coin the covenant of life and the covenant of redemption are two aspects of the one everlasting covenant. The plan of redemption was not an afterthought. Law and justice, grace and mercy are blended together in the nature of God. The everlasting covenant expresses the very character of God and is therefore immutable, as God Himself is. The covenant of life was based on love, for it is inseparable from the covenant of redemption where the Godhead took the consequence of transgression into their own hearts.

The requirements, the norms, and the value judgment of the covenant of life were fulfilled in the life and person of Jesus Christ; likewise, the covenant of redemption. In His love, and by grace and mercy, God substitutes Christ's obedience for man's disobedience, and He accepts Christ's death as a replacement for man's eternal death. This is the good news, the gospel. In Jesus Christ sinful man is brought into a new covenant relationship with God and becomes a child of God. Our standing with God is by grace, and the renewed life of obedience is also by the enabling grace of God accepted by man through faith. Theologically, Christologically, and soteriologically the church is constituted in the covenant of life and the covenant of redemption, and every aspect of ecclesiology will have to be viewed within the framework of the two covenants or the two aspects of the one everlasting covenant.

THE CHURCH OF THE COVENANTS

The Church in Eden. When God created man and woman He established the family. Being in a true relationship with God through the covenant of life they were the family of God. After the Fall it was possible to restore the relationship with God by entering the covenant of redemption; doing so, the family of God was renewed and became the people of God, which—as we will observe—historically became the church.

The church, according to the Protestant Fathers, antedates New Testament times.[1] In emphasizing the existence of the church, from the time of the Creation and the Fall, the Protestant Reformers sought to identify the church with the covenants of life and redemption or with the order of creation and with God's redemptive acts in past history. Further, that history—together with the principles and theological concepts that undergirded it—is contained in the Bible and is in the purest sense church history and ecclesiology under the heading of the family of God or people of God.

Since the centrality of faith is the same at all times, and the true church (the people of God) is likewise the same at all times, it became supremely important for the Protestant Reformers to be able to unfold true church history and ecclesiology for the reformed church.

Luther makes the Garden of Eden the beginning of the history of the church: "The church has always existed; there has always been a people of God from the time of the first person Adam to the very latest infant born, even granting that at times the church has been exceedingly weak and so dispersed that it was manifest nowhere."[2]

The Patriarchs and the Covenant. In the divine administration of the covenant, the Old Testament reveals successive covenants reaching their fulfillment in Jesus Christ; but in each instance the covenant was established by God's promise and grace and accepted by man through faith. Those who went into the covenant relationship with God made up the people of God, the church.

At the time of the Flood "the earth was corrupt in the sight of God, and the earth was filled with violence" (Gen. 6:11). In other words, the law or covenant of life had been transgressed with catastrophic consequences. "But Noah found favor in the eyes of the Lord" (Gen. 6:8), and God established His covenant with Noah (Gen. 6:18). By faith the ark was built; "Noah did according to all that the Lord had commanded him" (Gen. 7:5). Immediately after the flood "Noah built an altar to the Lord" (Gen. 8:20), and God said: "I establish My covenant with you" (Gen. 9:11).

God similarly established His covenant with Abraham (Gen. 17:1-7, 10). The Abrahamic covenant has global dimensions. God first said: "I am God Almighty; Walk before Me and be blameless. And I will establish My covenant between Me and you, and I will multiply you exceedingly." Next, Abraham was told that he would "be the father of a multitude of nations." That covenant would be "an everlasting covenant." Already when Abraham left his home country God had said: "And in you all the families of the earth shall be blessed" (Gen. 12:3). The covenant also had eternal dimensions. The Epistle to the Hebrews (chapter 11) records the faith of those who built altars during the first period of salvation history. About Abraham it is said: "By faith Abraham, when he was called, obeyed by going out to a place which he was to receive for an inheritance; . . . for he was looking for the city which has foundations, whose architect and builder is God" (Heb. 11:8, 10). No doubt the eternal city was the final goal for Abraham.

The covenant was based on a promise given by God and accepted by Abraham. We read that Abraham "believed in the Lord; and He reckoned it to him as righteousness" (Gen. 15:6). Later Abraham was asked to offer his son Isaac, the son of promise. When he was about to sacrifice his son, God intervened and said: "I know that you fear God, since you have not withheld your son, your only son, from Me" (Gen. 22:12). Then Abraham looked up and saw a lamb.

On Mount Moriah Isaac had asked, "Where is the lamb for the burnt offering?" And Abraham said, "God will provide for Himself the lamb" (Gen. 22:7-8). Isaac's question "Where is the Lamb?" was truly answered by John the Baptist when he saw Christ and said: "Behold, the Lamb of God who takes away the sin of the world!" (John 1:29).

When Jacob, as a sojourner, went to Haran and in a dream saw a ladder on which "the angels of God were ascending and descending" (Gen. 28:12) he said: "This is none other than the house of God, and this is the gate of heaven" (Gen. 28:17). Jacob called the place Bethel and promised: "And this stone, which I have set up as a pillar, will be God's house" (Gen. 28:22). In this connection God renewed His covenant with Jacob.

The People of Israel and the Covenant. The covenant made with Abraham, Isaac, and Jacob was renewed with Israel. The initiative was made by God, and the gracious and unmerited release from bondage in Egypt is the background for the covenant at Mount Sinai. The record reads: "Now then, if you will indeed obey My voice and keep My covenant, then you shall be My own possession among all the peoples, for all the earth is Mine. . . . And all the people answered together and said, 'All that the Lord has spoken we will do!' " (Ex. 19:5, 8). Then followed the issuing of the Ten Commandments and instruction about the tabernacle and its services.

The tabernacle contained the moral principles for life (the ark with the Ten Commandments), and the altar—on which the sacrifices were made—represented the work of atonement. The services in the tabernacle pointed to God's promises and grace. Over the ark with the Ten Commandments was the mercy seat, making the covenant one of grace by faith in the promise of forgiveness in the Lamb of God.

Christ and the Covenant. When Christ died on the cross as "the Lamb of God," the meaning of the temple services ceased. The covenant of grace was confirmed and rectified, and we can speak about the newness of the covenant of grace.

The prophet Jeremiah had spoken about this: " 'But this is the covenant which I will make with the house of Israel after those days,' declares the Lord, 'I will put My law within them, and in their heart I will write it; and I will be their God, and they shall be My people' " (Jer. 31:33). The New Testament asserts that this promise is fulfilled in the people of the New Testament (see Heb. 8:6-13). The Apostle Paul writes: "And if you belong to Christ, then you are

Abraham's offspring, heirs according to promise" (Gal. 3:29).

Christ is the mediator between God and man (1 Tim. 2:5) as well as the "guarantee of a better covenant" (Heb. 7:22). Zacharias, the father of John the Baptist, said that the time had come when God would "remember His holy covenant, the oath which He swore to Abraham our father" (Luke 1:72-73).

The prophet Isaiah had depicted a better covenant through a faithful servant different from all of the past (see Isa. 42:18 ff; 52:13; 53; 59:20-21). This was fulfilled in Christ. It was in the setting of the Passover and the crucifixion of Christ that the transition from the old covenant to the new took place. During the Passover meal Christ took the bread and said: "This is My body which is given for you," and "This cup which is poured out for you is the new covenant in My blood" (Luke 22:19, 20). The expression "new covenant" (1 Cor. 11:25; 2 Cor. 3:6; Heb. 8:13; 9:15) points to the fact that God summed up all things in Jesus Christ.

The Westminster Confession of Faith, which has influenced English speaking people more than any other creed, closes its discussion of the covenant by pointing out that the covenant of grace was in principle always the same, but differently administrated in the Old and New Testaments. In the former "it was administered by promises, prophecies, sacrifices," etc. pointing to Christ, but in the New Testament "when Christ the substance was exhibited, the ordinances in which this covenant is dispensed are the preaching of the word and the administration of the sacraments of Baptism and the Lord's Supper."[3] In other words, the church always was and always will be the custodian of the covenant.

THE REMNANT

Successive renewals of the covenant revealed the existence of a remnant within Israel. In the midst of all the calamities—including destruction and exile—that came upon the Israelites as a result of their disobedience to God's instruction, moral injunctions, and religious precepts, there was always a faithful remnant which constituted the true people of God. In some cases God postponed punishment and destruction for the sake of the remnant, but when disaster came God promised the ongoing of His redemptive purpose through the remnant, composed of His faithful and obedient children (Isa. 1:9, Zeph. 2:3). God's mercy, promises and instruction, and man's acceptance of them as well as their actualization in obedience to God, is constituted in the biblical concept of the remnant, which in turn is inseparable from the theology of the covenant.

The remnant also points out a twofold aspect of the church: the true and the false, or apostate. The struggles between Cain and Abel, Ishmael and Isaac, Esau and Jacob reflect contrasting religious attitudes in the history of Israel and Christianity.

In the story of Joseph the concept of the remnant is renewed. It is recorded how Joseph made himself known to his brethren when they visited Egypt in order to purchase grain. He said to them: "I am your brother Joseph, whom you sold into Egypt. And now do not be grieved or angry with yourselves, because you sold me here; for God sent me before you to preserve life . . . to preserve for you a remnant in the earth, and to keep you alive by a great deliverance" (Gen. 45:4, 7).

When we come to the kingdom of Israel we find reference to the remnant in the ninth century story of Elijah who spoke to King Ahab about the impending judgment. In his discouragement Elijah said to the Lord: "I have been very zealous for the Lord, the God of hosts; for the sons of Israel have forsaken Thy covenant, torn down Thine altars and killed Thy prophets with the sword. And I alone am left; and they seek my life, to take it away" (1 Kings 19:14). But God told Elijah that a remnant was left (1 Kings 19:18).

Prophets Amos, Micah, and Isaiah of the eighth century B.C., who predicted and proclaimed an imminent judgment, point to the remnant as survivors. God "may be gracious to the remnant of Joseph" (Amos 5:15), and "surely gather the remnant of Israel" (Micah 2:12; cf. 5:3). For the prophet Isaiah the theology of the remnant was so important that he gave his son the symbolic name: "a remnant shall return" (Shear-jashub, Isa. 7:3). The truth of this name is stated in these words: "A remnant will return, the remnant of Jacob, to the mighty God. For though your people, O Israel, may be like the sand of the sea, only a remnant within them will return; a destruction is determined, overflowing with righteousness" (Isa. 10:21-22).

After the return of some from the Babylonian captivity in the fifth century B.C., Nehemiah speaks of these as the remnant "who survived the captivity" (1:2, 3). Further, both Jeremiah (31:7; cf. 23:5-6) and Zechariah (8:11-12; cf. 12:8-10; 14:1-9) used the term remnant with reference to the messianic future. John the Baptist perceived his calling as that of gathering the repentant as a remnant who would be ready to accept the Messiah.

Christ came to the covenant people, and beginning with Abraham He could look back upon nineteen centuries of history. Throughout the Old Testament—generation after generation—God continually pleaded with His covenant people and the nations regarding the blessings of obedience and disastrous results, or curses, for disobedience. The agenda of the prophets consistently listed the moral issues of the time and their social and religious implications as well as the moral and spiritual remedies.

The story of Israel from Abraham to Christ is well known; it tells about the peoples' moral failure and disobedience resulting from their lack of trust in and loyal acceptance of God's promises. At the time of Moses the people erected an idol to worship. During the time of the judges they were brought under oppressive neighboring nations seven times. The united monarchy lasted only during the reigns of three kings, and was then divided into two kingdoms. The northern kingdom was conquered by the Assyrians and later the southern kingdom by the Babylonians. Only a remnant returned from captivity, and their personal and national behavior and understanding of God's promises showed but little improvement. Christ said, "How often I wanted to gather your children together, the way a hen gathers her chicks under her wings, and you were unwilling. Behold, your house is being left to you desolate!" (Matt. 23:37-38). These words were spoken by Christ just prior to his great prophetic discourse regarding the destruction of Jerusalem and "the end of the age" (Matt. 24:3).

Christ came, but all forsook Him; even Peter denied Him. Christ Himself became the remnant and the second Adam; a new humanity began with Him and a new beginning for the remnant: the New Testament church. Christ Himself, His disciples and the New Testament Church fulfilled "the witness" of the servant and the remnant spoken of by the prophet Isaiah (Isa. 42:1-6; 43:10; 44:8; 53; 61:1-8). This fact is part of the foundation of the church and its ministry. A study of this topic has pointed out that

> In the Old Testament, especially in the prophecy of Second Isaiah, the Remnant with which the Servant is associated and to some extent identified is to be a witnessing Remnant. It has a mission to declare God's nature to Israel and to the Gentiles, and to witness to the fulfillment of the predictions of God's prophet. But this ministry is evidently conceived of

as being exercised in the eschatological future. Then in St. Paul's writings the Remnant has carried out its function. . . . It seems therefore a clear deduction from Paul's teaching that the first disciples *were* the faithful Remnant and that their apostolate sprang from this fact. In other words, the apostles were apostles because they were the first Church.[4]

The significance of the remnant motif is categorically expressed by T. W. Manson in his well known work, *The Church's Ministry,* when he states: "Now the Church is the embodiment of the Remnant ideal." He explains: "The significant history of Israel is the history of the Remnant, that is, the history of the minority in Israel who remain loyal to the covenant and to their covenant God. This Remnant, always there even when unobserved by man, is manifested in times of religious crisis. The nature of the crisis determines the way in which it will show itself."[5]

In the Bible the last direct reference to the term "remnant" is found in connection with the description of the last anti-Christian struggle between Satan and the remnant church under the picture of the woman and her seed: "And the dragon was wroth with the woman, and went to make war with the remnant of her seed, which keep the commandments of God, and have the testimony of Jesus Christ" (Rev. 12:17, KJV). The same remnant is also described by the words: "Here is the perseverance of the saints who keep the commandments of God and their faith in Jesus" (Rev. 14:12). Both statements point out that the remnant before the second advent of Christ has the characteristics of the covenant relationship with God, as we have seen them to be from the beginning.

The very existence as the remnant makes it "a society within a society." However, it was the remnant which should share the covenant blessings with all nations. Accordingly, the remnant "is not an isolationist group, carefully fostering a private life of its own secluded from the contaminations of the world. It has to discharge a task in the world as well as to maintain its own inner life. It has to present the gospel to those outside; and it can only do that effectively as its members live according to Christ in their relations to one another."[6]

AN ESCHATOLOGICAL COMMUNITY

The Old Testament places the people of God, the church, in the center of a great cosmic drama which began back in eternity, the last scenes of which would take place at the coming of the Messiah. In the ancient world man had little concept of history, and what understanding he had was conceived as a circular movement of historical events reflective of the yearly agricultural cycle. The uniqueness of the Hebrew prophets' idea of history was a specific linear concept climaxing in the appearance of the Son of man.

A landscape painter may in the same painting portray in the foreground a village, with its houses and people, and in the background a valley, hills, sky, and sun, even though some are a very great distance away. Likewise the Old Testament writers, in describing the future, depicted the first and second advents of Christ, the first as the foreground and the latter as the background of salvation history or church history.

The nucleus of the Christian church came into being as an eschatological community: the new people of God. "Eschatological" in the sense that what Peter described taking place at Pentecost was "in the last days" (Acts 2:17), as the kingdom of God had truly been inaugurated in the Christ-events, and would be fully established at His return. After the resurrection the Christ-events were proclaimed by Christ Himself and later by the disciples as being the fulfillment of God's promise to Israel embodied in the covenant-remnant-eschaton concepts, thus the prophetic and apocalyptic message they proclaimed became constitutive for the church and thereby normative for the church at all times. In this connection notice the following:

> A large part of the Church's failure throughout the ages has just lain in her failure to understand the prophetic and apocalyptic preparation. When authority and compulsion seemed a sure and quick road to truth and unity, it was difficult to regard the Church as other than a worldly corporation, and to remember that she stood for God's rule in however few, and by God's way of the patient endurance of love, however long. It is the things Christ does not trust in, which men have been so slow to learn.[7]

The eschatological aspect of the Christian church and its message must have a definite bearing upon the form and purpose of ministries the church establishes. Having referred to experimentation with new types of ministries in a changing society and different cultures one present-day theologian writes that they "must be governed and limited by the awareness that 'the early Church did not plan its ministries according to the needs of the time but mainly according to the vision it held of the eschatological nature of the Church which was taken seriously at that time.' "[8]

THE CHRISTOLOGICAL FOUNDATION

The Apostle Peter in his defense before the Jewish Sanhedrin in Jerusalem makes the following statement about Christ: "He is the stone which was rejected by you, the builders, but which became the very corner stone. And there is salvation in no one else; for there is no other name under heaven that has been given among men, by which we must be saved" (Acts 4:11, 12). Previously, Peter had said: "Everyone who calls on the name of the Lord shall be saved" (Acts 2:21). On a subsequent occasion the apostles were flogged and ordered "to speak no more in the name of Jesus. . . . So they went on their way from the presence of the Council, rejoicing that they had been considered worthy to suffer shame for His name" (Acts 5:40, 41).

The Old and New Testaments, like the ancient people at large, placed great significance on a person's name, for it was bestowed in order to express attributes, personality, essence, and character. In the case of Jesus, God "bestowed on Him the name which is above every name, that at the name of Jesus every knee should bow, of those who are in heaven, and on earth, and under the earth, and that every tongue should confess that Jesus Christ is Lord, to the glory of God the Father" (Phil. 2:9-11). Christ asked His followers to pray "in My name" (John 16:23-24), and the Apostle Paul tells the believers: "And whatever you do in word or deed, do all in the name of the Lord Jesus" (Col. 3:17).

To believe and know the name of Jesus Christ means to apprehend the attributes that characterize the different titles bestowed upon Him— Messiah, Prophet, Priest, King, Servant, Redeemer, Judge, Lord, Savior, etc. These names personify in Christ the many facets of Christology which are perceived within the context of the biblical covenant-remnant-eschaton motif. The church and its ministries are founded in Christ as a person. He is par excellence the Apostle (Heb. 3:1), the Prophet (Matt. 21:11; Luke 24:19), the Priest (Heb. 5:6), the Shepherd or Pastor, the Bishop or Overseer (1 Peter 2:25), the Deacon (Luke 22:27), the Teacher (Matt. 23:8), the Servant (Matt. 12:18).

Since Christianity is experienced through one's relationship to Jesus Christ as a person, He Himself becomes the authority for His own teaching. Actually, Jesus placed Himself in the position of priority over His teaching. When He met man face to face His first question was, "Who do you say that I am?" (Mark 8:29). In light of the centrality of Christ Himself in the Christian faith, it is no wonder that His followers were "called Christians" (Acts 11:26). The total life and teaching of Christ laid the foundation in which the church was erected.

The New Testament maintains that one's Christian profession is only Christian in proportion to its correct theological understanding of Jesus Christ as a person and the practical application of this understanding. If we remove the Christ of Scripture from the church we will be left with an empty shell or a house built on sand and not on the rock (Matt. 7:24-27).

THE ENDOWMENT OF THE HOLY SPIRIT

We have observed that all the hopes and purposes of the church are constituted in Jesus Christ, but at the same time it must also be pointed out that their realization is rooted and grounded in the Holy Spirit.

In Christ's own life the Holy Spirit played an intimate and continuous role. We recall His conception by the Holy Spirit (Matt. 1:18, 20); at His baptism the Holy Spirit descended as a dove upon Him (Matt. 3:16); "and Jesus, full of the Holy Spirit, returned from the Jordan and was led about by the Spirit in the wilderness" (Luke 4:1). Returning from the wilderness to Nazareth "He entered the synagogue on the Sabbath, and stood up to read." He read from the prophet Isaiah: "The Spirit of the Lord is upon Me" (Luke 4:16, 18). The cross became possible through "the eternal Spirit" (Heb. 9:14), and it was the Spirit "who raised Christ Jesus from the dead" (Rom. 8:11).

Concurring with the prediction of John the Baptist that Christ would baptize "with the Holy Spirit" (Matt. 3:11), Jesus promised that the Holy Spirit would come to the individual believer and the church at large (John 14:26; 15:26; Acts 1:5).

John the Baptist's call to repentance and baptism, the baptism of Christ with the Holy Spirit descending upon Him, as well as the baptism of Christ's followers by the Holy Spirit on the day of Pentecost, became eschatological signs of the renewal of the covenant relationship with the remnant. The manifestation of the Holy Spirit also became a sign that the power of the kingdom of God was present in the church.

The fifth book of the New Testament bears the name: The Acts of the Apostles, but it records the acts of the Holy Spirit in community. He directs the activities and endeavors of the church (Acts 6:3; 8:29; 10:19-20; 16:6-8). The sign, that the first gentile converts were as acceptable as Jewish converts and were likewise of the new Israel, was that their experience was identical to the Jewish experience on the Day of Pentecost: "the Holy Spirit fell upon all those who were listening to the message" (Acts 10:44-47; cf. 11:15-18). Furthermore, Peter did not require that these gentiles be circumcised and become proselytes. By the Spirit they were joined to the true Israel of God. By the Spirit we find that "wonders and signs were taking place" (Acts 2:43; cf. 4:30; 5:12; 8:13; 14:3), and "people who were sick or afflicted with unclean spirits . . . were all being healed" (Acts 5:16; cf. 8:6-8; 16:16-18).

From the inauguration of the church we learn that those who became the nucleus of the church "all with one mind were continually devoting themselves to prayer," and as a result "they were all filled with the Holy Spirit." This cause-and-effect relationship between the believers and God are as constitutive for ecclesiology as Christology. This should not surprise us for the Holy Spirit is Christ's representative fulfilling His words, with which Matthew closes his Gospel: "I am with you always, even to the end of the age" (Matt. 28:20).

The church is in a unique sense the community of the Holy Spirit. No one can make the confession that " 'Jesus is Lord,' except by the Holy Spirit" (1 Cor. 12:3). Those "who are being led by the Spirit of God, these are sons of God" (Rom. 8:14). Church membership meant "the fellowship of the Holy Spirit" (2 Cor. 13:14; Phil. 2:1).

The various gifts the Holy Spirit bestowed on the followers of Christ (1 Cor 12:4, 11, 28; Eph. 4:11) were not for private possession but for the building up of the church. The building up of the church does not take place as it does in secular society and political systems, with their propaganda and orchestration of opposing views and ideas. On the contrary, motivation and methodology are found in the principles of the kingdom of God actualized in unity and love through prayer and the power of the Holy Spirit.

The Holy Spirit is a gift which fulfilled the hope of the Old Israel (as spoken by the prophets; see Joel 2:27-29), but transcended Israel of old and became the hallmark of the New Israel, the Christian community (see Acts 2:16-21). There is no substitute. Any gift or any "church" activity, not directed and empowered by the Holy Spirit, will be merely human. While humanitarian acts may be produced sociologically, such activities will not transcend into the spiritual realities of reconciliation. Only the Holy Spirit can endow the individual and the church with a life and activities that result in the fruits of the Spirit.

New Testament ecclesiology can only be realized by a congregation filled with the Holy Spirit. Here is found the key to solve any church problem and the source for fulfilling its glorious mission. The endowment of the Holy Spirit given to the church at its inauguration included methodology and motivation as well as power for actualization, and is constitutive for the church at any time and place.

EKKLESIA DEFINED

The English word "church," as its equivalent *kirche* (German), and *kirke* (Danish), is derived from the Greek *kuriakon* meaning "belonging to the Lord." The French *eglise* and the Spanish *iglesia* stem from the Latin *ecclesia*, which in turn is a translation of the Greek *ekklesia*. The latter is the word for "church" in the Greek New Testament. It is composed of two words: the preposition *ek* meaning "out" and *kaleo* (the verb form of the word) "to call."

The word *ekklesia* reminds us that the church is made up of those who are "called out" (the remnant motif) from the world into fellowship with Christ to whom they belong (*kuriakon*). Before the Jewish Council in Jerusalem the Apostle James said: "God first concerned Himself about taking from among the Gentiles a people for His name" (Acts 15:14). The Apostle Peter writes that the Christian is one called "out of darkness into His marvelous light" (1 Peter 2:9).

In the New Testament we find three qualifying expressions regarding the *ekklesia*. It speaks of the church as "of God" (1 Cor. 11:16), telling us that God is its originator. Next, *ekklesia* is described as "of Christ" (Rom. 16:16) reminding us that the church has Christology as its foundation. Thirdly, we find the expression that the church is "of the saints" (1 Cor. 14:33), pointing out that it is made up of those who have experienced salvation (soteriology).

In classical Greek *ekklesia* was a secular expression used for an official gathering or assembly of citizens, as in the Acts of the Apostles (19:32, 39-41). However, it is in the Septuagint (the Greek translation of the Hebrew Old Testament) that we find the religious roots of *ekklesia* and another historical link between the Old and New Testaments. The Septuagint translates the Hebrew *gahal* (meaning assembly, congregation, gathering) with *ekklesia* (See 1 Kings 8:14, 22; 1 Chron. 13:2).

Since the *ekklesia* of the Septuagint has the connotation mentioned above, we find that *ekklesia* is also rendered "congregation" (see Acts 7:38; Heb. 2:12). Luther in his translation of the New Testament preferred the word "congregation" instead of "church."

The *ekklesia* is the gathering of those who belong to Christ; therefore, the English word "church" (*kuriakon* from *kuriakes*, "belonging to the Lord") is proper. However, the word *ekklesia* (from *ek*, "out from," and *kaleo*, "to call") has the added emphasis of being called out from "the world" in order to belong to Christ. Further, historically the word "church" has the connotation of the larger structured Christian community with its developed hierarchy and institutionalism, as in the Anglican Church and the Roman Catholic Church. At the other end of the spectrum we have congregationalism in which the church is defined as the local assembly of Christians. The usage of the word *ekklesia* in the New Testament will clarify this issue.

The first and original *ekklesia* mentioned is the one in Jerusalem (Acts 5:11; 8:1, 3). Next, we notice that the local assemblies are named the *ekklesia,* as for example "the church of the Thessalonians" (1 Thess. 1:1; 2 Thess. 1:1). Others are at Antioch, Rome, Cenchrea, Ephesus, Caesara, Corinth, Laodicea, etc. The assembly in a home is called *ekklesia* (Rom. 16:5). Within a specified territory *ekklesia* (in the singular and plural) denotes the total number of churches as in Judea, Samaria, Galilee, Galatia, etc. (Acts 9:31, 14:23; Gal. 1:2).

Finally, *ekklesia* means the church universal, inasmuch as Christ is the head of His body, the total church (Col. 1:18, 24; Eph. 1:22; 3:10, 21). Christ said: "Where two or three have gathered together in My name, there I am in their midst" (Matt. 18:20). This means that the total essence of Christ (My name) is present in the local *ekklesia*, and not separated from but representative of, the essence of the universal church, which is one with the local *ekklesia*, whether it be a house church, a city church, or a provincial church. The *ekklesia* is universal for it exists that it may be the salt, leaven, and light of the whole world.

STRUCTURAL METAPHORS

The New Testament is rich in concepts, images, analogies, and metaphors providing us with a better understanding of the nature of the *ekklesia* and the meaning of ecclesiology, just as the name of Christ is descriptive of Christology and soteriology.

The Apostle Peter presents a small sample of *ekklesia* metaphors when he writes: "But you are a chosen race, a royal priesthood, a holy nation, a people for God's own possession, that you may proclaim the excellencies of Him who called you out of darkness into His marvelous light; for you once were not a people, but now you are the people of God; you had not received mercy, but now you have received mercy" (1 Peter 2:9-10). Each of these titles has its antecedents in the *ekklesia* of the Old Testament (see Ex. 19:6; Deut. 4:20; 7:6; 10:15; 14:2).

One of the most beloved psalms of the Old Testament is The Shepherd Psalm, telling us that the one who has God as his shepherd "will dwell in the house of the Lord forever" (Ps. 23:6). The shepherd-sheep image typifies God's relationship to His people. In the Gospel of John we find Christ describing at length (chapter 10) the *ekklesia* as a shepherd-sheep relationship, and He frames His description within Christology, soteriology, and ecclesiology.

Christ compares Himself to a vine and His followers to the branches (John 15). As an ecclesiological metaphor its antecedent is also found in the Old Testament. Isaiah writes: "The vineyard of the Lord of hosts is the house of Israel" (See Isa. 5:1-7; Ps. 80:8-11; Hosea 14:7). The Apostle Paul also described Israel as an olive tree (Rom. 11:17-24; see also Jer. 11:16). These images—olive tree and vine—point up one essential characteristic of the true *ekklesia*. It has potential for fruitfulness only when it has its existence in Christ.

In the Bible, marriage is used as an analogy to express the relationship between God and His people, Christ and the *ekklesia* (Isa. 62:5; Eph. 5:25-33). A pure woman is used to illustrate the *ekklesia* and as such she is the bride of Christ (2 Cor. 11:2). The false or apostate church is depicted as "the mother of harlots" (Rev. 17:5). The marriage between Christ and His bride is used with a specific emphasis on eschatological preparedness. In this regard the parable of the ten virgins is pertinent (Matt. 25:1-13), and likewise the announcement of the marriage feast described in the closing chapters of the Bible. When the time for the inauguration of the everlasting kingdom came we are told "His bride has made herself ready" (Rev. 19:7).

Most of the images depicting the *ekklesia*, (we have referred only to a few; one exegete lists more than eighty[9]) as well as concepts explaining the essence of the *ekklesia*, advocate the idea that the church is not a corporation or institution, but a living, supernatural, divine organism existing in an individual and corporate relationship with Christ. This in turn means that the total life of the church with its functions and ministries (services) depend upon Him and are derived from Him as its head. Two major and distinct metaphors, the *ekklesia* as a temple and as the body of Christ, will be considered later.

THE CHURCH IS ONE

The unity or oneness within the local church and the universal church was constantly in the mind of Christ and the apostles. The oneness of the church has its source in the unity of the Godhead. From the constitutive relatedness of the Trinity grows a three-dimensional relationship like a triangle: God to man, man to man, and man to God. All three dimensions are necessary and form an inseparable unity. Within this relational triangle the church is designed to live and develop its mission of reconciliation.

In Christ's great intercessory prayer, offered just prior to His crucifixion, He asks that His followers "all be one; even as Thou, Father, art in Me, and I in Thee, that they also may be in Us; that the world may believe that Thou didst send Me" (John 17:21). It should be observed that Christ repeats His constitutional prayer for the church when He petitions, "that they may be one, just as We are one; I in them, and Thou in Me, that they may be perfected in unity, that the world may know that Thou didst send Me, and didst love them, even as Thou didst love Me" (John 17:22-23). Christ here points out that the visible expression of this perfect unity is the key witness of the church's redemptive role to the world. Being reconciled to God the church is to live in oneness before the world as a reconciling community inwardly and outwardly. The Apostle Paul writes: "God was in Christ reconciling the world to Himself, not counting their trespasses against them, and He has committed to us the word of reconciliation. Therefore, we are ambassadors for Christ, as though God were entreating through us; we beg you on behalf of Christ, be reconciled to God" (2 Cor. 5:19-20).

In connection with the shepherd-sheep analogy, Christ said to his audience: "And I have other sheep, which are not of this fold; I must bring them also, and they shall hear my voice; and they shall become one flock with one shepherd" (John 10:16).

Prior to its inauguration the nucleus of the church was "all with one mind" (Acts 1:14) and afterwards "those who believed were of one heart and soul" (Acts 4:32). Accordingly, Christ's prayer had been fulfilled, and Paul later could say of the believers, "You are all one in Christ Jesus" (Gal. 3:28).

The Apostle Paul's First Epistle to the Corinthians is, to a large degree, an appeal to the display of a unity that was both inward and outward. After his opening remarks he writes: "Now I exhort you, brethren, by the name of our Lord Jesus Christ, that you all agree, and there be no divisions among you, but you be made complete in the same mind and in the same judgment" (1 Cor. 1:10). The exhortation was caused by the emergence of a certain nasty spirit among the believers. Paul had been informed "that there are quarrels among you. Now I mean this, that each one of you is saying, 'I am of Paul,' and 'I of Apollos,' and 'I of Cephas' and 'I of Christ.' Has Christ been divided?" (1 Cor. 1:11-13). The Church in Corinth had lost the consciousness of its center of unity, which is Christ. The same has been repeated over and over again in the history of the church.

Paul always seeks to heal any division, whatever its nature may be, by Christocentric exhortations. Knowledge and faith, which unite the church, are "in Christ Jesus, who became to us wisdom from God, and righteousness and sanctification, and redemption" (1 Cor. 1:30). Further, it does "not rest on the wisdom of men, but on the power of God," neither is it a "wisdom of this age" but taught by the Word and the Spirit (1 Cor. 2:5-6).

In the first part of the Epistle to the Ephesians Paul deals with the blessings of redemption in a moving and Christ-centered way, climaxing with the words: "To Him be the glory in the church and in Christ Jesus to all generations forever and ever. Amen" (Eph. 3:21). In this Christological setting Paul expresses his appeal for unity. He writes: "Preserve the unity of the Spirit in the bond of peace. There is one body and one Spirit, just as also you were called in one hope of your calling; one Lord, one faith, one baptism, one God and Father of all who is over all and through all and in all" (Eph 4:3-6). This statement could rightfully be named the Pauline Magna Carta of church unity.

The Apostle Paul presents the organic Christ-centered unity of the church by the body metaphor. The church is defined as Christ's body with Him as its head (Col. 1:18, 22; Eph. 1:22; 5:23, 29), and as such He is the Lord of the church and by His Spirit directs all its activities; the church is completely dependent upon Him.

While Paul stressed that in the Christ-unity of the church no class distinction is found, but social equality, he at the same time tells us in two major passages (Rom. 12:4-8; 1 Cor. 12:12-31) that there are functional differences in the church, illustrated by the different functions of the members of the physical body. Every part is important and belongs to the body; if one part is lacking the body can't function properly. What seems "to us to be less admirable we have to allow the highest honour of function. . . . God has harmonized the whole body by giving importance of function to the parts which lack apparent importance, that the body should work together as a whole with all the members in sympathetic relationship with one another" (1 Cor. 12:23-25, PME).

Organic Christ-centered unity as a mark of the church will also be noticed when we deal with the catholicity and apostolicity of the church. But first we will turn to the church of the saints.

THE CHURCH IS HOLY

The church is comprised of "saints" (1 Cor. 1:2; 2 Cor. 1:1; Eph. 1:1; Phil. 1:1; Col. 1:2). "Saints" is translated from the same Greek word as "sanctify" and "holy," making them synonymous. Its biblical meaning is that of consecrated persons and things dedicated for divine worship or set apart for the gods (classical Greek), and for God (the biblical usage); the one who is set apart for God belongs to Him, and reflects His character. In view of this we find that at the time of the Protestant Reformation, discipline was implied in teaching and practices as a mark of the church. It was mentioned directly in some of the confessions.[10] A new life begins for the one God calls to Himself. We read again from the pen of Paul: ". . . those who have been chosen of God, holy and beloved, put on a heart of compassion, kindness" etc. (Col. 3:12). Here the topic of "being chosen" and "holy" is placed in the middle of ethical exhortations when those who are truly baptized "have put on the new self who is being renewed to a true knowledge according to the image of the One who created him." In this renewal "Christ is all, and in all" (Col. 3:10-11).

In the history of redemption, as recorded in the Bible and in church history, we find over and over again a prophetic message presented as a protest against a lack of ethical relevance in the life of the church. The church is holy because it lives under a new order, the Spiritual reign or kingdom of God. A "new man" is said to be "created in Christ Jesus for good works" (Eph. 2:10); therefore, "if any man is in Christ, he is a new creature; the old things passed away; behold, new things have come" (2 Cor. 5:17).

Growth of the Christian life is being "conformed to the image" of Jesus Christ (Rom. 8:29). To "have put on a new self" means "being renewed to a true knowledge according to the image of the One who created him" (Col. 3:10). In the covenant relationship with Christ the church will mirror the character of God; it will be holy, or the church of the saints.

THE CHURCH IS CATHOLIC

The word "catholicity" conveys the meaning of totality or universality and is practically equivalent to the word "ecumenical" (sometimes spelled oecumenical), which expresses the idea of "worldwide" or "the whole inhabited world."

In examining the word *ekklesia* in the New Testament we noticed that it was applied to the local church as well as to the universal church. The Fathers of the ancient church expressed the universality of the church by the word "catholic." However, the meaning of the word was enlarged to include the connotation of possessing the true Christian teaching. Accordingly, the medieval church claimed that catholicity could only apply to the Roman Catholic Church, as the universal custodian of Christian doctrine and tradition.

Historical Protestantism has always asserted its faithfulness in life and doctrine to the early ancient church. Its confessions claimed catholicity, inasmuch as they draw extensively from the ancient church Fathers and the early general councils. The Protestant Reformers of the sixteenth century asserted this catholicity. Jaroslav Pelikan writes that according to both Luther and Calvin "the church had been Christian and catholic before the papacy; therefore it could be both Christian and catholic without the papacy. In the name of such Christian catholicity they were willing to challenge Rome." He then adds: "Recent research on the Reformation entitles us . . . to say that the Reformation began because the reformers were too catholic in the midst of a church that had forgotten its catholicity."[11] Luther, in his invective against the Catholic Duke Henry of Brunswick, said: "I shall prove that we have remained with the true, ancient church, yea, that we are the true, ancient church. But you have fallen from us, that is, from the ancient church, and set up a new church in opposition to the old."[12]

The conflict between the Protestant Reformers and Rome grew out of the Reformers' claim and adherence to catholicity, so well expressed in the following statement: "Nothing so illustrates the tragic character of the Reformation as this: the Roman church excommunicated Luther for being too serious about his catholicism, while it retained within its fellowship the skeptics and the scoffers who did not bother to defy its authority."[13]

Pelikan here implies that the papal claim to universal supremacy was challenged on the basis of the church's catholicity. Indeed, both the Orthodox Churches and the Anglican Churches challenge papal supremacy on this point, observing further that God has given Peter to the church, not the church to Peter.

In his book, *Unitive Protestantism*, John T. McNeill emphasizes the noncatholicity of Roman Catholicism. He writes:

> The Reformation was a revolt, not against the principle of unity and catholicity, but against the privileged and oppressive monarchy of Rome—an uprising not merely of national, but of catholic feeling, against what had become a localized and over-centralized imperialism in Christianity, which made true catholicity impossible. . . . The parish was not a congregation, but an administrative unit. The governmental aspect of unity was not supported by an adequate religious bond. The Roman Church had substituted the idea of 'Roman obedience' for the earlier conception of catholicity expressed in a universal free communion. . . . In the Reformation the Christian people were taught to think, to believe, and to sing together, and given a new vision of the high and universal fellowship which is the church catholic.[14]

In view of the different perceptions of catholicity as perceived by Roman Catholics, Eastern Orthodox, and Protestants it is important to notice that the ancient church and the churches which grew out of the Reformation in the sixteenth century affirmed that catholicity, in order to be genuine, should be apostolic, that is, faithful to the teaching of the apostles and the practices of the New Testament church.

THE CHURCH IS APOSTOLIC

Apostolicity as a constitutive mark of the church is stated une-quivocally by the Apostle Paul when he writes that the church is "built upon the foundation of the apostles and prophets, Christ Jesus Himself being the corner stone" (Eph. 2:20). Christ as the corner stone is an obvious reference to Christ's own words: "The stone which the builders rejected, this became the chief corner stone" (Matt. 21:42; repeated by Peter in Acts 4:11, 1 Peter 2:7).

The new Jerusalem, the abode of the glorified church, has "twelve gates" representing the church of the Old Testament, and "twelve foun-dation stones" with "the names of the twelve apostles" (Rev. 21:12, 14). Apostolicity is faithfulness to the teaching of, and witness about, Jesus Christ as proclaimed by the apostles. Accordingly, Paul writes that in its truest sense "no man can lay a foundation other than the one which is laid, which is Jesus Christ" (1 Cor. 3:11).

In this connection it should be noted that the New Testament im-ages the church as a building, sanctuary, or temple of God. The con-text for Paul's statement of Christ as the corner stone is that of the church as a living temple composed of the people of God (Eph. 2:17-22).

The church as a temple is described as a living organism, similar to the analogy of the church as a body. Accordingly, Paul speaks of "the building up of the body of Christ;" and "the growth of the body for the building up of itself in love" (Eph. 4:12, 16). In similar fashion Peter uses the image of the temple: "You also, as living stones, are being built up as a spiritual house for a holy priesthood, to offer up spiritual sacrifices acceptable to God through Jesus Christ" (1 Peter 2:5). The church or the body of Christ in the collective sense, and even the body of the individual Christian in the individual sense is, like a temple, the dwelling place of the Holy Spirit (1 Cor. 3:16; 6:19).

The apostles were building up the church by the authority given to them by Christ and attested by the Holy Spirit. Paul speaks about "our authority, which the Lord gave for building you up" (2 Cor. 10:8); further, "it is in the sight of God that we have been speaking in Christ; and all for your upbuilding, beloved" (2 Cor. 12:19). In his closing remarks to the Corinthians he speaks about "the authority which the Lord gave me, for building up and not for tearing down" (2 Cor. 13:10).

The building of the universal church into one living temple was accomplished by the apostles' constant traveling and by writing, whereby they had opportunity to give counsel and nourish mutual assistance and oneness in life and doctrine. The apostolic churches had common practices (1 Cor. 11:16, 14:33); no single church was to act as if "the word of God" began or ended with them (1 Cor. 14:36); likewise, the churches were to live "according to the tradition" which they had received from the apostles (2 Thess. 3:6). The apostles were conscious of the fact that they had received by Jesus Christ the true knowledge of God's redemptive purposes as compared with Rabbinical teaching. They, therefore, spoke about Christianity as "belonging to the Way"; other statements read: "concerning the Way"; "I [Paul] persecuted this Way"; "according to the Way"; "exact knowledge about the Way." (Acts 9:2; 19:23; 22:4; 24:14, 22). Using the analogy of "the Way," the apostles no doubt also had in mind Christ, who calls Himself "the way, and the truth, and the life" (John 14:6).

The early ancient church recognized that the church, in order to be apostolic, must be based on the teaching of the apostles. In this recognition they followed the example of the first Christians, who "were continually devoting themselves to the apostles' teaching" (Acts 2:42). The Gospels and apostolic writings became the rule, or measuring rod, for life and doctrine. It is in the succession of apostolic proclamation, or the teaching of the Word, that apostolicity is preserved, not in a mechanical succession of bishops.

The Protestant Fathers, who revived the original meaning of apostolicity, emphasized the apostolic reality when they coined the phrase "the Bible alone." For the Protestant Reformers the Bible was an unregulated regulator. Any creed or confessional statement had to be submitted to the judgment of the Bible. According to authentic Protestantism and the *sola Scriptura* principle, the formulation of faith (dogma), as it developed, must be identical with the apostolic formulation revealed in Holy Scripture.

In the study of ecclesiology, "apostolicity" as a mark of the church has generally been considered either as apostolic succession of the bishops or as apostolic teaching as found in the New Testament (we have emphasized the latter). However, it should not be overlooked as has often been the case, historically and theologically, that "apostolicity" is the mark of the church in its missionary outreach. The apostles were the witnesses of the life and teaching of Christ to the non-Christian world. For the church to be apostolic it must be a missionary church.

THE GOSPEL RIGHTLY TAUGHT

Even though the Protestant Reformation has been viewed from the particulars of political, social, nationalistic, liberal, and economical forces at work, it was essentially religious in character. Within the sphere of religion the primary issue was religious certainty and authority and how to articulate the true meaning of Scripture.

In 1513 Luther began to lecture for more than two years on the book of Psalms. Important are his remarks on the subject of righteousness by faith in his comment on Psalms 31 and 71, where he stated his rediscovery of the gospel: "The righteous man shall live by faith" (Rom. 1:17). Psalm 31:1 reads, "In Thee, O Lord, I have taken refuge; let me never be ashamed; in Thy righteousness deliver me." (See also Ps. 71:1-2.) The text opened his eyes to consider faith as trust in God's righteousness and not his own works or his own righteousness.

In 1515, 1516, and 1517 Luther began to lecture on the Epistles to the Romans, Galatians, and Hebrews respectively. The key which opened the Bible for him was the centrality of Christ he had discovered in the Psalms. We refer to this as the Christ-alone principle. A principle is defined as (1) a source or cause from which a thing comes, (2) a settled rule, and a truth which is general and upon which others are founded. Thus defined "Christ alone" is a principle. Accordingly, the Apostle Paul writes about the "master plan of salvation for the church through Jesus Christ" (Eph. 3:21, LB), and that "we have redemption" according to God's "kind intention which He purposed" in Christ (Eph. 1:7, 9).

The Christ-alone principle can be compared to the central point of a circle. We may also say that Christ is the hub of the wheel. As from a star many rays radiate, so from the hub we have spokes: forgiveness, conversion, new birth, repentance, justification, sanctification, atonement, regeneration, adoption, resurrection, glorification, etc. Each is an attempt to describe what happens to the believer when, through "the Bible alone," he places by "grace alone" his "faith alone" in "Christ alone." The rim keeps them all together in Christ, who is the totality of the soteriological message. We may call this illustration the wheel of salvation.

We must remember that repentance and faith introduce an individual into a personal relationship with Christ, and in this relationship we have the theology of experience where two persons give themselves to one another; we by faith, Christ by grace.

The Lutheran Reformation of the sixteenth century grew out of Luther's personal experience with "Christ alone." The same can be said of John Wesley's "conversion experience" and its relationship to the Wesleyan revival and the founding of Methodism in England during the eighteenth century. On May 24, 1738, John Wesley, at that time thirty-five years of age, went to a small chapel in Aldersgate Street, London, where the Moravian brethren, who were followers of Zinzendorf and influenced by German Pietism, held worship. The speaker read Luther's preface to the Commentary on Romans. What followed can best be told in Wesley's own words: "About a quarter before nine, while he was describing the change which God works in the heart through faith in Christ, I felt my heart strangely warmed. I felt I did trust in Christ, Christ alone, for salvation: and an assurance was given me, that He had taken away my sins, even mine, and saved me from the law of sin and death."[15] Here we find expressed not only Wesley's kinship with Luther and Paul, but with all believing souls in every age.

When the Protestant confessions or creeds defined the "one holy church" as "the congregation of saints in which the gospel is rightly taught" (Augsburg Confession, Art. vii), it was understood that correct teaching and preaching adhered to the four principles: "the Bible alone," "Christ alone," "grace alone," and "faith alone." These four concepts served as theological principles. "The Bible alone" is the framework within which the church moves; it is the primary source from which the church forms its concepts and makes its decisions. Within that framework is another principle that is a settled rule, a source, a truth on which all others are founded: "Christ alone." Within "Christ alone" we find two other principles: one from Christ to man "by grace alone" and one from man to Christ "by faith alone." Thus the uniqueness, necessity, and all-sufficiency of Christ became predominant in each mark of the church.

THE SACRAMENTS RIGHTLY ADMINISTERED

The medieval church developed an elaborate sacramental system composed of seven sacraments: Baptism, Confirmation, the Eucharist, Penance, Extreme Unction, Order, and Matrimony. The Protestant Reformers opposed the Roman Catholic sacramental system, which they believed brought the faithful into bondage to the priestly hierarchy. They asserted that, tried by Scripture, there are only two sacraments: Baptism and the Lord's Supper. They also criticized the denial of the cup to the laity.

For the purpose of the present study we do not need to go into the theological niceties of the sacraments, but only wish to point out that one's concept of the sacraments has a direct bearing on ecclesiology, especially the concepts of the Christian ministry and ordination as it later will be noticed.

2 THE PRIESTHOOD OF BELIEVERS

Jesus Christ . . . made us to be a kingdom, priests to His God and Father; to Him be the glory and the dominion forever and ever. Amen. —Apostle John

We are all priests, as many of us are Christians. We are all consecrated priests through baptism.
—Martin Luther

The New Testament never uses the term "priesthood" or "priest" (hiereus) to designate the ordained ministry or the ordained minister. In the New Testament, the term is reserved, on the one hand, for the unique priesthood of Jesus Christ and, on the other hand, for the royal and prophetic priesthood of all baptized. The priesthood of Christ and the priesthood of the baptized have in their respective ways the function of sacrifice and intercession. As Christ has offered himself, Christians offer their whole being "as a living sacrifice". As Christ intercedes before the Father, Christians intercede for the Church and the salvation of the world. Nevertheless, the differences between these two kinds of priesthood cannot be overlooked. While Christ offered himself as a unique sacrifice once and for all for the salvation of the world, believers need to receive continually as a gift of God that which Christ has done for them.
—World Council of Churches on Ministry

As an introduction three preliminary observations of basic significance for our topic will be made. 1) In the nations of the ancient world, including Israel, priests formed a distinct class, but such is not the case in the church of the New Testament. Here the word "priest" is never used to designate an official position or order of ministry, but 2) the titles "priest" and "high priest" are only applied to Jesus Christ. 3) Further, the New Testament tells us, unambiguously, that the members of the church are "a holy priesthood," "a royal priesthood, a holy nation, a people for God's own possession," and Jesus Christ "has made us to be a kingdom, priests to His God and Father" (1 Peter 2:5,9; Rev. 1:6; 5:10). The beginnings of our subject are found in the Old Testament.

ISRAEL A KINGDOM OF PRIESTS

The Covenant and Priesthood. Three months after the Israelites left Egypt Moses reminded them that God had brought them out of bondage and entered into a covenant relationship with them. He then asked Moses to tell the people: "Now then, if you will indeed obey My voice and keep My covenant, then you shall be My own possession among all the peoples, for all the earth is Mine; and you shall be to Me a kingdom of priests and a holy nation" (Ex. 19:5-6; Deut. 4:20; 14:2). The concept of the priesthood of the people was part of the covenant at Sinai. The people responded to God's invitation. "All that the Lord has spoken we will do!" (Ex. 19:8).

Next follows the issuance of the Ten Commandments and detailed instruction about the tabernacle, its services, and redemptive purpose. In other words, God's ethical standards and the pattern for all aspects of their worship were presented to the people. What we have referred to as the covenant of life and the covenant of grace and redemption was thus expressed. The renewal of the everlasting covenant became the framework for the people becoming "a kingdom of priests and a holy nation." Israel did not consider itself a mere state; it was a theocracy, a commonwealth under God and a creation of the everlasting covenant.

The Sanctuary and its Priests. The sanctuary with its worship and sacrificial system was the center for the life of the covenant community and the vehicle by which they expressed their covenant faith. The sanctuary made the plan of redemption and the possibility of worshiping God tangible. The gospel, the good news in Jesus Christ, can be fully understood only when it is seen in the light of the Old Testament sanctuary and the Epistle to the Hebrews, which in the New Testament deals with Christ's high priestly work in the heavenly sanctuary, after which the earthly is patterned.

Also, at the time of Moses and in connection with the establishment of the covenant, the official priesthood was instituted. Aaron was the first high priest and from then on the priests were all of the family of Aaron. They were responsible for the worship and sacrifices, first in the tabernacle and later in the temple. The family of Aaron belonged to the tribe of Levi; those of the tribe who were not of the family of Aaron assisted the priests and were responsible for maintenance of the temple complex. They were called Levites.

The Epistle to the Hebrews defines the work of the high priest as an obligation "to offer sacrifices for sin" (Heb. 5:3). The very definition of priesthood presupposes the sinfulness of man and leads us, in turn, to the significance of the covenant of life and redemption as expressed in the *Evangelical Dictionary of Theology:*

> Law and priesthood are simultaneous in origin and inseparable in operation (Heb. 7:11 ff.). The reason for this is that the Israelites, like the rest of mankind, were sinners and therefore when confronted with the law, which is God's standard of righteousness, lawbreakers. Certainly the God-given law is holy and just and good and spiritual (Rom. 7:12, 14) and as such marks out the way of life: by faithfully keeping its precepts a man shall live (Lev. 18:5; Neh. 9:29; Matt. 19:16-17; Rom. 10:5; Gal. 3:12). But man's radical problem is that he is a sinner. The Law shows him up for what he is, a lawbreaker, and "the wages of sin is death" (Rom. 6:23; cf. Ezek. 18:4, 20; Gen. 2:17). Consequently Paul writes, "The very commandment which promised life proved to be death to me" (Rom. 7:10)—not that there is anything wrong with the law; the fault is in man who breaks the law (Rom. 7:13). Hence the necessity for the formulation of the law to be accompanied by the institution of a priesthood to mediate redemptively between God and the sinner who has broken his law, and who needs to be restored from death to life.[1]

Because of the mediatory and representative nature of the Aaronic priesthood, it has correctly been pointed out that "in Israel, the priesthood was not a vocation but an office."[2] The vocation of the priesthood, on the other hand, the call to minister reconciliation, intercession and sanctity to others, was expected by each member of Israel, beginning with the parents at home, but extended to the local community and the total family of nations.

A Priesthood for all Nations. God had intended that through the covenant with Israel as a "kingdom of priests" (Ex. 19:5-8) the covenant blessings would reach all nations; that is, blessings that result from being reconciled to God through the covenant of redemption and by obedience to the divine constitutional principles of life (the covenant of life). Referring to "strangers" and "foreigners," the prophet

Isaiah says to Israel: "You will be called the priests of the Lord; You will be spoken of as ministers of our God" (Is. 61:6). However, Israel failed, not in building a sanctuary, neither in performing the worship and rituals connected with it, but in becoming a priesthood at large.

The people did not remain in covenant relationship with God and thus forfeited the calling to mediate the covenant blessings to the nations at large. The petition of the Lord's Prayer, "Thy kingdom come, Thy will be done, on earth as it is in heaven" (Matt. 6:10), expressed an intercessory ministry which Israel had been asked to fulfill (Isa. 59; 62; Ez. 20:30-32; etc.) but failed to do. Indeed, the maladies they experienced were the result of not performing this task; however, God constantly sought to call them back to their ministry (Isa. 52; 59; 62; Dan. 9:2-9; etc.). Finally, the promises and hopes for Israel were then proclaimed as fulfilled in Christ and through Him to a new Israel who would become a royal and holy priesthood (see Isa. 42:1-4; 53; 55:3-5; 56:3-8; 61).

CHRIST THE TRUE HIGH PRIEST

The End of the Earthly Sanctuary. The moment Christ died on the cross "the veil of the temple was torn in two from top to bottom, and the earth shook" (Matt. 27:51). At that moment the priesthood of Aaron came to an end and the perfect priesthood conceived in the one person Jesus Christ began as predicted: "The Lord has sworn and will not change His mind, 'Thou art a priest forever according to the order of Melchizedek' " (Ps. 110:4).

Christ's priesthood is compared to that of Melchizedek, whom Abraham met after he had entered into a covenant relationship with God (Gen. 14:18-20); it is forever (Heb. 7).

Christ's High Priestly Ministry. As a high priest Christ presented His own blood "within the veil," in the heavenly sanctuary made atonement, and "obtained eternal redemption" (Heb. 6:20; 8:3; 9:7, 12, 24). By dying on the cross Christ "offered one sacrifice for sins for all time"—"once for all." Further, "for by one offering He has perfected for all time those who are sanctified" (Heb. 10:12, 14; 7:27).

Christ The High Priestly Mediator. Compared with the earthly sanctuary Christ "obtained a more excellent ministry, by as much as He is also the mediator of a better covenant" (Heb. 8:6). Christ is also said to be "the mediator of a new covenant" (Heb. 9:15), and "has become the guarantee of a better covenant" (Heb. 7:22). This was a fulfillment of the prophetic word of the Old Testament: "For this is the covenant that I will make with the house of Israel. After those days, says the Lord: I will put My laws into their minds, and I will write them upon their hearts. And I will be their God, and they shall be My people. And they shall not teach everyone his fellow citizen, and everyone his brother, saying, 'Know the Lord,' for all shall know Me, from the least to the greatest of them. 'For I will be merciful to their iniquities, and I will remember their sins no more'" (Heb. 8:10-12; Jer. 31:31-34). The total witness of the New Testament is that the ascended and glorified Christ is the only mediator between God and man. The title "mediator" is a technical, legal expression, "designating an arbitrator or guarantor."[3] Paul writes: "For there is one God, and one mediator also between God and men, the man Christ Jesus, who gave Himself as a ransom for all" (1 Tim. 2:5-6).

Christ said: "I am the way, and the truth, and the life; no one comes to the Father, but through Me" (John 14:6). The author of the Epistle to the Hebrews accordingly encourages believers with the words: "Let us therefore draw near with confidence to the throne of grace, that we may receive mercy" (Heb. 4:16).

Having in great detail dealt with the topic, "Jesus the High Priest," Oscar Cullmann writes that "the High Priest concept describes most fully and adequately the New Testament understanding of Jesus." Referring to the Epistle to the Hebrews he says that "it is clearly the central theme of a canonical writing of the New Testament."[4]

In his *Institutes of the Christian Religion* Calvin writes: "Christ is the only Pontiff and Priest of the New Testament: to him all priestly offices were transferred, and in him they closed and terminated" (IV.xviii.14).

The Son of Man and the Priesthood of Believers. While Christ fulfilled and perfected the Aaronic priestly ministry, He never made any direct reference to Himself as priest and neither sought the prerogatives of the priesthood. According to the narrative of the four Gospels "the only title Jesus applied to himself" was that of the Son of Man. Further, (from the pen of Oscar Cullmann) the titles "Son of Man" and "Second Adam" are "internally united and always belong essentially together."[5]

Being in full harmony with the will of God (covenant of life) Christ became the perfect image of God. As the True Man or the Second Adam He fulfilled the covenant concept of Exodus 19:6 and exemplified how, in a fallen world, those who have entered into covenant relationship with God will be a "holy nation" and "kingdom of priests" in a reconciling ministry.

At the age of twelve Christ told His parents: "Did you not know that I must be busy with my Father's affairs" (Luke 2:49, JB). Christ's whole life was dedicated to the kingdom of God as He Himself taught: "But seek first His kingdom and His righteousness," and then the things of this world "shall be added" (Matt. 6:33). The kingdom of God is not a territory, but the rule of God. Christ proclaimed and exemplified "the gospel of the kingdom" (Matt. 4:23; 9:35); that is, the good news about the redemptive covenant relationship with God. Christ also said, "My kingdom is not of this world" (John 18:36).

The contrast between the ministry of the official priesthood and that of Christ has succinctly been expressed by Professor A. Glasser of Fuller Theological Seminary:

> In his ministry Jesus sought none of the prerogatives of the priests "who alone could offer sacrifices." He neither demonstrated nor authorized formal priestly mediation. In his actual contact with people, however, he maintained the heart of the priestly concept—approaching God on behalf of others—and by precept and example exalting the idea of a ministering priesthood. He demonstrated that kingdom ministry meant personal interest in others, expressed by intercessory prayer and spontaneous thanksgiving. He prayed that Peter's faith might not fail (Luke 22:31, 32). He prayed for his disciples on the night of his crucifixion (22:40). He prayed for his crucifiers while he hung on the cross (23:34). By his example and teaching official religious status was succeeded by a personal interest and concern for one's fellow man. In the example of Jesus the priestly function was person-motivated and person-centered.[6]

When Christ was baptized by John the Baptist He identified Himself with the covenant-remnant-eschaton motif (which we observed in Part One). At His baptism Christ received the power of the Holy Spirit. Next followed the temptation in the wilderness, in which Christ remained obedient in His covenant relationship with God. To the tempter He said: "You shall worship the Lord your God, and serve Him only" (Matt. 4:10).

After the temptation Christ entered His public ministry. He came to His home town, Nazareth. He entered the synagogue on the Sabbath and was asked to read from the Scriptures and to speak. Christ read from Isaiah 61:1-2, according to Luke: "The Spirit of the Lord is upon Me, because He anointed me to preach the gospel to the poor. He has sent Me to proclaim release to the captives, and recovery of sight to the blind, to set free those who are downtrodden, to proclaim the favorable year of the Lord." Christ then said: " 'Today this Scripture has been fulfilled in your hearing.' And all were speaking well of Him, and wondering at the gracious words which were falling from His lips" (Luke 4:18-22).

It is most significant that at the beginning of His ministry Christ identified Himself with Isaiah chapter 61, where the result of proclaiming the "good news" (Isa. 61:1)—or gospel (Luke 4:18)—would result in a new people who would "be called the priests of the Lord" and "be spoken of as ministers of our Lord" (Isa. 61:6). Accordingly, Peter could speak about "a chosen race, a royal priesthood, a holy nation, a people for God's own possession" (1 Peter 2:9).

In a study of 1 Peter 2:4-10 (*The Elect and the Holy*) Professor John Hall Elliott makes the following summary observation:

> The formation, election, and sanctification of this community is an eschatological salvific event. This act of salvation and "recreation," according to I P [1 Peter], involves the consummation of all that God had planned for His Israel. The focal point of this event is Jesus Christ. People become participants in the event of salvation and rebirth in that they hear His word and confess Him to be the *kurios* [Lord]. They who believe in Jesus as the Elect and Precious One of God are gathered together as the Elect and Precious People. Through Jesus Christ, i.e. on the basis of His life and death as the spotless Lamb, those who come to Him in faith are made holy. They become the possession of His Spirit. This Spirit transfigures the *basileian* [kingdom] and the *hierateuma* [priesthood] of the Old Dispensation into a House (hold) in which He resides, into a Body of Priests which He sanctifies.[7]

THE COMMUNITY OF BELIEVERS A ROYAL PRIESTHOOD

A Spiritual Temple of Believers. The immediate effect of Christ's high priestly office makes it possible for the individual believer to have direct access to the throne of grace (Heb. 10:19-22). Collectively, the believers, when filled with the Holy Spirit, become the temple of God. Through Christ we have "access in one Spirit to the Father. So then you are no longer strangers and aliens, but you are fellow citizens with the saints, and are of God's household, having been built upon the foundation of the apostles and prophets, Christ Jesus Himself being the corner stone, in whom the whole building, being fitted together is growing into a holy temple in the Lord; in whom you also are being built together into a dwelling of God in the Spirit" (Eph. 2:18-22).

The Christian as a "priest" brings his whole life as a sacrifice to God. Paul writes: "I urge you therefore, brethren, by the mercies of God, to present your bodies a living and holy sacrifice, acceptable to God, which is your spiritual service of worship. And do not be conformed to this world, but be transformed by the renewing of your mind, that you may prove what the will of God is, that which is good and acceptable and perfect" (Rom. 12:1-2). After this statement Paul enumerates the spiritual gifts given to the members of the church as the body of Christ (see also 1 Cor. 12). Further from the pen of Paul: "For we are the temple of the living God; just as God said, 'I will dwell in them and walk among them; and I will be their God, and they shall be My people. Therefore, come out from their midst and be separate,' says the Lord. 'And do not touch what is unclean; and I will welcome you. And I will be a father to you, and you shall be sons and daughters to Me,' says the Lord Almighty" (2 Cor. 6:16-18).

Priest, sacrifice, and temple are all entities in the spiritual experience of the priesthood of believers as the Apostle Peter tells us: "And coming to Him as to a living stone, rejected by men, but choice and precious in the sight of God, you also, as living stones, are being built up as a spiritual house for a holy priesthood, to offer up spiritual sacrifices acceptable to God through Jesus Christ. . . . You are a chosen race, a royal priesthood, a holy nation, a people for God's own possession, that you may proclaim the excellencies of Him who has called you out of darkness into His marvelous light" (1 Peter 2:4-5, 9).

The Ministry of Reconciliation. The practical effect of Christ's high priestly office upon ecclesiology is twofold: The church has no need of a priestly mediatory order (for example, with supernatural authority and power to change the bread and wine of the Lord's Supper into a sacrifice), for all believers are priests by the fact that they are one with Christ in a holy and royal priesthood of reconciliation.

The Apostle Paul writes: "Now all these things are from God, who reconciled us to Himself through Christ, and gave us the ministry of reconciliation, namely, that God was in Christ reconciling the world to Himself, not counting their trespasses against them, and He has committed to us the word of reconciliation. Therefore, we are ambassadors for Christ, as though God were entreating through us; we beg you on behalf of Christ, be reconciled to God" (2 Cor. 5:18-20).

Christ's last command to His followers was, "Go into all the world and preach the gospel to all creation" (Mark 16:15; Matt. 28:18-20; Acts 1:8). After Christ's ascension the priesthood of believers "went out and preached everywhere" (Mark 16:20; Acts 2); they entered into the work of priestly intercession. Paul writes: "First of all, then, I urge that entreaties and prayers, petitions and thanksgivings, be made on behalf of all men, for kings and all who are in authority, in order that we may lead a tranquil and quiet life in all godliness and dignity. This is good and acceptable in the sight of God our Savior, who desires all men to be saved and to come to the knowledge of truth" (1 Tim. 2:1-4). The followers of Christ were empowered to fulfill the words of Christ: "You are the light of the world" (Matt. 5:14).

When the Apostle Peter speaks about the believers as "a royal priesthood" the reason is given, "that you may proclaim the excellencies of Him who has called you out of darkness into His marvelous light" (1 Peter 2:9). That all believers take part in sharing with others the "marvelous light" of the gospel is no doubt reflected in the numerous terms in the New Testament for the activity of witnessing; for example, announce, admonish, confess, explain, proclaim, teach, preach, etc. Christ has provided once and for all, the sacrifice; so the believer does not bring an external sacrifice but a sacrifice of praise and thanks: "Through Him then, let us continually offer up a sacrifice of praise to God, that is, the fruit of lips that give thanks to His name. And do not neglect doing good and sharing; for with such sacrifices God is pleased" (Heb. 13:15-16). Thus the believers share in the universal priesthood of the Savior Jesus Christ.

Through baptism and the endowment of the Holy Spirit the believers have entered into covenant relationship with Jesus Christ, and the essential characteristics of the nature of the fellowship of believers, the church, (as dealt with in Part One) have become living realities in their lives. Their lives are changed into the image of Christ, and they endeavor to minister as He ministered on earth.

We have previously defined the church—the *ekklesia*—as those

who have been "called out" and "belong to the Lord." Eduard
Schweizer, in his discussion of the priesthood of believers, refers to
the meaning of "church" as "the act of gathering together. . . . That
means, however, that 'church' is not originally an abstract theological
term, but one that denotes an actual happening. . . . The Church is
spoken of as something that really 'takes place.' "[8]

At the First Assembly of the World Council of Churches in
Amsterdam, in 1948, Karl Barth gave a lecture with the title, "The
Church—The Living Congregation of the Living Lord Jesus Christ."
In it he refers to the church as a "congregation," and defines this latter as "event"; another way of saying that in the fellowship of believers
something "takes place." To this could be added that what "takes
place," or "the event," makes the congregation or the fellowship into
a priesthood of believers.

We will enumerate some of the aspects which Barth emphasizes
in defining the "congregation" as "the event."

> 1) The congregation is the *event* which consists in gathering
> together (congregatio) those men and women (fidelium) whom
> the living Lord Jesus Christ chooses and calls to be witnesses
> to the victory He has already won, and heralds of its future
> universal manifestation.

> 2) The congregation is that *event* in which the absolute
> sovereignty of Jesus Christ . . . finds its proper answer and
> response in the perfect freedom of obedience of those who
> have been called, called out, and called together by Him, and
> summoned to gratitude and to service.

> 3) The congregation is that *event* in which these men . . .
> unite together over against the world; yet only in order that
> they may identify themselves with the need and the hope of
> the world.

> 4) The congregation is the *event* in which the witness of
> apostles and prophets to Jesus Christ, deposited in Scripture,
> as such, becomes present, effective and fruitful.

> 5) The congregation is the *event* in which the communion
> of the Holy Ghost also establishes, with divine power, a

human fellowship.

6) The congregation is the *event* in which the Sacraments are powerful as the one reality by which men live: Baptism, which incorporates human beings into this special relation to Jesus Christ, and the Lord's Supper, which keeps them in this state of grace, that is, of "belonging to Him", and enables them to fulfill their mission to others.

7) The congregation is the *event* in which the divine mission of Jesus Christ is represented and attested.

8) The Renewal of the Church: The life of the Church is preserved, and saved in one way alone: by the renewal of her life as an "*event*", and thus by the renewal of her "gathering" as a congregation. A church that is not thus engaged in a reformation corresponding to the way in which she was originally "formed", has already fallen into the abyss of non-existence, or, in other words, she has fallen into the hopeless condition of a nominal church, or an empty ecclesiastical shell.[9]

That something really "takes place" and makes "the event" in the fellowship of believers was expressed by Christ Himself when He said: "I say to you, that if two of you agree on earth about anything that they may ask, it shall be done for them by My Father who is in heaven. For where two or three have gathered together in My name, there I am in their midst" (Matt. 18:19-20). When and where Christ is present by the Holy Spirit "things take place" and "events" happen, as when He personally was present on earth. At the close of His earthly ministry of intercession and reconciliation He could say to the Father: "I glorified Thee on the earth, having accomplished the work which Thou hast given Me to do" (John 17:4). Christ radiated the character of God, thus man beheld the glory of God (John 1:14). Further, Christ came to sanctify the fellowship of the believers "that He might present to Himself the church in all her glory" (Eph. 5:26-27).

Testimony of the Early Church. In the second century we find church leaders re-echoing the New Testament belief in the royal priesthood of the believers. The apologist Justin Martyr (d.c. A.D. 165) wrote: "... being inflamed by the word of his [Christ's] calling, we are the true highpriestly race of God." Another apologist, Aristides, wrote (about A.D. 146), "that all Christians could trace their genealogy from the High Priest Jesus Christ." Irenaeus (d.c. A.D. 200) expressed himself in these words: "All who are justified through Christ have the sacerdotal order." Tertullian (d.c. A.D. 220) asked the question with the answer implied: "Are not even we laics priests? It is written in Revelation 1:6: 'A kingdom also and priests to his God and Father, hath he made us.' "[10] It should be observed that the four church leaders wrote respectively from Rome, Athens, Gaul, and Carthage.

The ecclesiology of the early church in all its aspects, including organization and administration, enhanced the doctrine of the priesthood of believers. As we will observe later, oneness and equality within functional difference was realized, all for the sake of the ministry of reconciliation.

Baptism: the Ordination to Priesthood. For all believers baptism is the mode of entry into the priesthood. They are "ordained priests" by their baptism; they enter into the new covenant relationship with Christ. Tertullian wrote that in baptism the believers "are thoroughly anointed with a blessed unction" just as in the old dispensation priests "on entering the priesthood" were "anointed with oil from a horn."[11] In the early part of the sixth century, similar picture is given by St. Laurentius: "From that day and that hour in which thou camest out of the font thou art become to thyself a continual fountain, a daily remission. Thou hast no need of a doctor, or of a priest's right hand. As soon as thou descendedst from the sacred font thou wast clothed in a white robe and anointed with the mystic ointment; the invocation was made over thee, and the threefold name came upon thee, which fills the new vessel (that thou wert) with this new doctrine."[12]

At the time of the Protestant Reformation Luther expressed the same concept. He asserts that "we are all consecrated priests through baptism" and "we are all priests, as many of us as are Christians."[13] "It is enough that you are consecrated and anointed with the sublime and holy chrism of God, with the word of God, with baptism, . . . then you are anointed highly and gloriously enough and sufficiently vested with priestly garments." Therefore, "the Holy Spirit in the New Testament diligently prevented the name *sacerdos,* priest or cleric, from being given to any apostle or to various other offices, but it is solely the name of the baptized or of Christians as a hereditary name with which one is born through baptism."[14] Accordingly, Luther asserts: "All Christians are truly of the spiritual estate."[15]

Anointment to the Priesthood. At baptism the believer is anointed by the Holy Spirit as the priests and kings in Old Testament times were anointed with oil. At the baptism of Christ the Spirit of God descended upon Him (Matt. 3:16). Peter on the day of Pentecost said: "Repent, and let each of you be baptized in the name of Jesus Christ for the forgiveness of your sins; and you shall receive the gift of the Holy Spirit" (Acts 2:38).

Just before the ascension Christ promised, "You shall be baptized with the Holy Spirit" (Acts 1:5). Over and over again we read in the Acts of the Apostles (which could be named the Acts of the Holy Spirit) that "they were all filled with the Holy Spirit" (Acts 2:4; 4:8, 31; 6:5; 7:55; 8:19; 9:17; 11:16, 24; 13:9; 15:8). In this connection it should be noted that almost always when being filled with the Holy Spirit is mentioned, in the same verse or the next verse mention is made of witnessing. This in accordance with Christ's own words recorded in the prologue of the Acts of the Apostles: "You shall receive power when the Holy Spirit has come upon you; and you shall be My witnesses both in Jerusalem, and in all Judea and Samaria, and even to the remotest part of the earth" (Acts 1:8).

By baptism and the anointment by the Holy Spirit the believers became "living stones" in the temple and "a spiritual house for a holy priesthood" (1 Peter 2:4-5). Therefore, the Holy Spirit in the New Testament, far from being given exclusively to any apostle or office-holder in the church, was given to all baptized believers, making their baptism an "ordination" to the priesthood of believers. Accordingly, the Apostle Paul could write to the believers that they were "in the Spirit, if indeed the Spirit of God dwells in you. But if anyone does not have the Spirit of Christ, he does not belong to Him" (Rom. 8:9). He admonishes them by saying: "Walk by the Spirit, and you will not carry out the desire of the flesh" and encourages them to have a life demonstrating "the fruit of the Spirit" (Gal. 5:16, 22). He also identifies the believers as those "who are spiritual" (Gal. 6:1). "Now we have received, not the spirit of the world, but the Spirit who is from God, that we might know the things freely given to us by God, which things we also speak, not in words taught by human wisdom, but in those taught by the Spirit, combining spiritual thoughts with spiritual words" (1 Cor. 2:12-13).

George Huntston Williams makes the following summary statements about the ancient church from A.D. 30 to 313: "To sum up, the laic in the ancient Church had an indelible 'ordination' as priest, prophet and king, no longer in bondage to the world, but freed through Christ to know the truth in the illumination of the Spirit, to exercise sovereignty over the inner temple of self, to join in the corporate thanksgiving of the redeemed, and to forgive the brethren in Christ's name."[16]

LAITY AND CLERGY

In analyzing the concept of the priesthood of believers further it will be profitable to notice the history and usage of the two words "laity" and "clergy."

The Laos of God. The terms "laity" and "laymen" are generally used of the body of believers in contrast to, or to distinguish them from, the clergy—the official, professional, career ministers of the church. However, this distinction is not present in the New Testament. While the New Testament speaks about the priesthood of believers, it has been noted that it never uses the word "priest" to designate a public or official position in the church.

In the New Testament church members are also designated as the *laos* of God. Our term "laity" is derived from the Greek word *laos*, "people." We have observed that in the Old Testament Israel was chosen to be "a kingdom of priests" to the nations of the world (see Ex. 19:4-6), hence the importance of intercession as noted earlier. Israel failed in their individual and collective role as priests to the gentiles, but the people (*laos*) of the New Testament became the new "royal priesthood" (1 Peter 2:9) and constituted, collectively, a priestly kingdom (Rev. 1:6). Regarding the *laos* of God we read: "God first concerned Himself about taking from among the Gentiles a people for His name"; "I will call those who were not My people, 'My people'"; "I will be their God, and they shall be My people"; Christ "gave Himself for us, that He might redeem us from every lawless deed and purify for Himself a people for His own possession"; "you are a chosen race, a royal priesthood, a holy nation, a people for God's own possession" (Acts 15:14; Rom. 9:25; 2 Cor. 6:16; Titus 2:14; 1 Peter 2:9).

The Clergy of God. Our English word "clergy" comes from the Greek *kleros*, with the meaning of "inheritance," "possession," "portion," or "lot" (see Mark 15:24; Acts 1:17, 26; 8:21; 26:18; Col. 1:12).

In the Old Testament the people of God are called "His own possession" or "inheritance" (Deut. 4:20-21). Likewise, in the New Testament the church as the body of Christ is God's *kleros*. The technical
use of the word *kleros*, or clergy, as we know it from the Middle Ages,
first began in the third century.

Already in the middle of the third century we find the appointed
and representative ministry of the New Testament changed, so it was
compared to the Aaronic priesthood. Cyprian, bishop of Carthage,
writes about the Lord's Supper as a sacrifice in the hands of bishops:
"The Lord's passion is the sacrifice which we offer." He likewise emphasizes episcopal apostolicity and finds the church fulfilled in the
bishop: "Whence you ought to know that the bishop is in the Church,
and the Church in the bishop."[17]

The sharp change which took place in the third century regarding the priesthood of believers has been pinpointed in these words:
"It is evident, however, that though the ancient doctrine of the
priesthood of all believers might still occasionally be remembered,
it had purely theoretical value. In practical Christian life the clergy,
by the middle of the third century, were a distinct, close-knit spiritual
rank, on whom the laity were religiously dependent."[18]

VOCATION AND CALLING

In the New Testament the words for "vocation" and "calling"
are from the same Greek term, *klesis*. Thus, the Pauline exhortation:
"Work worthy of the vocation" has also been translated: "Walk worthy of the calling" (Eph. 4:1 in KJV, NASB, JB).

In the Middle Ages only the clergy had a vocation or calling (from
the Latin *voco*, calling), but the laity had no divine calling. Before
the Protestant Reformation, the clergy, in the main, were the professionals both in the church and in the state. Herein lies the background
for using the word vocation for "professionals," and a sociological
distinction was made. However, such was not the case in the early
church.

Vocation in the Early Ancient Church. We are so used to identifying Christianity with church buildings and beautiful cathedrals that
we forget that it was only toward the close of the second century that
simple church buildings began to be erected, and then only in large
cities. To be objective in our evaluation of the apostolic and post-
apostolic period in the second century, we must exclude many of the

later professional associations with the word "priest" and "bishop." Those appointed to serve the church were chosen by the people and were themselves "lay people."

Cyprian, who became bishop of Carthage (A.D. 248-58), did much to depreciate the concept of the priesthood of believers and enhance the power of the bishop. In spite of his great influence we must not forget that "He was simply the chief pastor of the Christian congregation at Carthage and of its outlying mission districts. He had no diocese and never exercised diocesan rule. He had no cathedral, not even a church. His congregation met in the audience hall of a wealthy Carthaginian burgher."[19]

In order to have a realistic historical picture of the early church a lengthy quotation from Thomas M. Lindsay will suffice:

> The office-bearers of the early Church were clergy in virtue of their call, election, and setting apart by special prayer for sacred office; but they worked at trades, carried on mercantile pursuits, and were not separate from the laity in their every-day life. We find bishops who were shepherds, weavers, lawyers, shipbuilders, and so on, and the elders and deacons were almost invariably men who were not supported by the churches to which they belonged. . . . The power of the laity in the early Church did not depend simply on the fact that they chose the office-bearers and had some indefinite influence over councils, as some modern writers put it, but on the fact that in the earliest times none of the office-bearers, and for many centuries few of them, depended upon the Church as a whole to provide them with the necessities of life. They were clergy, as has been said, in virtue of their selection for office and of their solemn setting apart to perform clerical functions; but they had daily association with the laity in the workshop, on the farm, in the warehouse, in the law-courts, and in the market-place. They held what must seem to be a very anomalous position to mediaeval and modern episcopalians. . . . But the practice had its value in the early centuries and has its importance now. It knit clergy and laity together in a very simple and thorough fashion, and brought men, whose life and callings made them feel as laymen do, within the circle of the hierarchy which ruled, and so prevented the hiearchy degenerating into a clerical caste.[20]

Vocation in the Protestant Reformation. The Protestant Reformation of the sixteenth century was religious in character but had social, political, and economic consequences. Among other things it became a revolt against medieval and Roman Catholic values in the area of vocation. It all began with Martin Luther's formulation of the doctrine of the priesthood of believers, which made null the dichotomy between clergy and laity. Likewise, a new era was initiated by his belief that each person should serve God according to his station in life, no matter how humble; and he should discharge his occupation as a Christian vocation or calling.

Commenting on Luther's concept of the priesthood of believers, Philip Schaff makes the following pertinent observation:

> This principle, consistently carried out, raises the laity to active co-operation in the government and administration of the church; it gives them a voice and vote in the election of the pastor; it makes every member of the congregation useful, according to his peculiar gift, for the general good. This principle is the source of religious and civil liberty which flourishes most in Protestant countries. Religious liberty is the mother of civil liberty. The universal priesthood of Christians leads legitimately to the universal kingship of free, self-governing citizens, whether under a monarchy or under a republic. The good effect of this principle showed itself in the spread of Bible knowledge among the laity, in popular hymnody and congregational singing, in the institution of lay-eldership, and in the pious zeal of the magistrates for moral reform and general education.[21]

The dictum, "Things that affect all must be dealt with by all," is part of the concept of the priesthood of believers.

If a Christian, according to Luther, has accepted God's calling (*voco*), his work should be discharged as a vocation (calling) in which he serves God and his neighbor. He realizes that the " 'poor, dull, and despised works' are adorned with the favor of God 'as with costliest gold and precious stones.' " The mundane things of life become vehicles for the Spirit of God. Said Luther:

> If you are a craftsman you will find the Bible placed in your workshop, in your hands, in your heart; it teaches and

preaches how you ought to treat your neighbor. Only look
at your tools, your needle, your thimble, your beer barrel,
your articles of trade, your scales, your measures, and you
will find this saying written on them. You will not be able
to look anywhere where it does not strike your eyes. None
of the things with which you deal daily are too trifling to tell
you this incessantly, if you are but willing to hear it; and there
is no lack of such preaching, for you have as many preachers
as there are transactions, commodities, tools, and other im-
plements in your house and estate; and they shout this to your
face, "My dear, use me toward your neighbor as you would
want him to act toward you with that which is his."[22]

This Protestant work-ethic is an expression of the New Testament
doctrine of the priesthood of believers, reminding us that Jesus Christ
during the major part of His life was Jesus the Carpenter from
Nazareth. The concept has had a spiritual, moral, and social impact
of paramount importance upon the West, both in its Lutheran, Reformed, and Free Church traditions. Likewise, we find here the roots and
inspiration to the founding and early history of America. Here reference
should be made to Calvin's presbyterianism. In his presbyterian form
of church organization Calvin gave a significance to the individual
"which of necessity leads to a democratic conception and development of the entire ecclesiastical system."[23] In the various councils in
Geneva, laymen, teachers, and ministers decided together on
disciplinary matters. Calvin also gave to the local congregation a voice
in the choice of its officers. Nevertheless, it was only with the
presbyterian and congregational forms of church government, in a
society with separation of church and state, that religious liberty and
modern democracy could be fully developed.

MEDIEVAL PRIESTHOOD

Growing Importance of Rome. Reference has been made to the
general change which took place regarding the concept of the
priesthood of believers in the third century. This change also meant
that the stage was set for the realization of the claim to universal
supremacy and jurisdiction by the bishop of Rome. The exercise of
his power and authority further added to the depreciation of the
priesthood of believers. We will therefore briefly sketch the historical

development of the medieval church. The stage was not primarily set by the theological concept of Rome as the See of Peter, even though this argument was used, but by the political situation—as A. B. Hasler points out: "As a matter of fact, however, it was not Apostolic origins but political position that determined who got authority in the Church."[24]

The establishment of Constantine's state-church made the church "Roman" in a non-theological, non-ecclesiological sense. During the Middle Ages the papacy sought to realize the Roman ideal of one people, one religion, one language, and one supreme ruler, who was a representative of the divine. The Roman judicial system and governmental structure were taken over into the organization and governance of the church. Pagan Rome literally grew into Papal Rome. The situation has been summarized in these words:

> The reconciliation of the Roman Empire with Christianity under Constantine the Great (ca. 280-337) and the establishment of Christianity as the state religion altered the nature of churchly offices. A church hierarchy grew up that corresponded to the state's. Church officials received numerous privileges, some of them rising to the rank of senators. Civil and religious laws were now often identical. Canon law entered upon a boom period. After the partial breakdown of the Roman Empire, high church officials also took over political functions.[25]

Referring to the fact that "it was the emperor who had the greatest interest in settling doctrinal disputes" and who "convoked ecumenical councils and largely dictated their results," Hasler closes with the observation: "But as yet no one said anything about infallibility. If anybody was infallible it was the emperor."[26]

In the person of Pope Leo the Great (A.D. 440-461) the idea of the papacy became reality. He has been called "the Father of the Papacy."[27] Immediately upon assuming the episcopacy he began to assert the authority of his See by formulating the Petrine theory. In an early sermon he speaks of Peter always being recognized in Peter's See.[28]

Peter "was ordained before the rest in such a way that from his being called the Rock, from his being pronounced the Foundation, from his being constituted the Doorkeeper of the kingdom of heaven, from his being set as the Umpire to bind and to loose, whose judgments shall retain their validity in heaven, from all these mystical titles we might know the nature of his association with Christ." This work of Peter was still carried on by his successor. Pope Leo could therefore say: "And so if anything is rightly done and rightly decreed by us, if anything is won from the mercy of God by our daily supplications, it is of his work and merits whose power lives and whose authority prevails in his See." In other words, in each pope Peter as the chief apostle is "reincarnated." The sermon was given on the anniversary of his elevation to the pontificate and he points out that the occasion was in honor of St. Peter for "in my humble person he may be recognized and honoured." Leo could therefore say: "When therefore we utter our exhortations in your ears, holy brethren, believe that he is speaking whose representative we are: because it is his warning that we give, nothing else but his teaching that we preach."[29]

Pope Gregory the Great (A.D. 590-604), "the last of the Latin fathers and the first of the popes, connects the ancient with the mediaeval church."[30] He contended strongly for the supremacy of Rome and exercised constant supervision over bishops in all parts of the East and the West. The spiritual and temporal authority he exercised gave birth and form to the papacy of the Middle Ages. In addition to his "multitudinous duties, he was virtual King of Italy." Not only head, he was also "the first Pope to become in act and in influence, if not in name, the temporal sovereign of the West."[31]

Between 1073 and 1302 the papacy made its most lofty claims to universal supremacy and also attained its maximum power. Pope Gregory VII (1073-1085) summed up his concept of the pope in a document entitled *Dictatus Papae*. This document makes the pope God's representative on earth, with absolute power over the church and secular rulers:

That the Roman church was founded by God alone,

That the Roman pontiff alone can with right be called universal.

That he alone can depose or reinstate bishops. . . .

That he alone may use the imperial insignia. . . .

That it may be permitted to him to depose emperors. . . .

That a sentence passed by him may be retracted by no one; and that he himself, alone of all, may retract it. . . .

That he himself may be judged by no one. . . .

That the Roman church has never erred; nor will it err to all eternity, the Scripture bearing witness. . . .

That he who is not in peace with the Roman church shall not be considered catholic.

That he may absolve subjects from their fealty to wicked men.[32]

To a large degree Gregory VII succeeded in realizing the lofty ideals of the *Dictatus Papae*

On various occasions in the history of the Roman Catholic Church we find the title "Vicar of Christ" used with reference to the bishops, but Pope Innocent III (A.D. 1198-1216) claimed the title exclusively for himself, as holder of the unique chair of St. Peter.[33] In a letter to the patriarch of Constantinople in 1199 he stated: "The pope is the vicar of Christ, yea of God himself. Not only is he intrusted with the dominion of the Church, but also with the rule of the whole world. Like Melchizedek, he is at once king and priest. . . . So are they also to his vicar."[34]

Pope Boniface (A.D. 1294-1303) declared in his bull *Unam sanctam*: "There is one body of the one and only church, and one head, not two heads, as if the church were a monster. And this head is Christ and his vicar, Peter and his successor."[35] This document expressed the proudest, most ambitious and highest claim regarding the universality of papal power and jurisdiction:

And we must necessarily admit that the spiritual power surpasses any earthly power in dignity and honor, because spiritual things surpass temporal things. . . . Therefore if the temporal power errs, it will be judged by the spiritual power, and if the lower spiritual power errs, it will be judged by its superior. But if the highest spiritual power errs, it can not be judged by men, but by God alone. . . . We therefore declare, say, and affirm that submission on the part of every man to the bishop of Rome is altogether necessary for his salvation.[36]

Influence of Greek Philosophy. We find that the medieval world was, to a large degree, indebted or enslaved to Greek ideas. The Greek dichotomy of spirit and matter led to the concept that the highest element of man is spirit, while the body belongs to man's lower existence. The free man, the Hellene, was the bearer of the spirit, and his activities were in the realm of the mind. Work performed for the necessities of life was considered degrading, and belonged to the servant and the slave. In addition, physical work was depreciated.

Christianity was to a large degree conquered by Aristotelian theory and scale of values, which became the base for theological, political, and social concepts, including that of vocation. The theology and ecclesiology of the medieval church reached its peak in the writings of Thomas Aquinas, who was philosophically an Aristotelian. While in the Greek society the free man found his "spiritual activities" in the social and political sense; the medieval "spiritual man" found it in the religious sense; and it was epitomized in the priest, the monk, and the nun. Based on Aristotelian philosophy, the church created a homogeneous society—religiously, politically, and socially. But the scale of values moved from the serf and peasant at the lowest level of life (busy with the material and animal life), to the highest life (the spiritual pursuits of the religious person), reaching its apex in the pope. The Greek dichotomy of spirit and matter was maintained, but it must be emphasized that this opposition between the two is neither biblical nor Christian.

Thomas Aquinas. In order to better understand the difference, and subsequent conflict, between the basic ideological principles of Roman Catholicism and those of its opponents, especially as it relates to the priesthood of believers, it will be helpful to consider, however briefly, the thoughts of Thomas Aquinas (c. 1225-1274).

During the thirteenth century a number of universities were founded and scholasticism reached its highest intellectual achievement in the Middle Ages. In this, the Franciscan and Dominican friars or monks had a great share.

Through social work and preaching, as confessors and inquisitors, teachers and missionaries, the friars were the strength of the papacy during the thirteenth century. The Dominicans had a still more lasting influence when Thomas Aquinas made the papal claim of supremacy a part of Catholic theology: "As for the Church itself, Rome is the mistress and mother of all churches. To obey her is to obey Christ. This is according to the decision of the holy councils and the holy Fathers. The unity of the Church presupposes a supreme centre of authority. To the pope, it belongs to determine what is of faith. Yea, subjection to him is necessary to salvation." Accordingly, it has been stated that "high churchmanship could no further go."[37]

Aquinas also says that "the secular power is joined to the spiritual, as in the pope, who holds the apex of both authorities, the spiritual and the secular."[38]

Thomas Aquinas defended ecclesiastical preeminence as a corollary to the doctrine that the basic truths are those of faith, and that salvation, man's chief concern, is in the hands of the church. The church is a necessary instrument for achieving man's chief end, and its hegemony is thus given a somewhat Aristotelian justification. If a ruler ignored the decrees of the church he should be excommunicated and his subjects absolved from the necessity of obedience. The authority of the priest was temporal as well as spiritual; the pope was to be obeyed implicitly in all matters of civil welfare as well as in those which related to salvation.

The true end of man is, through a virtuous life, to obtain eternal life. But this cannot be attained through human virtue alone; otherwise the will of the king, as the supreme political power, would be sufficient. But inasmuch as this objective transcends earthly life, it must be reached through the ministry of the priesthood. Although the king is supreme in temporal affairs, even he is subject to the priest. Theologian Reinhold Seeberg writes regarding Aquinas' political theory: "The church attains its summit in the pope. With Aristotle, it was held: 'But the best government of a multitude is that it be ruled by one.' "[39]

Thomas Aquinas aimed to harmonize reason and revelation, to reconcile the doctrine of the church and rational philosophy, which classic learning had revived. Aquinas represented the scholastic philosophy which is antiindividualistic. We will later return to this point.

In 1567 Pope Pius V declared Thomas Aquinas to be the "Doctor of the Church." As late as 1879 Pope Leo XIII pronounced, in his encyclical of that year, that the theology of Thomas Aquinas is "the standard of Catholic orthodoxy."[40] He was also made patron of Catholic universities, and upon the occasion celebrating his canonization in 1923, Pope Pius XI reemphasized his authority as the theologian of the Roman Catholic Church.

The Decline of the Papacy. The thirteenth century brought the central medieval period of the papacy to its highest level but also saw the beginning of its decline. In 1305 the archbishop of Bordeaux was elected pope and took the name Clement V. He never crossed the Alps into Italy, and in 1309 moved the papal court from Rome to Avignon, a city along the river Rhone in France, where the papal court remained until 1377. This period has been called the Babylonian Captivity of the papacy because it nearly equalled in length the seventy years of exile of the Jews in Babylon. During this period there were seven popes, all French.

In 1378 began the Great Schism which lasted until 1417. During these years there were two series of popes, one at Rome and the other at Avignon, each duly elected and with a set of cardinals, and both under reciprocal excommunication. One part of Europe adhered to Rome, the other to Avignon. In 1409 Cardinals from the two papal courts met at the Council of Pisa to elect a new pope instead of the two rival popes. The new pope, who took the name Alexander V, set up court at Bologna. Neither of the two other popes would resign, thus there were now three duly elected popes, each with his own papal court and cardinals.

The nations of Europe divided their allegiance among the three papal courts, where each of the rival popes was proclaiming eternal condemnation over his rivals. The whole of Christendom was really under ban, since each of the popes excommunicated the other two and their followers. This situation lasted until the Council of Constance, 1414-1418. Here an internal struggle took place between the papists and the conciliarists. The latter sought to transform the papacy from an absolute monarchy into a constitutional monarchy, or system, in which power was not seated in one person but in a group of men, as for example, the bishops and cardinals. For the conciliarists the highest authority would then be a general council composed of delegates duly elected and rightly representative of all Christendom. The Conciliar Movement with its religious, political, and social consequences is the most important aspect of ecclesiastical history in the fifteenth century.

The Council of Constance healed the schism. It was a victory for the Conciliar Movement, but before long the pope and the papalist party undid the conciliar idea.

PRECURSORS OF A NEW ORDER

The Conciliar Movement failed to transform the papacy, yet it marked the end of the medieval papacy as a universal power in European society. The Renaissance popes were, to a large degree, preoccupied with the politics of the Italian city states.

The city states of Florence, Venice, Milan, and Naples had grown strong and become centers for commerce and culture, and in this process competed with the Papal States. Between them we find continued political interaction with intrigue, conflict, and aggression. The Renaissance popes, like other rulers of this period, patronized the arts and the humanities. Nepotism became widespread in filling positions in the papal government. What Leo X—pope at the time of Luther but who never perceived the depth of Luther's attack on the church— said when he became pope, other Renaissance popes could have said, "Now we have the papacy, let us enjoy it."

The waning of the influence of the hierarchy and its structure made possible new advances in religious experience and thinking as well as in science. We think of Copernicus and Galileo in the field of astronomy, and Lorenzo Valla and Nicholas of Cusa in linguistic and historical studies. Comparing the Latin Vulgate with the Greek New Testament, Valla demonstrated its many inadequacies.

New religious experience in the life of the individual was reflected in lay piety and new devotional literature. Meister Eckhart (1377) and Thomas á Kempis in the fifteenth century are typical examples. Next to the Bible, á Kempis' *Imitation of Christ* has been the world's most influential devotional book for half a millennium. It is also next to the Bible in number of copies, editions, and translations.

By preaching and education, John Van Ruysbrock, a disciple of Eckhart, and Gerard Groot, one of Ruysbrock's disciples, led out in a spiritual renewal in the Netherlands. Groot founded the Brethren of the Common Life, a fine example of the *devotio moderna* (the new devotion) of the time. The Brethren of the Common Life established, or reformed, several hundred schools, some of which had between one and two thousand students.

The influence of the Brethren of the Common Life was far-reaching. Paving the way for the Reformation of the sixteenth century, they inspired the lives of men such as Martin Luther, John Calvin, and Martin Bucer.

The *devotio moderna* of the Netherlands left a heritage which influenced the Puritans in the sixteenth and seventeenth centuries, and the Pilgrim Fathers. We now turn to two "thinkers" who created philosophical, theological, and political concepts which became important for a renewal of the concept of the priesthood of believers. These concepts have remained with us to the present. To know the religious, social, and political climate in which these concepts were formulated is important for a correct evaluation of Roman Catholicism, Protestantism, modern democracy, and the doctrine of the priesthood of believers.

Marsilius of Padua (c. 1290-1349). In the fourteenth century a new note was sounded in the ongoing struggle between pope and emperor, between church and state. "He who struck it was Marsilius of Padua, a thinker whose influence, though greater after his death than in his lifetime, was that of a portent."[41] His book *Defensor Pacis* (Defender of Peace), set forth most of the ideas which were to become "the creative forces of the modern era." He has been characterized as "a precursor of the Reformation, a theorist of popular sovereignty and constitutional systems, a herald of the modern sovereign state."[42] He "arrived at the fully matured principle of religious toleration."[43] According to Ephraim Emerton, former professor of Ecclesiastical History at Harvard University, "His book has often been called the most remarkable literary product of the Middle Ages, and I am inclined to accept this verdict." He was "the herald of a new world, the prophet of a new social order."[44]

Marsilius completed *Defensor Pacis* on June 24, 1324. Its aim was to explain "the principal causes whereby civil peace or tranquillity exists and is preserved, and whereby the opposed strife arises and is checked and destroyed."[45] The one singular cause which Marsilius sets forth as the root of strife and the hindrance of peace is "the belief, desire, and undertaking whereby the Roman bishop and his clerical coterie, in particular, are aiming to seize secular rulerships and to possess excessive temporal wealth."[46]

In his discussion of the state, Marsilius rejects the idea that the sovereignty of the state rests with "a certain few" rather than with "the whole body of citizens or the weightier multitude thereof." He asserts that "the people, or the multitude composed of all the groups of the polity or city taken together, is more ample than any part of it taken separately, and consequently its judgment is more secure than that of any such part." He further explains: "For the few would not discern or desire the common benefit equally as well as would the entire multitude of the citizens. Indeed, it would be insecure, as we have already shown, to entrust the making of the law to the discretion of the few."[47]

The same principle that formed the basis of Marsilius' political structure is equally valid for the church: the people themselves are the source of all power.

According to Marsilus "the truest and the most fitting" meaning of the word "church" is "the whole body of the faithful who believe in and invoke the name of Christ, and all the parts of this whole body in any community, even the household."[48] He points out that the word "church" was used in his time for those who preside over the church. He writes: "This usage was long since brought about by the church of the city of Rome, whose ministers and overseers are the Roman pope and his cardinals. Through custom they have brought it about that they are called the 'church' and that one says the 'church' has done or received something when it is these men who have done or received or otherwise ordained something."[49]

Contrary to this concept Marsilius asserts that it is "the believers of Christ, who are the 'church.' "[50] George H. Sabine comments that "even the laity, Marsilio says, are churchmen (*viri ecclesiastici*)," an expression suggestive of Martin Luther's phrase, "the priesthood of the Christian man."[51]

In his first discourse Marsilius argues that the source of authority in the state rests with the people. In his second discourse he applies the same principle to the church. Gewirth elaborates on the concept of the church as it had become identified with the pope: "Marsilius' doctrine of the church subverts this entire hierarchic structure. He weakens the continuum between priesthood and God, reverses the superiority of clergy over laymen, and equalizes priests, bishops, and pope in that respect in which their authority had been considered essentially unequal. This revolution is accomplished by the different interpretation which he places upon the definition of the church as the *universatis fidelium*."[52] Marsilius draws the conclusion that it is "by virtue of the words of Scripture, therefore, no bishop or church is the head or leader of the rest, as such." But "the only absolute head of the church . . . is Christ himself."[53] He nullifies the sacerdotal power of the priesthood. A sinner is forgiven completely without an intermediate agency: ". . . in the sinner who is truly penitent, that is, who is contrite and has the intention of confessing, God alone performs certain things before the confession and before all action on the part of the priest. These things are the expulsion of guilt, the restoration of grace, and the forgiving of the debt of eternal damnation."[54]

It is significant that Marsilius' basic principle, which later became the foundation principle for the modern democratic states—that the source of all power is the people—was born in reaction against papal supremacy. This principle is according to Marsilius, the defender of peace both in the state as well as in the church. Accordingly, one of the authorities on the political ideas of Marsilius writes: "The permanent significance of Marsilius' ideas is to be found not merely in his opposition to the papal and ecclesiastic institutions of medieval Christendom, but in the entire doctrinal structure which he adduces in support of such opposition."[55]

Many before and after Marsilius spoke against the universal supremacy of the papacy, but it was the ideological structure of *Defender of Peace* relating to the basic principles on which the papacy rested its authority, which on one hand made advocates of the papacy curse it, and on the other made it considered a most important work by those who saw in the supremacy of the pope the source of a corrupt church and the root of strife in the state. The reactions to *Defender of Peace* testify to the impact of its ideology. Pope Clement VI (1342-1352) declared "that he had never read a more shockingly heretical book than the *Defensor pacis*."[56] When the popes later condemned such men as Wyclif, Hus, Luther, among others, they charged them with having gotten their ideas from Marsilius. As late as in the Canon Law of 1917 the editor, after having referred to the pope's "supreme and full power of jurisdiction in the whole Church," comments: "All those who pervert the essential divine organization of the Church as a perfect society of the monarchical type, necessarily deny the power of the Roman Pontiff. The so-called democrats of the later middle ages (Marsilius, Jandunus, Wiclif, and Hus) were deliberately bent on destroying the pure notion of papal power."[57]

On the other hand, a man such as Matthias Flacius, professor at Jena from 1557 and a strict Lutheran, wrote in his *Catalogus testium* that, among pre-Reformation works, "there is no more sound, scholarly, bold and pious book against the papal power."[58] Leaders of the

Protestant Reformation would no doubt agree with Flacius, and in our early discussion of Marsilius we made reference to twentieth-century historians who lauded him.

William of Occam (c. 1290-1349). Occam gave a great blow to medieval scholastic theology, as represented by Thomas Aquinas. He taught that the philosopher and theologian must begin with the individual. Only the individual is real. His critical theory of knowledge "is closely bound up with his political theory."[59]

With this basic concept Occam arrived at the principle of representation, also basic for Marsilius: "That which touches all must be acted on by all." It is interesting to note that in arriving at this conclusion his basic concepts are theological and scriptural, according to which one must begin with the individual inasmuch as only the individual is real. Stephen C. Tornay, an authority on the philosophy of Occam, writes that Occam thus "presents a strong evaluation of the human personality as against the corporate political body, reflecting Ockham's emphasis on the concrete and individual in his theory of knowledge as against the general and universal."[60]

Occam strongly emphasizes that the apostolic principle, which should be followed by the pope and the bishops, is that of serving the church spiritually.[61] "It belongs to the pope, even as to all bishops in general, as the canons bear witness, to further the reading, speaking, preaching of the word of God and divine worship and all those things that are necessary and proper to Christians for the attainment of eternal life and do not exist among unbelievers." Since the clergy cannot be occupied with secular matters, Occam encourages the idea that laymen care for secular business connected with the administration of the church.[62]

Characteristic is Occam's constant appeal to Scripture as the final source of authority. No doctrine not rooted in Holy Scripture should be acknowledged as catholic and necessary to salvation; neither the church nor the pope could make new articles of faith. In this way he contributed to upsetting the medieval theory of the seat of authority and assailed the traditional doctrines of his time. In the introduction to his last treatise he wrote: "Yet let all men hold this as certain: that in matters of faith and of knowledge, one evident reason or one authority of Scripture reasonably understood will move me more than the assertion of the whole world of mortal men. . . ."[63]

Occam was a distant voice of the Protestant Reformation; no wonder Luther called him "my dear master," and said "I am of the

Occamist faction." Occam "stands in a direct relation to the greatest event of the succeeding age, the Reformation. . . . He was no forerunner for Luther as a Reformer, but he was one of the factors without which the Reformation would have been impossible."[64]

A Historical Sequel. Marsilius' and Occam's ideas of representation in the church are of the highest significance. They influenced John Wyclif (c. 1327-84) and John Hus (c. 1369-1415) to become reformers. Both advocated the doctrine of the priesthood of believers, and became the morning stars of the Protestant Reformation. The English Reformation, especially Puritanism, quickly took roots, where the soil had been prepared by the followers of Wyclif, the so-called Lollards, known as the "Poor Preachers."

In the light of what we have observed it is understandable that Luther, with the other Protestant Reformers, had to re-evaluate ecclesiology and as a consequence renewed the apostolic and early church's understanding of the holy and royal priesthood of all believers.

Church historian Philip Schaff tells us that the "social or ecclesiastical principle of Protestantism is the general priesthood of believers, in distinction from the special priesthood which stands mediating between Christ and the laity."[65] This principle means that all the believers are active participants in the total life of the church; they should be anchored in the Word of God by studying it for themselves and offer prayers at the throne of grace both for themselves and in intercession for others. The believers are endowed with different spiritual gifts by which they serve the body of Christ, thus the totality of believers (men and women alike) constitute the priesthood of God.

ROMAN CATHOLICISM AND VATICAN COUNCIL II

The Voice of Hans Küng. As a highly distinguished and influential theologian, both among Catholics and Protestants, Hans Küng's voluminous work *The Church* reflects the current search for a better understanding of ecclesiology, not least the significance of the role of the laity, even within the Roman Catholic Church. Dealing with the latter topic he writes:

> The fundamental error of ecclesiologies . . . was that they failed to realize that all who hold office are primarily (both temporally and factually speaking) not dignitaries but

> believers, members of the fellowship of believers; and that compared with this fundamental Christian fact any office they may hold is of secondary if not tertiary importance. Bluntly put: the believer who holds no office is a Christian and member of the Church of Christ; a man who holds office without faith is no Christian and not a member of the Church. The Church must be seen first and foremost as a fellowship of faith, and only in this light can ecclesiastical office be properly understood.

> Does this mean that the community precedes ecclesiastical office, or that the community rather than the office is the higher authority? There is no question of having to make such a choice in the New Testament, where we find both community and office represented as equal authorities, both subject to a highest authority, namely Jesus Christ, the Lord of the Church, acting in time through his Spirit."[66]

From the time of the atoning death and sacrifice of Christ on the cross, the only valid sacrifices are "sacrifices of thanks and praise for what Christ has perfected; not sacrifices of external gifts, but the offering of oneself. In this way sacrifice is a concrete act of witness and confession of faith, as well as service of love." With this in mind Küng writes: "If then *all* believers have . . . to make sacrifices through Christ, this means that *all* believers have a priestly function, of a completely new kind, through Christ the one high priest and mediator. The abolition of a special priestly caste and its replacement by the priesthood of the *one* new and eternal high priest has as its strange and yet logical consequence the fact that *all* believers share in a universal priesthood."[67]

Decrees of Vatican Council II. Several of the many documents and decrees issued during the Second Vatican Council try in one form or another to give the "lay people" a more prominent place within the church.[68] However, a special "Decree on the Apostolate of the Laity" was issued. In the introduction we read:

> Wishing to intensify the apostolic activity of the People of God, this most holy Synod earnestly addresses itself to the laity, whose proper and indispensable role in the mission of the Church it has already called to mind in other documents.

The layman's apostolate derives from his Christian vocation, and the Church can never be without it. Sacred Scripture clearly shows how spontaneous and fruitful such activity was at the very beginning of the Church (cf. Acts 11:19-21; 18:26; Rom. 16:1-16; Phil. 4:3).[69]

We further read: "Our own times require of the laity no less zeal. In fact, modern conditions demand that their apostolate be thoroughly broadened and intensified. . . . An indication of this manifold and pressing need is the unmistakable work of the Holy Spirit in making the laity today even more conscious of their own responsibility and inspiring them everywhere to serve Christ and the Church."[70]

In the English translation and edition by Walter M. Abbott, S.J. a preface was written to this Decree. The opening paragraph speaks for itself. It reads:

Although a "lay apostolate" has existed in the Church since the days of our Lord in Jerusalem, it was not until the Second Vatican Council that the Church's official thinking on the matter was stated in a conciliar decree. As one layman put it pungently, "The lay apostolate has been simmering on the 'back burner' of the Church's apostolic life for nearly two thousand years, and finally the Fathers of this Council moved it up to the 'front burner' and turned the heat up all the way." Everyone hopes it will 'come to a boil' soon because so much of the Church's mission depends on an apostolic laity. Indeed, the renewal of the Church, called for by the documents of the Council, depends in great part on a laity that fully understands not only these documents but also their own co-responsibility for the mission of Christ in the Church and in the world.[71]

The decree on the laity grew out of the central document of Vatican II: Dogmatic Constitution on the Church. Here chapter 4 deals with "The Laity." It follows the chapters on "The Mystery of the Church" and "The People of God," which points out that the church is the body of Christ and the people of God. Chapter 3 gives a description of "The Hierarchical Structure of the Church, with Special Reference to the Episcopate." Here it is stated that the bishop "has no authority unless it is simultaneously conceived of in terms of its head," the pope, Peter's successor, and Vicar of Christ. As such "the Roman Pontiff has full, supreme, and universal power over the Church. And he can always exercise this power freely."[72]

It is most significant that after the description of church (chapters 1 and 2) and before dealing with the laity (chapter 4) we find the section on the hierarchical structure of the church. The place of the laity must be seen in the light of the latter, likewise the nature of the church. Accordingly, the chapter on the laity begins with these words: "Having set forth the functions of the hierarchy, this holy Synod gladly turns its attention to the status of those faithful called the laity."[73]

The Second Vatican Council and the Roman Catholic Church do not accept the "priesthood of all believers." Their involvement is defined as the "apostolate of the laity." Priesthood only belongs to the clergy.

The structure of the Roman Catholic Church maintains a tension between the believer and the hierarchy, as well as within the hierarchy itself. It is therefore understandable that Hans Küng and many theologians with him are disappointed with their church in the post-Vatican II era. To a large degree the same is also the case among Catholics in America, which, as a country, has constitutive principles different from Roman Catholicism, both ecclesiologically and politically.

The early church became a specific and unique historical phenomenon for the believers fulfilled the calling and covenant of "a chosen race, a royal priesthood, a holy nation, a people for God's own possession" (1 Peter 2:9). This was to be a normative experience for the church at any time and place.

Ecclesiology can only be true to the New Testament when the proper place—theologically, Christologically, soteriologically and pneumatologically—is given to the doctrine of the priesthood of believers.

3 THE MINISTRY: NEW TESTAMENTAL PERSPECTIVES

Now concerning spiritual gifts, brethren, I do not want you to be unaware. . . Now there are varieties of gifts, but the same Spirit. And there are varieties of ministries, and the same Lord. And there are varieties of effects, but the same God who works all things in all persons. But to each one is given the manifestation of the Spirit for the common good.
—Apostle Paul

The remarkable fact is that the word "priest" is not used once anywhere in the New Testament for someone who holds office in the Church; . . . It is remarkable, too, that in his preaching Jesus does not use the image of the priest. . . . On no occasion did Jesus describe himself or his disciples as priests. —Hans Küng

THE NATURE OF THE MINISTRY

Usage of the Terms "Ministry" and "Minister." The New Testament refers to the work of the church mostly by the word "ministry." The Apostle Paul speaks about "varieties of ministry," as noted previously, but with reference to the total body of believers (1 Cor. 12:1, 4-7). Speaking about the household of Stephanas Paul writes that "they have devoted themselves for ministry to the saints" (1 Cor. 16:15). Paul himself and other church workers are also spoken of as "ministers" called to "the work of the ministry" (1 Cor. 12:5; 2 Cor. 3:6-8; Col. 1:7, 25; 2 Cor. 5:18; 1 Tim. 1:12; Eph. 4:12). Paul encouraged Timothy to be "a good servant of Christ Jesus" and "fulfill your ministry" (1 Tim. 4:6; 2 Tim. 4:5). He also refers to Apollos, Tychicus, and Epaphras respectively as "servants through whom you believed," "faithful minister in the Lord," and "faithful servant of Christ" (1 Cor. 3:5; Eph. 6:21; Col. 1:7). As will be seen, the New Testament includes women in the terms "ministry" and "minister."

The Ministry a Service, the Minister a Servant. The words "ministry" and "minister" are translated respectively from the Greek *diakonia* and *diakonos*, meaning "service" and "servant." As already observed, English translations of the New Testament use these two words interchangeably. Accordingly, it is a mistake to read one's concept of priest into the word "minister" as found in some New Testament translations. Furthermore, the word is used for both men and women.

As in the New Testament, the basic secular meaning of *diakonia* and *diakonos* is that of the service rendered by a waiter (Luke 17:8; John 12:2). To be a minister of Christ means to be a servant (*diakonos*). Christ said: "Let him who is the greatest among you become as the youngest, and the leader as the servant. For who is greater, the one who reclines at the table, or the one who serves? Is it not the one who reclines at the table? But I am among you as the one who serves" (Luke 22:26-27).

The New Testament usage of *diakonia* and *diakonos* has theological, Christological, and soteriological connotations. The Apostle Paul writes: "Therefore if any man is in Christ, he is a new creature; the old things passed away; behold, new things have come. Now all these things are from God, who reconciled us to Himself through Christ, and gave us the ministry of reconciliation" (2 Cor. 5:17-18). The New English Bible reads, "service of reconciliation."

The ministry or service of reconciliation begins with the covenant of redemption. "God so loved the world, that He gave His only begotten Son." In similar fashion Christ gave Himself in self-denying love. "Have this attitude in yourselves which was also in Christ Jesus, who, although He existed in the form of God, did not regard equality with God a thing to be grasped, but emptied Himself, taking the form of a bond-servant" (Phil. 2:57). Christ is the bond-servant, that is, the minister par excellence.

The ministry of Christ's mother, the Virgin Mary, is often overlooked. Her response to the divine revelation concerning her role as the mother of our Lord through the coming of the Holy Spirit into her life is salutary: "Behold, the bondslave of the Lord; be it done to me according to your word. . . . And my spirit has rejoiced in God my Savior. For He has had regard for the humble state of His bondslave" (Luke 1:38, 47-48). Somewhat similarly, the church was born on the day of Pentecost through the outpouring of the Holy Spirit upon God's "bondslaves, both men and women" (Acts 2:18).

The apostles Paul, James, Peter, Jude, and John were true ministers of Christ, they called themselves "bond-servants of Jesus Christ"

(Rom. 1:1; 2 Cor. 4:5; Titus 1:1; Jas. 1:1; 2 Peter 1:1; Jude 1; Rev. 1:1). In all these passages the words "bond-servant" and "bondslaves," which include both men and women, are translated not from the Greek *diakonos*, but from *doulos*, meaning a slave. As a slave belongs fully to his master and has nothing he can call his own, so a minister (servant) and the ministry (service) belong to Jesus Christ. It involves one's total dedication to Christ in the service of reconciliation and for the concern of one's fellowmen.

A New Value System. An ambitious mother sought for her two sons the two highest positions within the government of the country. She expected that the fulfillment of the hope of a great and glorious kingdom like that of David was imminent, and believed with many that the hope of the kingdom would be realized by Jesus of Nazareth. So the mother of James and John came to Jesus with a bold request. "She said to Him, 'Command that in Your kingdom these two sons of mine may sit, one on Your right and one on Your left.' " In response Jesus taught His followers that service is a basic principle of the kingdom of God and the nature of the Christian ministry. Said Jesus: "You know that the rulers of the Gentiles lord it over them, and their great men exercise authority over them. It is not so among you, but whoever wishes to become great among you shall be your servant, and whoever wishes to be first among you shall be your slave; just as the Son of Man did not come to be served, but to serve" (Matt. 20:21, 25-28).

The kingdom of God is not a spatial domain but the rule of God. In this fallen world it involves, as proclaimed in the Sermon on the Mount, a 180-degree turnaround in value concepts.

As we study the lives of the disciples of Christ it becomes obvious that the concept of self-forgetful service as the highest realization of self, and manifesting itself in true success and achievement, was something new for them and contrary to human behavior. That was not the kingdom they expected. It is therefore no wonder that Christ spoke about the need of "conversion" and to "be born again" in order to be able to see and to enter the kingdom of God (John 3:3, 5). In addition, in this same Gospel we find some of His most insightful instructions on service—by parable (ch. 12) and by example (ch. 13). Christ illustrated the growth and realization of the servant image and the kingdom of God in the parable of a seed planted in the soil (John 12:23-26). The seed disintegrates but gives birth to a new life; thus, by losing self in service, a new life begins, resulting in the fullest realization of the very self of man. In the following chapter He washes the disciples' feet and speaks further of servanthood. Indeed, the story of the disciples' subsequent obedience to Him and their effective service on behalf of others is challenging evidence of their self-realization through the recreative power and grace of God, which brought a complete change in attitude and practice on every level of their inner life and outer world.

As Hans Küng points out, in the New Testament "words in secular Greek for civil and religious authorities are consistently avoided in connection with the ministries of the Church;" that is, Greek words which imply "hierarchy," "primacy," "rank," "power," and "authority," or describe the "honour," "dignity," and "total power of office." The same is pointed out by M. Warkentin as follows: "The vocabulary of New Testament leadership permits no pyramidal forms; it is a language of horizontal relationships, of leaders and followers, of those set before others as models (1 Cor. 11:1; 2 Thess. 3:9; 1 Tim. 4:12; 1 Pet. 5:3), of mutual service one to another for the sake of the kingdom." In this connection reference is made to the book *The Church in Search of It Self* by Robert Paul, who writes: "The credibility of the Church has a direct relationship to the *way* authority is exercised and manifested in the Church: what the Church does and the way it does it demonstrate to everyone what manner of Spirit rules the Church."[1]

THE APOSTOLATE

The Meaning of Apostleship. Apostleship has its beginning in Christ Himself. Paul writes: "Therefore, holy brethren, partakers of a heavenly calling, consider Jesus, the Apostle and High Priest of our confession. He was faithful to Him who appointed Him" (Heb. 3:1-2). As the Father appointed Christ an apostle, so Christ "appointed twelve, that they might be with Him, and that He might send them out to preach" (Mark 3:14). The Gospel of Matthew calls "the twelve" disciples and designates them as apostles (Matt. 10:1, 2). By choosing twelve Christ no doubt had in mind Israel composed of twelve tribes. Another statement of Jesus to the disciples, though symbolic, makes this obvious: "You also shall sit upon twelve thrones, judging the twelve tribes of Israel" (Matt. 19:28). Indirectly, Christ intimates that the New Israel is also structured.

The word "apostle" is a translation of the Greek word *apostolos*, a compound of the *apo*, "off" and *stello*, "to send." An *apostolos* is therefore a messenger, an ambassador, an envoy, or a delegate.

After Christ had appointed the twelve apostles we read: "Now after this the Lord appointed seventy others, and sent [*apostello*] them" (Luke 10:1). The appointment of seventy again reflects that Christ no doubt had in mind a new Israel as a continuation of the old Israel. Moses had appointed seventy elders to assist him (Ex. 24:1; Num. 11:16) and at the time of Christ the Jews had a council of seventy (71 with the high priest), the Sanhedrin. As in the case of the Twelve there seems to have been in the mind of Christ—in embryo—a certain functional structure. This is further supported by the fact that the word "apostle" is used as a title in the Gospel narratives (Luke 17:5, 22:14, 24:10), and Matthias was carefully chosen to fill the place of Judas (Acts 1:23-26).

The Uniqueness of the Twelve. The position of the twelve apostles was unique. Christ had personally called them, taught them, and associated with them in His personal ministry. They had witnessed His crucifixion, resurrection and ascension. Although the mandate to proclaim the good news was primarily given to them (Acts 1:2), from what followed on the day of Pentecost we can infer that it was an obligation equally felt by all the disciples, women as well as men (Acts 2:4, 7).

The Twelve were in a true sense Christ's personal ambassadors. Their primary task was to preach the gospel, then to teach, to oversee, to organize or unify, and pray that the brethren might receive the Holy Spirit. This is the picture we have from the story of the beginning of the primitive church (Acts 1:2-26; 2:37-42; 5:12; 6:1-8; 8:14-24).

The ministry of the Twelve was foundational for the universal church. The unique position of the Twelve was confined to the apostolic period of the primitive church. The church is "built upon the foundation of the apostles and prophets, Christ Jesus Himself being the corner stone, in whom the whole building, being fitted together is growing into a holy temple in the Lord; in whom you also are being built together into a dwelling of God in the Spirit" (Eph. 2:20-22).

Apostolic succession is not to be found in the establishment of an apostolic office, order or position, but functionally in proclaiming, as Christ's ambassadors, the gospel. However, the essence of the various functions and offices or orders of church ministry, as it developed within New Testament time, is rooted in the apostleship of the Twelve. The different ministries which Paul mentions in his list of spiritual gifts were to a large degree bestowed upon the Twelve. In this sense, and only in this sense, can we speak—like the Protestant Fathers—about apostolic succession and apostolicity.

THE CHARISMATIC MINISTRY

Spiritual gifts. The Apostle Paul deals with the different functions of the ministry in terms of spiritual gifts (Rom. 12:6-8; 1 Cor. 12:1, 8-10, 28-30; 14:1; Eph. 4:11-12). Peter in his First Epistle likewise deals with this important theme (4:10-11). These were gifts of divine grace (the Greek word "charisma" means a free gift, favor, or benefit). Therefore, when we speak about a charismatic ministry we speak about a service graciously endowed by the Holy Spirit. All ministerial functions are "Spirit-given."

The Apostle Paul gives us two lists of charismatic ministries. The one in 1 Corinthians reads: "And God has appointed in the church, first apostles, second prophets, third teachers, then miracles, then gifts of healings, helps, administrations, various kinds of tongues" (1 Cor. 12:28). The second list enumerates apostles, prophets, evangelists, pastors, and teachers (Eph. 4:11).

The Missionary-Apostle. We have observed that the unique apostleship of the Twelve ceased with their death. However, the term apostle has a secondary usage; its application widens: Christ Himself was the apostle par excellence; the Twelve had a unique apostleship; Paul was an apostle on a par with the Twelve and his writings were included in the New Testament; Christ "appointed seventy others" (Luke 10:1) and later said that He would send "prophets and apostles" (Luke 11:49).

To illuminate the term "apostle" in the New Testament let us briefly note its usage within Judaism. The Hebrew equivalent to the Greek *apostolos* is *shaliach*, from a verb meaning "to send." We are told: "What characterizes the *shaliach* of all periods is their commissioning with distinctive tasks which take them greater or lesser distances away from the residence of the one who gives them."

Whether the *shaliach* is a messenger of a corporate body or of an individual, his commission is representative in nature. The rule laid down stipulated: "The one sent by a man is as the man himself." The *shaliach* could not transfer his task to another; in other words, there was no socalled "apostolic succession." In contrast to the apostles of the New Testament the *shaliach* functioned only within Judaism and was not a Jewish missionary.

We are also informed that "as representatives of the scribes, and in their name again of all Israel, we have to mention supremely the rabbis who were sent out to the whole *diaspora* by the central authorities; for them the designation *shaliach* became an official title in the true sense. Their commission was many-sided enough, but it was always made possible by the authority which stood behind them in the person of those who sent them."[2] After the destruction of Jerusalem (70 A.D.), their work became more extensive. For example, they took up a collection for the scribes in Palestine, helped to appoint teachers in the local synogogues, and carried messages and decisions of the Jewish council (Sanhedrin). Before he became a Christian Paul, the rabbi, was sent as a *shaliach* to Damascus with letters stating the purpose of his commission (Acts 9:1-2).

It should also be noted that the envoys were generally not sent alone but in pairs or more, together. This reminds us of Christ who sent the disciples out "two and two" (Luke 10:1), and Paul and Barnabas who were commissioned by the church in Antioch (Acts 13:2). In this connection another incident from the life of Paul and Barnabas should be noticed. It is recorded (Acts 11:27-30) that the prophet Agabus told the church in Antioch that "a great famine" would come. The members of the church in Antioch "determined to send a contribution for the relief of the brethren living in Judea. And this they did, sending it in charge of Barnabas and Saul to the elders." In other words, Paul and Barnabas were the envoys (*apostolos/ shaliach*) to the elders in Jerusalem, who were in charge of the relief work.

It has been pointed out that the *shaliach* was not only a messenger for the Jewish court, but also a representative of the synagogue congregation. While in the first case his task may be defined as administrative, in the latter it was liturgical, being "the representative of the synagogue in its corporate worship." T. W. Manson writes: "It was his task to lead the prayers of the congregation; and in the early synagogue the term did not designate an office but a function, which might be performed by any member of the synagogue who was able and willing." He quotes Rabban Gamaliel: " 'The agent of the congregation fulfills the obligation that rests upon the many.' " Professor Manson continues: "It comes to this that the *shaliach* of the synagogue congregation is only a useful functionary for the purpose of corporate and public worship. He does nothing that the individual worshiper is not able and obliged to do for himself. He is the voice of the congregation, through whom all speak."[3]

Later we will observe the Protestant Reformers' concept of a representative ministry and will find that they express themselves in terms similar to those we have just noticed. Within Judaism only the priests were permitted to offer sacrifices, but in the New Testament no priest is needed forasmuch as Christ Himself is both sacrifice and priest. However, as missionaries the apostles of the New Testament were representatives of the Christian community.

From its very inception the church was a witnessing and missionary community, and its activities and ministry must necessarily be evaluated from the perspective of outreach. The apostles were called "our brethren . . . messengers [Greek *apostoloi*] of the churches, a glory to Christ" (2 Cor. 8:23). In one sense Paul belonged to the Twelve although "untimely born" (1 Cor. 15:8-11), and in another to the wider group which includes Barnabas, Andronicus, Junias, Silvanus, Timothy, Appollos and Epaphroditus. Directly and indirectly these are referred to as apostles and representatives of the church. (See Acts 13:2, 3; 14:14; Gal. 2:9; Rom. 16:7; 1 Cor. 4:6, 9; 1 Thess. 1:1; Phil 1:1; 2:25). The Revelation refers to "saints and apostles and prophets" (Rev. 18:20). The apostles of the New Testament are not officers of the congregation, but like the prophets and teachers, they are establishing and nurturing congregations (1 Cor. 12:28; Eph. 2:20; 3:5-7; 4:11-12). The final outcome "of apostolic work is a local congregation; and the local congregation, as part of the Body of Christ, itself enters into the apostolic ministry."[4]

Prophets. At the advent of Christ the spirit of prophecy was renewed when Zacharias prophesied about the birth of his son John the Baptist, who would be "the prophet of the Most High" (Luke 1:67, 76). Simeon had the gift of prophecy; he and the prophetess Anna gave testimonies regarding "the child Jesus" (Luke 2:25-38). The people considered Christ as a prophet: "He is a prophet, like one of the prophets of old." "They began glorifying God, saying, 'A great prophet has arisen among us!' and, 'God has visited His people!' " (Mark 6:15; Luke 7:16).

Christ made reference to "prophets and apostles" (Luke 11:49) and also said: "I am sending you prophets" (Matt. 23:34).

On the day of Pentecost Peter said: "You shall receive the gift of the Holy Spirit" and the words of the prophet Joel should be fulfilled: "Your sons and your daughters shall prophesy" (Acts 2:38, 17). We have already referred to this event when defining the ministry in terms of "bondslaves." The full text reads: "Even upon My bondslaves, both men and women, I will in those days pour forth of My Spirit and they shall prophesy" (Acts 2:18). More than two decades later Paul tells us that in the churches both men and women were prophesying (1 Cor. 11:4-5).

Acts of the Apostles mentions the following prophets by name: Agabus, Barnabas, Simeon, Lucius, Manaen, Saul of Tarsus, Judas, and Silas (Acts 11:28; 13:1; 15:32). Reference is also made to the fact that the four daughters of Philip, the evangelist, were prophetesses (Acts 21:8-9).

It appears that some were prophets and teachers by virtue of being apostles (missionaries). Others were itinerant prophets and teachers. Christ may have had in mind the itinerant prophets in the primitive church when He said: "He who receives a prophet in the name of a prophet shall receive a prophet's reward" (Matt. 10:41). Christ's statement is at least applicable to the situation in the early church. In general, prophets and teachers were found in the local churches. In Antioch, "while they were ministering to the Lord and fasting," it was through prophets and teachers that the Holy Spirit said, " 'Set apart for Me Barnabas and Saul for the work to which I have called them' " (Acts 13:1-2). God had called Paul and Barnabas, but the church, under the inspiration of the Holy Spirit, commissioned them. The unity between the church and the prophet is expressed in the phrase "saints and prophets" (Rev. 16:6; 11:18). The term "prophet" specifies more than making predictions. The Old Testament prophets included the role of revivalist. They were also adept at applying biblical principles to the situations in which Israel found itself. In the New Testament the role of prophet included speaking to the believers "for edification and exhortation and consolation" (1 Cor. 14:3).

The congregation was endowed with the Spirit to discern if the message of the prophet and teacher was from God. Paul says: "You judge what I say" (1 Cor. 10:15), and "Do not quench the Spirit; do not despise prophetic utterances. But examine everything carefully" (1 Thess. 5:19-21). John writes: "Beloved, do not believe every spirit, but test the spirits to see whether they are from God; because many false prophets have gone out into the world" (1 John 4:1). Enumerating the various gifts in the congregation, Paul also mentions the one of discernment (1 Cor. 12:10).

According to the second century church manual, Didache, also named Teaching of the Twelve Apostles: "Not everyone who speaks in a spirit is a prophet, except he have the behaviour of the Lord. From his behaviour, then, the false prophet and the true prophet shall be known."[5] The Book of Revelation tells us that God's remnant "hold to the testimony of Jesus" which "is the spirit of prophecy" (Rev. 12:17; 19:10).

Teacher. Christ not only makes reference to "prophets and apostles" but also mentions teachers: "I am sending you prophets and wise men and scribes" (Matt. 23:34). In the New Testament, Christ is the teacher par excellence. The Gospels record few references to Christ preaching, but numerous instances of His teaching. He was "teaching in their synagogues" and "the cities and the villages" (Matt. 4:23; 9:35); He was "teaching them as one having authority" and they were "astonished at His teaching" (see for example Matt. 7:28-29; 22:22; Mark 11:18). Nicodemus, one of the Jewish rulers, said to Christ: "Rabbi, we know that You have come from God as a teacher" (John 3:2).

In another connection it will be observed that at the time of Christ the teacher had a prominent role within Judaism. Thinking of Christ's promise of sending "wise men and scribes" and the church as Christ's representative, it is not surprising that Paul speaks about "teachers" as part of the charismatic ministry (1 Cor. 12:28).

The teachers were "wise men" and had the "gift" of knowledge. They edified the congregation (1 Cor. 14:26); they instructed candidates for baptism, and others in the basics of Christianity (Gal. 6:16). Paul's writings give a clear indication how he as a teacher instructed the congregation in the rudiments of the Christian faith and built up the membership in knowledge and understanding (See 1 Cor. 11:23 ff; 15:3-8, 51-58; 2:6 ff.; 7:6, 10, 14; 2 Thess. 2:15). Paul could, with good reason, say: "Retain the standard of sound words which you have heard from me" (2 Tim. 1:13), and to the Romans he expresses thankfulness because they had been obedient to his "form" (standard or pattern) "of teaching" (Rom. 6:17).

Paul no doubt expected each church to have teachers, so the members no longer should "be children, tossed here and there by waves, and carried about by every wind of doctrine, by the trickery of men" (Eph. 4:14). James refers to the seriousness of being a teacher: "Let not many of you become teachers, my brethren, knowing that as such we shall incur a stricter judgment" (James 3:1). The role of teacher remained after the apostolic age.

Evangelists. In the Epistle to the Ephesians Paul lists "evangelists" among the spiritual gifts (Eph. 4:11). An "evangelist" is a messenger of the good news, the gospel. Evangelists are mentioned in only two other places in the New Testament. Writing to his young co-worker Timothy, Paul says: "Preach the word; . . . reprove, rebuke, exhort, with great patience and instruction. For the time will come when they will not endure sound doctrine; but wanting to have their ears tickled, they will accumulate for themselves teachers in accordance to their own desires; and will turn away their ears from the truth, and will turn aside to myths. But you, be sober in all things, endure hardship, do the work of an evangelist, fulfill your ministry" (2 Tim. 4:2-5).

When, at the close of his third missionary journey, Paul came to Caesarea (A.D. 58) he stayed in "the house of Philip the evangelist, who was one of the seven" (Acts 21:8). We first meet Philip in Acts, chapter six (A.D. 35). He was one of the Seven chosen to assist the congregation with "the daily serving of food" to the widows (Acts 6:1). After the stoning of Stephen, when believers had to flee from Jerusalem, Philip went to Samaria, where he proclaimed Christ, conducted a healing ministry, and cast out unclean spirits (Acts 8:5-8). Next we find him on the road to Gaza where he meets the Ethiopian eunuch, brings him to faith in Christ, and baptizes him. Thereafter, he preaches in various cities and finally in Caesarea, where Paul stayed in his home.

It appears that the work of an "evangelist" was a function and not an office. The apostles were entrusted with "the gospel of Christ," and thus fulfilled an evangelistic function (Gal. 1:6-7).

Pastors. In Ephesians Paul lists "pastors" after "evangelists" and before "teachers" (Eph. 4:11). The word for "pastor" is translated from the Greek word for a shepherd. Ministerial shepherding originated in Christ. From the prophetic word the high priests and scribes believed that the Messiah would "shepherd My people Israel" (Matt. 2:6). When Christ came, He speaks of Himself as "the good shepherd" (John 10:11) and is referred to as "the great Shepherd of the sheep" (Heb. 13:20), "the Shepherd and Guardian of your souls" (1 Peter 2:25), and "the Chief Shepherd" (1 Peter 5:4). As such Christ said to Peter: "Shepherd My sheep" (John 21:16).

Only in Ephesians is the word "shepherd" used in connection with the ministry, but elsewhere three times as a verb. The first time— by Jesus to Peter—where it is synonymous with the word "tend" (John 21:15-17). Paul addressed the elders of the church in Ephesus, who came to Miletus to see him on his way to Jerusalem, as shepherds:

"Be on guard for yourselves and for all the flock, among which the Holy Spirit has made you overseers, to shepherd the church of God" (Acts 20:28). Their duty was to "oversee" and to "shepherd."

Like Paul, the Apostle Peter uses the words "to shepherd" when he addresses the elders. He writes: "Therefore, I exhort the elders among you, as your fellow elder and witness of the sufferings of Christ, and a partaker also of the glory that is to be revealed, shepherd the flock of God among you, exercising oversight not under compulsion, but voluntarily, according to the will of God; and not for sordid gain, but with eagerness; nor yet as lording it over those allotted to your charge, but proving to be examples to the flock" (1 Peter 5:1-3).

No doubt the work of the local pastor and teacher may also have been combined in one individual, who was both shepherd and teacher of the flock of God. It should be noticed that the Greek of Eph. 4:11 uses a conjunctive particle *de* ("on the other hand", "also") to introduce each special gift (as separate from one another) until it comes to "pastors and teachers." For this reason it could be translated "pastors who are teachers" as though there was a blur in the distinction between these two. Keeping in mind that that word "pastor" is derived from the Greek word for "shepherd," the Living Bible reads: ". . . still others have a gift for caring for God's people as a shepherd does his sheep, leading and teaching them in the ways of God."

Post-Apostolic Period. At the turn of the first century a letter known as First Epistle of Clement to the Corinthians was sent from the church of Rome to that of Corinth. In it we are told that the apostles preached "from district to district, and from city to city."[6] An anonymous letter named the Epistle of Barnabas (c. A.D. 130) describes the twelve apostles as "twelve evangelizers."[7]

In writings from the early or middle second century we also find the term apostles used to describe traveling missionaries. These apostles were greatly respected: "Let every Apostle who comes to you be received as the Lord." There must have been a growing number of apostles, for in order to distinguish between a true and false apostle the following counsel was given: "But let him not stay more than one day, or if need be a second as well; but if he stay three days, he is a false prophet. And when an Apostle goes forth let him accept nothing but bread till he reach his night's lodging; but if he asks for money, he is a false prophet."[8]

In general, the title "apostle" disappeared from the vocabulary of the Christian ministry and was replaced by the word "missionary."

However, missionaries who pioneered the gospel in some countries were honored by the title "apostle." Wherever the Greek language is still used, as in the Greek Orthodox Church, missionaries are named "holy apostles."

In the middle of the second century reference is made to the three ministries: "The thirty-five are the prophets of God and his servants, and the forty are apostles and teachers of the preaching of the Son of God."[9] The charismatic ministries mentioned in the New Testament continued into the second century. We have observed that Christ and John listed "prophets and apostles" (Luke 11:49, Rev. 18:20). Paul says: "I was appointed a preacher and an apostle (I am telling the truth, I am not lying) as a teacher of the Gentiles in faith and truth" (1 Tim. 2:7, 2 Tim. 1:11). In Revelation we notice that "the woman Jezebel, who calls herself a prophetess . . . teaches" (Rev. 2:20).

The author of the Epistle of Barnabas writes: "I hasten to write in devotion to you, not as a teacher, but as it becomes one who loves to leave out nothing of that which we have."[10] In Didache the teacher is described as one with an itinerant ministry; like the prophets, they were honored but should also be tested, whether or not they were genuine.[11] Christian apologists such as Justin Martyr and Tatian (middle of the second century), were no doubt itinerant teachers, but teachers were also found in the local congregations. Eusebius, a church historian in the time of Constantine, refers to "the presbyters and the teachers of the brethren in the villages."[12]

JEWISH RELIGIOUS LIFE

Before we turn to the next section dealing with ministerial administration, let us note certain aspects of Jewish religious life which may have a bearing upon our subject.

Declining Importance of Priesthood and Levites. The religious and spiritual influence and authority of the priesthood were not of paramount significance at the time of Christ. The priests, when not performing routine rites in the temple, were engaged in common secular business and work, like the people in general. The succession of Aaron's descendants in the high priestly office ended after the Maccabean revolt (160 B.C.), when the Maccabees appointed the high priest from their own family. That ceased when Herod (35 B.C.) executed the high priest, who from then on was appointed by the civil authorities, generally from among the Sadducees, a small group of aristocrats. As administrators of the temple the high priests had a strong political influence.

After the Babylonian captivity only a comparatively small number of Levites returned. In the Gospels there are only two references to the Levites; one in the parable of the Good Samaritan (Luke 10:30-37), and another telling us that the Jews sent priests and Levites to John the Baptist with the inquiry, "Who are you?" (John 1:19). We are told of only one Levite who became a follower of Christ (Acts 4:36), while "a great many of the priests were becoming obedient to the faith" (Acts 6:7).

On account of the nature of their work the Levites were of less importance than the common priest. Serving mainly as gatekeepers and musicians, their religious influence was negligible.

The Importance of the Synagogue. As recorded in the Gospels and the Acts of the Apostles, Christ, the twelve apostles, and early Christians all felt a close relationship with the synagogue. New Testament eccelesiastical structures and ministerial practices were not created in a vacuum. Names and structures of the time were often used, but given a new Christian content. For example, after having traced the development of Christian worship and liturgy during the first four centuries Professor C. W. Dugmore came to the conclusion: "It has become clear that the Church's debt to the Synagogue in the matter of worship is great indeed."[13] H. K. Booth in his study writes: "The synagogue became the pattern for the early church. Many of the Pauline churches were started in the synagogues, and the records we possess of the apostolic age show how closely these churches adhered to the synagogue in organization and worship."[14] The same author also writes: "But the one distinctive feature of the synagogue which must be kept in mind was its democracy. The officers were elected by the people; the service was informal and in it the people could participate both in response and discussion; both scripture and prayer were offered not by a priestly hierarchy of celebrants, but by any layman chosen by the congregation."[15]

The religious affairs of a local Jewish community, including the control of the synagogue, were in the hands of a board, or council, of elders (Luke 7:3-5). It has been brought to our attention that "the older communal order of the local Jewish community is continued in the constitution of the synagogue. To the local board, usually made up of 7 members, there corresponds in places with a separate Jewish cultic community the synagogal council."[16] The council appointed the "ruler of the synagogue," who in turn was responsible for arranging the church service, including choosing the readers and the one who should deliver an address. He also appointed the *chazan* or sexton who assisted him during worship and "was custodian of the building."[17]

Wherever there were Jews, in the time of Christ and the apostolic church, we find one or more synagogues. The historical beginning of the synagogue goes back to the time of exile and the return, and is closely related to the development of the Sanhedrin.

The Sanhedrin. When Ezra and Nehemiah returned to Jerusalem with a group of the exiles from Babylon, they called an assembly (Neh. 7-10) which has been named "the Great Synagogue." This assembly was replaced by a standing assembly which then became a Council, the so-called Sanhedrin. It was believed to be a resemblance of the councilors or elders established by Moses (Num. 11). Both at the time of Moses and Christ the Council was representative of all Israel. The sources do not give a uniform picture of its history, structure, and authority. No doubt it varied during the Persian, Hellenistic, Maccabean, and Roman periods.

The significant aspects of the Sanhedrin at the time of Christ have been summarized as follows: "The sanhedrins existed everywhere. In villages they had seven members, in larger places twenty-three. Jerusalem is said to have had two consultative sanhedrins of three members each, while over all was the Great Sanhedrin of seventy-one (including the high priest *ex officio*). From the lowest to the highest the functions of all these bodies were of the most general character, combining without distinction executive, legislative and judicial duties."[18]

The Great Sanhedrin in Jerusalem consisted of three groups, listed in the Gospel narratives, as the chief priests, scribes, and elders (Matt. 27:41; Mark 11:27; 14:43, 53; 15:1). The chief priests were retired high priests, the elders had their seats as lay nobles, and the scribes at the time of Christ were mainly from the Pharisees and represented the developing theology of Judaism. In the New Testament we read that Christ and the apostles were brought before the Council.

It is understandable that after the destruction of Jerusalem the influence of the rabbi further increased, but at the same time the administrative function of the Sanhedrin decreased. It was reorganized as a religious council or court at Jamnia, near Joppa, and its head (the *nasi*) was considered the "patriarch."

The Elder, Scribe and Rabbi. In the light of the historical and theological development of Judaism, the importance of the elders and the scribes became obvious. We have previously mentioned that the religious and spiritual influence of the priesthood was negligible.

When Simon Maccabeus (ca. 150 B.C.) was appointed as high priest instead of a descendant of Aaron it was said "until a true prophet should arise."[19] There was a Messianic expectation—the coming of the ideal prophet, priest, and king. The significance of these titles for Christ and Christology has been mentioned earlier. John the Baptist pointed out the eschatological expectation of the time when he said: "The time has come at last—the kingdom of God has arrived. You must change your hearts and minds and believe the good news" (Mark 1:15, PME).

As a reaction to Hellenistic and Roman culture and influence, as well as priestly aristocracy, the elders and Pharisaic scribes came into vogue. The study of, and obedience to, the Torah became of paramount importance. While the priests traced their lineage back to Aaron, the elders and scribes traced their succession back to Joshua and Moses and the seventy elders chosen by Moses. We should notice that when God told Moses, "Assemble seventy elders from Israel, men known to you as elders and officers in the community" (Num. 11:16, NEB), the Greek Old Testament reads "scribes" instead of "officers." Thus the scribes could trace their lineage back to the time of Moses, and had established a line of succession.

The rabbis were considered the custodians and interpreters of the law of Moses and the oral traditions, and thus the biblical scholars and theologians of their time, and had religious authority to speak for God as Moses did. When the temple was destroyed the scribes or rabbis were ready to be the "new priests" in Judaism. It has been expressed in these words: "Rabbinic Judaism claimed that it was possible to serve God not only through sacrifice, but also through study of Torah. A priest is in charge of the life of the community, but a new priest, the rabbi. The old sin-offerings still may be carried out through deeds of loving-kindness; indeed, when the whole Jewish people will fully carry out the teachings of the Torah, the Temple itself will be rebuilt."[20] We will return to the importance of the rabbis in our study of ordination.

THE APPOINTED MINISTRY

It is generally agreed that during the New Testament period, there were two appointed ministries: "deacon" (Greek, *diakonos*) and "elder-overseer" (*presbuteros-episkopos*). "Presbyter" is another name for "elder," as "bishop" is for "overseer." Before we examine these two ministries let us note the appointment of the Seven in Acts, chapter six.

The Council of the Seven. The story of how to solve a major practical problem in the emerging church reads as follows: "Now at this time while the disciples were increasing in number, a complaint arose on the part of the Hellenistic Jews against the native Hebrews, because their widows were being overlooked in the daily serving of food. And the twelve summoned the congregation of the disciples and said, 'It is not desirable for us to neglect the word of God in order to serve tables. But select from among you, brethren, seven men of good reputation, full of the Spirit and of wisdom, whom we may put in charge of this task. But we will devote ourselves to prayer, and to the ministry of the word.' And the statement found approval with the whole congregation; and they chose Stephen, a man full of faith and of the Holy Spirit, and Philip, Prochorus, Nicanor, Timon, Parmenas and Nicolas, a proselyte from Antioch. And these they brought before the apostles; and after praying, they laid their hands on them" (Acts 6:1-6).

It is interesting to notice the procedures of this church business meeting. The Twelve called the congregation together and made a suggestion which "found approval with the whole congregation." After the congregation had chosen seven persons, they were presented to the Twelve and after prayer hands were laid on them. Two of the Seven, Philip and Stephen, were evangelists. The words "deacon" and "elder" are not used.

The pragmatic situation of Acts 6:1-6 and the terminology used reflect, or compare with, actual events under Moses, which serve as an analogy. Then and now the people of God (the covenant-remnant people) were on march into a realization or fulfillment of God's promises which would bring them "even to the remotest part of the earth" (Acts 1:8). The setting of Acts 6 is within salvation history.

The promise was given to Abraham that his descendants would multiply (Gen. 22:17) and so they did in Egypt (Ex. 1:7, 10, 20). Now, the New Israel did the same: ". . . the disciples were increasing in number" (Acts 6:1), and "continued to increase greatly," even "a great many of the priests" became followers (Acts 6:7).

Through the leadership of Moses God multiplied signs and wonders in Egypt (Ex. 7:3). Stephen, one of the Seven and the one listed first, "full of grace and power, was performing great wonders and signs among the people" (Acts 6:8).

We read that when "the whole congregation of the sons of Israel" complained and murmured over the lack of food, Moses and Aaron called the people together (Ex. 16:2, 6); likewise, "the twelve summoned the congregation" (Acts 6:2).

The Twelve, like Moses (Num. 11), felt the weight of administration too heavy and in both cases the responsibility was distributed respectively to seven and seventy.

No reference is made in Acts 6 to elders or deacons. After the event of Acts 6:1-6 Stephen, "full of grace and power, was performing great wonders and signs among the people" (Acts 6:8), defended the faith before the Council, and suffered martyrdom (Acts 7). Philip went into evangelistic work, and some 20 years later we find him living in Caesarea. On a brief visit, Paul and his companions stayed in Philip's home. The record of this event mentions that Philip was "one of the seven" (Acts 21:8).

The Seven have been referred to as deacons, elders, and the "apostolate of the Seven".[21] They have been classified as deacons because they overlooked the distribution of alms. However, they were not named deacons and neither functioned as deacons did in association with elders in the time of Paul.

We are told that the church in Antioch sent alms to the church in Jerusalem by "the elders" (Acts 11:30), indicating that those in charge were elders; accordingly, it is thought that the Seven could be elders.

At least two of the Seven were actively involved in evangelism and missionary work, and thus also had the characteristics of an apostle missionary. This points in the direction of an apostolate of the Seven. We will return to this point after we ask why seven were chosen.

Among the different answers we find the following: "the number was fixed upon because of the seven gifts of the Spirit" (Isa. 11:2; Rev. 1:4); it represented "the different elements of the church: three Hellenists, three Hebrews, one Proselyte"; Jerusalem "may have been divided into seven districts"; it originated from "the Hebrew sacred number—seven"; the house churches in Jersualem may have been "seven in number."[21]

A more likely answer may be found in the organizational structure within Judaism. We have noticed that the Great Sanhedrin had seventy-one members, but there were also councils of twenty-three and seven members, the latter being named "the seven" of a city. Josephus, the Jewish historian at the time of Christ, refers to "seven men to judge in every city." If these could not "give a just sentence" then the case should be brought to the Sanhedrin in Jerusalem.[23]

According to Jewish sources (Talmudic literature) seven men made up an administrative council in the local towns and as such they were involved with the administration of the synagogue.[24]

It should also be noticed that a local Jewish community of 120 could choose seven as a council.[25] Luke makes a point of the fact that when Peter spoke to the first Christian community the gathering was "of about one hundred and twenty persons" (Acts 1:15). Did Luke make the reference to 120 for the purpose of pointing out that the followers of Christ were enough in number to establish a community?

The early primitive church lived as a Jewish Christian community within the framework of Jewish society. We see in the church-council of Jerusalem an analogy to the Jewish Council, and the council of the Seven also has its analogy in Judaism. The Christian councils have their own content and significance, but the analogy can help us locate their purpose in a historical setting.

The administration and judicial aspects or work of the Seven resemble in principle that of the Seven of the city, which in turn was related to the major Council in Jerusalem. The Seven represented the interests of the Hellenistic Jews who had become Christians. The apostolate of the Twelve demonstrated that the ministry is one of service (*diakonia*) and involved missionary outreach; the same is the case with the Seven, who have accordingly been described as the apostolate of the Seven. At the time when the apostolate of the Twelve ceased and the Council of Jerusalem came to an end, no doubt the council of the Seven likewise discontinued.

In the light of what has been observed, it is not surprising that the late A. M. Farrer in his book *The Apostolic Ministry* writes: "The supposition that the Seven are regarded by St. Luke as deacons is a very old error."[26] In this connection it is interesting to notice that Roman Catholic theologians, who have always endorsed the old traditions, also admit that "it is disputed whether the term *diakonos*, as used in Acts 6, designates exactly the same thing as the later ecclesiastical office of deacon."[27]

Further, it should also be observed that Vatican II's document on the church and its ministry makes no reference to Acts 6. Hans Küng explains: "With reference to the term 'deacon', and again in contrast with Trent, the traditional text for the biblical foundation of the diaconate, namely Acts 6:1-6, is no longer quoted. The commission's reasoning runs as follows: 'As far as Acts 6:1-6 is concerned, exegetes are no longer completely convinced that the men spoken of here correspond to our deacons, although they have traditionally been regarded as their forerunners. For this reason the text is not quoted in the Constitution.' "[28] We will comment further on the Seven when we deal with the question of ordination.

The Office of Deacons. We have previously pointed out that *diakonos* primarily denotes "a servant," the verb *diakoneo*, "to serve," and *diakonia* "service." Reference is made to Christ as a *diakonos* (Rom. 15:8); who came not "to be served, but to serve" (*diakoneo*) (Matt. 20:28). The followers of Christ are His "servants" (*diakonoi*) (John 12:26) and in the relationship to one another they should be servants (*diakonoi*) (Matt 20:26; 23:11). Those engaged in preaching and teaching are called servants (*diakonoi*) of Christ (1 Cor. 3:5; 2 Cor. 3:6; 6:4; 11:23; Eph. 3:7; 6:21; Col 1:7, 23, 25; 4:7; 1 Tim. 4:6). The office of deacon reminds us that any ministry and ministerial office is diaconal in purpose and structure, just as the church itself was established for the sake of service along with worship (celebration), instruction, and mutual support.

Two Pauline references indicate that the office of deacon was established in churches and had an origin and function different from the Seven. In the only description of the qualifications of a deacon their work is not spelled out (1 Tim. 3:8-13), as is the case with an overseer (*episcopos,* "bishop") where the qualifications are similar (1 Tim. 3:1-7). When addressing the church in Philippi (Phil. 1:1) Paul merely lists "overseers and deacons" without any comment.

The pair, overseer-deacon, may have been patterned—although not exactly—after the Jewish synagogue, where the worship was entrusted to two officers, while the total administration of the synagogue was in the hands of a committee of elders. In the story of Christ's visit to the synagogue in Nazareth, where He was given the opportunity to read the Scripture reading, we are told that "he closed the book and gave it back to the attendant" (Luke 4:20).

The leading elder or overseer of the synagogue was called *archisynagogos* (ruler of the synagogue). Jairus, whose daughter Christ raised from the dead, was such a person (see Mark 5:22, 35, 36, 38; Luke 8:49). Translators refer to him as "a ruler," "president," "official," and "leader" of the synagogue (KJV, NEB, NASB, LB).

In Hebrew the *archisynagogos* is the head or leader (*rosh*) of the assembly, and the other his servant or assistant (*chazzan*). In the synagogue some were also appointed as collectors and distributors of alms, but they had no responsibility for the worship service.[29]

Deaconesses-Fellow Workers. There is no conclusive evidence in the New Testament regarding an office of deaconess. The only place where the word *diakonos* applies to a woman is in the closing chapter of Romans, where some versions translate it as "servant," others as "deaconess." The text reads: "I commend to you our sister Phoebe, who is a servant of the church which is at Cenchrea; that you receive her in the Lord in a manner worthy of the saints, and that you help her in whatever matter she may have need of you; for she herself has also been a helper of many, and of myself as well" (Rom. 16:1-2).

In view of the fact that the help Phoebe rendered is not spelled out, it seems most natural to use the word "servant" for the varied services she rendered. However, a linguistic inconsistency is found even by the use of the word "servant," for in many instances the same translators use the word "minister" when *diakonos* refers to a male. It may be more appropriate to think of Phoebe as a fellow worker like Prisca, who is characterized as such in the following verse. This also seems plausible from the fact that Phoebe is described as "a helper" (Greek *prostatis*, a "leader," "champion," "patroness," "protectress"). In the New Testament it is found only here, and is feminine in gender. As a verb it is used in the New Testament to express one who "leads," "has charge over," "manages," "rules" (Rom. 12:8, 1 Thess. 5:12; 1 Tim. 3:4, 5, 12; 5:17). Outside the New Testament the masculine form *prostatas* is used as a title for "the office bearer in a heathen religious association." In the Greek Old Testament *prostatas* is translated "chief," "ruler," and "chief officer" (1 Chr. 27:3; 29:6; 2 Chr. 8:10)."[30]

There is no doubt that Phoebe was "a good friend" and "a great help," as *prostatis* is translated, respectively, in the New English Bible and the New International Version. However, Paul no doubt had more in mind when he used the word *prostatis*. One thing seems apparent: Paul does not refer to an office of deaconess as later conceived by the church. Likewise, the statements in 1 Timothy 3:17 and 5:9-10 are rather obscure and ambiguous in regard to a supposed order of deaconess. This does not mean that the church was wrong when it later created such an order, so long as it was in harmony with the theology and ecclesiology of the New Testament.

Other women who extended help are mentioned, but the nature of their help is not described; yet, the help was significant enough to mention them by name. Prisca (or Priscilla), together with her husband Aquila, Paul calls "my fellow workers in Christ Jesus, who for my life risked their own necks, to whom not only do I give thanks, but also all the churches of the Gentiles; also greet the church that is in their house" (Rom. 16:3-5).

According to Luke, Paul became acquainted with this couple when he came to Corinth (Acts 18:1-3). Later, they traveled with Paul and settled in Ephesus. By profession they were tentmakers like Paul, but also active in evangelistic work. We are told that Apollos, who was teaching about Jesus but "acquainted only with the baptism of John," received instruction from Prisca and Aquila about "the way of God more accurately" (Acts 18:24-26).

The significance of this wife-husband team is seen by the fact that Paul in his greetings to the church in Corinth writes: "Aquila and Prisca greet you heartily in the Lord, with the church that is in their house" (1 Cor. 16:19). Years later Paul requested Timothy to "greet Prisca and Aquila" for him (2 Tim. 4:19).

Paul mentions three other women by name: "Greet Mary, who has worked hard for you. . . . Greet Tryphaena and Tryphosa, workers in the Lord. Greet Persis the beloved, who has worked hard in the Lord" (Rom. 16:6, 12)). The women mentioned in Romans 16 can properly be described as fellow workers "in the Lord."

Elders in the Jersualem Church. It appears that the church in Jerusalem was administered somewhat similarly to the Jewish Council and the synagogue. James, the brother of Jesus and the leader, was associated with elders. We are told that the church in Jerusalem sent Barnabas to Antioch for a special mission. The Christians in Antioch decided "to send a contribution for the relief of the brethren living in Judea." The money was sent "in charge of Barnabas and Saul to the elders" (Acts 11:29, 30).

When Paul came to Jerusalem after his third missionary journey Luke records that "the brethren received us gladly. And now the following day Paul went in with us to James, and all the elders were present. And after he had greeted them, he began to relate one by one the things which God had done among the Gentiles through his ministry" (Acts 21:17-19). It appears that the apostles, together with elders, made up a council for the growing church in its missionary outreach.

When the question arose about circumcision "the brethren determined that Paul and Barnabas and certain others of them should go up to Jerusalem to the apostles and elders concerning this issue. . . . And the apostles and elders came together to look into this matter" (Acts 15:2, 6). After Paul had given his report, "It seemed good to the apostles and the elders, with the whole church, to choose men from among them to send to Antioch with Paul and Barnabas—Judas called Barsabbas, and Silas, leading men among the brethren, and they sent this letter by them, 'The apostles and the brethren, who are elders, to the brethren in Antioch' " (Acts 15:22-23). On the issue of circumcision, so important as to threaten the total disruption of the new movement, consultation was absolutely essential.

The Establishment of Local Elders. Outside of Jerusalem, we find that in the churches Paul founded during his first missionary journey he appointed elders "in every church" (Acts 14:23). Writing to Titus, Paul reminded him that he had left him in Crete that he "might set in order what remains, and appoint elders in every city as I directed you" (Titus 1:5). On Paul's third missionary journey "from Miletus he sent to Ephesus and called to him the elders of the church" (Acts 20:17). Reminding them of his work among them he exhorted them: "Be on guard for yourselves and for all the flock, among which the Holy Spirit had made you overseers, to shepherd the church of God which He purchased with His own blood" (Acts 20:28). Here the elders (*presbyteroi*) are called "overseers" (*episcopoi*), and as such they should "shepherd the church of God." In greater detail Peter wrote: "Therefore, I exhort the elders among you, as your fellow elder and witness of the sufferings of Christ, and a partaker also of the glory that is to be revealed, shepherd the flock of God among you, exercising oversight not under compulsion, but voluntarily, according to the will of God; and not for sordid gain, but with eagerness; nor yet as lording it over those allotted to your charge, but proving to be examples to the flock. And when the Chief Shepherd appears, you will receive the unfading crown of glory" (1 Peter 5:1-5; see also Eph. 4:11).

Presbyter-Bishop. The term elder or presbyter (Greek *presbyteros*) and overseer or bishop (*episcopos*) are used interchangeably (see Acts 20:17,28; Titus 1:5-9). In his letter to Timothy Paul wrote: "Let the elders who rule well be considered worthy of double honor, especially those who work hard at *preaching* and *teaching*" (1 Tim. 5:17). The King James Version reads: ". . . they who labor in the word and doctrine." The word "rule" (Greek *troestemi*) means "to lead," "attend to" (indicating care and diligence), "to superintend," "preside over," conveying the idea of overseeing. 1 Timothy 3 describes the qualifications of overseers (bishops and deacons) but does not use the word elders (presbyters). In 1 Timothy 5 only "elders" are mentioned, thus the two words are used interchangeably.

We have observed that the Apostle Peter exhorted "the elders" and refers to himself "as your fellow elder" (1 Peter 5:1). The Apostle James only refers to elders (not bishops) when he writes: "Is anyone among you sick? Let him call for the elders of the church, and let them pray over him, anointing him with oil in the name of the Lord" (James 5:14). In the second and third Epistle of John the author speaks about himself as "the elder" (2 John 1; 3 John 1).

Elders were overseers, but no doubt, as members of the body of Christ, they had individual gifts—shepherding, preaching, teaching, administration, etc. (see Rom. 12:3-8; 1 Thess. 5:12)—which were recognized and used in their role as elders. Eldership, as an appointment to minister (*diakonio*), seems reflected in the fact that there are elders in heaven who also serve the church on earth (see Rev. 5:5, 8; 7:13).

What we so far have obsesrved regarding the ministry in the New Testament will be considered further as we take note of theological and historical developments related to the ministry of the church.

4 THE MINISTRY: HISTORICAL—THEOLOGICAL OBSERVATIONS

The history of the church presents from the beginning a twofold development of good and of evil, an incessant antagonism of light and darkness, truth and falsehood, the mystery of godliness and the mystery of iniquity, Christianity and Antichrist. According to the Lord's parables of the net and of the tares among the wheat, we cannot expect a complete separation before the final judgment, though in a relative sense the history of the church is a progressive judgment of the church, as the history of the world is a judgment of the world.—Philip Schaff

AN HISTORICAL NOTE

Whenever ministerial functions and offices developed outside the framework of the nature of the ministry and the doctrine of the priesthood of believers—as described in the New Testament—or evolved contrary to the principles embodied therein, then the structure of the church and the ministry changed. We will note that "as the history of the world is a judgment of the world," so "in a relative sense the history of the church is a progressive judgment of the church."[1]

Changes gradually took place during the second century, and by the middle of the third century the concept of the ministry, and thereby the doctrine of the church, was greatly altered, especially through the work and writings of Cyprian. To him the essence, foundation, and unity of the church are found in the bishop, as his famous dictum says: "You ought to know that the bishop is in the Church, and the Church in the bishop; and if any one be not with the bishop, that he is not in the Church." From now on ecclesiastical offices constituted more and more the basic nature and structure of the church. As a result church history in general, and ecclesiology in particular became, to a large degree, the story of a growing power of the bishop not only administratively but also theologically, until it found its apex in the pope as the vicar of Christ. The future outcome of Cyprian's teaching was institutionalized churches contrary to the New Testament pattern.

The doctrine of the church and its ministry as presented by Cyprian "produced a greater change in contemporary Christian thought than any movement before the Reformation."[2] We will first seek to sketch the development of the ministry up to the time of Cyprian, keeping in mind that scholars generally agree "that in the New Testament the terms bishop and presbyter seem interchangeable, nor is there anything to show how the former term came to be used for an office that had taken on apostolic functions."[3]

In order that the general reader may become acquainted with the pertinent historical material and obtain direct impression of the source material, we will quote directly and let the sources speak for themselves.

A TRANSITION PERIOD (A.D. 100-200)

Clement of Rome. The earliest Christian writing of any extent outside the New Testament was written under the name First Epistle of Clement to Corinth.[4] The introductory salutation makes it clear that the letter was sent from one church to another, not from one bishop or church leader to another.

The letter was sent by three members of the Roman church prompted by the fact that some presbyters had unjustifiably been dismissed causing disunity in the church of Corinth. We find that the words bishops and presbyters are used interchangeably as in the New Testament. Speaking about the apostles of Christ Clement writes: "They went forth in the assurance of the Holy Spirit preaching the good news that the kingdom of God is coming. They preached from district to district, and from city to city, and they appointed their first converts, testing them by the Spirit, to be bishops and deacons of the future believers" (xlii.3-4). He makes reference to the title of bishops, but what follows indicates that it was used for the function of presbyters for one reads: "Blessed are those Presbyters who finished their course before now, and have obtained a fruitful and perfect release in the ripeness of completed work, for they have now no fear that any shall move them from the place appointed to them. For we see that in spite of their good service you have removed some from the ministry which they fulfilled blamelessly" (xliv.5-6). It is further substantiated from the following statements: "It is . . . shameful . . . that on account of one or two persons the stedfast and ancient church of the Corinthians is being disloyal to the presbyters." "Only let the flock of Christ have peace with the presbyters set over it." "You therefore, who laid the foundation of the sedition, submit to the presbyters" (xlvii.6; liv.2; lvii.1).

Ignatius of Antioch. A decade or two after the Epistle of Clement, we find that Ignatius of Antioch wrote several letters while he was on his way to Rome where he suffered martyrdom (c. A.D. 110-115).[5] Six of these were addressed to churches in Asia Minor and one to Polycarp of Smyrna. In these letters we are introduced for the first time to a threefold ministry: bishop, elders, and deacons. This structure is referred to as a threefold ministry, monarchical episcopate or monepiscopacy, where one person, a bishop, is in charge assisted by elders and deacons. This is different from the twofold ministry we have met and will meet. When the designation monarchical episcopate is used in connection with Ignatius it must be understood that it is not synonymous with the episcopacy a century later.[6]

It should be noticed that in the letters of Ignatius the word "bishop" is always used in the singular, with the presbyter in the plural. Further, the work of the bishop (*episcopos*) is always described with relationship to the presbytery (*presbyterion*). Ignatius expresses the hope that the church "may be joined together in one subjection, subject to the bishop and to the presbytery." He mentions the "justly famous presbytery" (Ephesians ii.2; iv.1).

In the letter to the Magnesians he writes: "Be zealous to do all things in harmony with God, with the bishop presiding in the place of God and the presbyters in the place of the Council of the Apostles, and the deacons, who are most dear to me, entrusted with the service of Jesus Christ." In the next paragraph he repeats: "As then the Lord was united to the Father and did nothing without him, neither by himself nor through the Apostles, so you do nothing without the bishop and the presbyters" (Magnesians vi.1; vii.1).

The same concept is expressed to the Trallians: "You should do nothing without the bishop, but be also in subjection to the presbytery, as to the Apostles of Jesus Christ our hope." Further, "Whoever does anything apart from the bishop and the presbytery and the deacons is not pure in his conscience" (Trallians ii.2; vii.2).

In the letter to the Romans no reference is made to a bishop—the same was the case in the letter of Clement of Rome—but this statement is made: "Remember in your prayers the Church in Syria which has God for its Shepherd in my room. Its bishop shall be Jesus Christ alone,—and your love" (Romans ix.1). He expresses a clear difference between a bishop and the apostles when he writes: "I do not order you as did Peter and Paul; they were Apostles" (Romans iv.3).

A threefold ministry is also mentioned to the Philadelphians. As there is one Eucharist so "there is one bishop with the presbytery and the deacons." "Give heed to the bishop, and to the presbytery and deacons" (Philadelphians iv.1; vii.1).

Ignatius closes his message to the Smyrnaeans with this greeting: "I salute the godly bishop, and the revered presbytery, and the deacons my fellow servants, and you all, individually and together, in the name of Jesus Christ" (Smyrnaeans xii.2). In his personal letter to Polycarp of Smyrna, whom he addresses as "a bishop," he also advises the Christian community when he writes: "Give heed to the bishop, that God may also give heed to you. I am devoted to those who are subject to the bishop, presbyters, and deacons" (Polycarp vi.1).

The main impression we have from the letters is the great burden Ignatius has for the unity, sanctity, universality, and apostolicity of the church. To preserve this unity the local church has an overseer (bishop), presbyters, and deacons. The bishop (overseer) is chairman of the presbytery, the first among equals (*primus inter pares*) and not as in later centuries the absolute number one (*primus absolutus*). With good reason we can speak about a presbyter-bishop. In the light of this it is understandable that the Lord's Supper, baptism and "agape" meals could not be performed without the bishop or by one whom he appoints (Smyrnaeans viii.2). The presbyter-bishop was, it seems, the presiding host at the Lord's Supper. We may even designate him as the senior pastor.

Before we leave Ignatius, note the following:

> But if there be no sacerdotalism, no apostolic succession, no one-man rule, and no diocese; if every Christian community is to be organized under a leader, who is called a bishop and sometimes a pastor, who presides over a court of elders, and has under him a body of deacons; . . . if nothing is to be done without the consent of the pastor or bishop, neither sacrament nor love-feast, nor anything congregational— then while the resemblance to modern episcopacy, with its diocesan system, is but small, there is a very great amount of resemblance to that form of ecclesiastical organization which

re-emerged at the Reformation and which is commonly called the presbyterian, though it might be more appropriately
named the conciliar system of Church government.[7]

Polycarp. We not only have Ignatius' letter to Polycarp of
Smyrna (died as martyr c. A.D. 156) but also a letter from Polycarp
to Philippi.[8] The opening sentence reads: "Polycarp and the Elders
with him to the Church of God sojourning in Philippi." While he speaks
in detail about the qualifications of presbyters and deacons, he does
not mention bishops at all (v, vi). On the contrary, he states: "Be subject
to the presbyters and deacons as to God and Christ" (v.3).

We have observed that Ignatius refers to Polycarp as a bishop and
to a threefold ministry in the church of Smyrna. However, Irenaeus
(d. c. A.D. 200) tells us that he had visited Polycarp's house as a boy
and refers to him as "that blessed and apostolic presbyter."[9] According to the record of Irenaeus, Polycarp visited Rome in order to discuss
with Anicetus the question of the date for celebrating Easter; Rome
and the Eastern churches celebrated on different dates. Anicetus is
described as the leader (not bishop) of the church in Rome and the
successor of "the presbyters before Soter, who presided over the
church." We are also told: "Nor did Polycarp persuade Anicetus to
observe it, for he said that he ought to keep the custom of those who
were presbyters before him."[10] Anicetus and Polycarp did not reach
an agreement, but celebrated the Lord's Supper together and separated
amicably. In another connection we will observe that 40 years later
another meeting took place between the leaders of the churches of
Rome and Ephesus and for the same reason, but the outcome was different. With special interest we will notice that at that time the title
presbyter was replaced with bishop.

The Apologist Justin Martyr. Justin Martyr, who suffered martyrdom in Rome (c. A.D. 165), was a native of Samaria. He lived
for some time in Ephesus and later settled in Rome. He became a
Christian apologist. He regularly refers to the "president" (Greek
proestos). This could be another word for "overseer." It has been suggested that "this usage may have been dictated by a concern to avoid
specifically ecclesiastical language in addressing the pagan world."[11]

In the description of the local church service and the celebration
of the Lord's Supper Justin tells us that after Scripture reading the
"president" gives a discourse and the congregation stands up and prays.
"There is then brought to the president of the brethren bread and a

cup of wine mixed with water."[12] This seems to be another picture of an elder-pastor who as "overseer" (bishop) presides in the church, and is the host of the Lord's Supper.

Hermes of Rome. Also counted among the Apostolic Fathers is Hermes of Rome (c. A.D. 100-140). He is remembered for his book, The Shepherd, which is composed of a series of visions, moral instructions, and ten parables.[13] His references to the ministry are scanty, but the structure presented indicates similarity to that of Clement where the words bishop and presbyter are used interchangeably as in the New Testament. It is presbyters who preside in the church (Vision II.iv.2.). Twice he mentions bishops but in the plural because it is used interchangeably with presbyter. The church is built on a foundation of "the Apostles and bishops and teachers and deacons who . . . served the elect of God in holiness and reverence as bishops and teachers and deacons" (Vision III.v.1). Bishops are listed together with "hospitable men who at all times received the servants of God into their houses gladly and without hypocrisy; and the bishops ever ceaselessly sheltered the destitute and the widows by their ministration, and ever behaved with holiness" (Similie IX.xxvii.2).

The Church Manual Didache. Reference has previously been made to the Teaching of the Twelve Apostles, also referred to as the Didache.[14] Here reference is made to a charismatic ministry and bishops and deacons, reminding us of the ministry found in the writings of Paul.

We find traveling teachers, apostles, and prophets with instruction on how to treat them and test them. The apostles are traveling missionaries and are not expected to stay more than two days, and "if he ask for money, he is a false prophet" (Didache xi.6). A true prophet and teacher may settle down in a church, but practical arrangements should be made for their sustenance (Didache xi, xii, xiii). Regarding the local ministry we read: "Appoint therefore for yourselves bishops and deacons worthy of the Lord, meek men, and not lovers of money, and truthful and approved, for they also minister to you the ministry of the prophets and teachers. Therefore do not despise them, for they are your honourable men together with the prophets and teachers" (Didache xv.1-2).

The words "bishops" and "deacons," no doubt, are used as by Paul (Phil. 1:1; Acts 20:17, 28), where bishops are synonymous with elders. The word "bishop" is therefore in the plural. In the writings of Ignatius we observed that the word "bishop" was used in the singular, referring to the presbyter-bishop among a group of presbyters and deacons.

Irenaeus of Gaul. At the close of the second century we find Irenaeus, a native of Asia Minor, in the church of Lyons in Gaul (present-day France) from 177 to his death (c. A.D. 200). Here he wrote the work Against Heresies in which we find reference to the ministry. In this connection it is interesting to notice that church historian Eusebius, at the time of Constantine, refers to Irenaeus as "a presbyter of the diocese at Lyons."[15] We have already referred to Irenaeus' statement regarding Polycarp being a presbyter.

In Irenaeus' struggle against the gnostic heresy his great argument is that the Christian church is genuine where apostolic succession is found in teaching and in office-bearers: presbyters-bishops. A few brief quotations from Against Heresies speak for themselves:

> When we refer them to that tradition which originates from the apostles, [and] which is preserved by means of the successions of presbyters in the Churches (III.ii.2). The faith preached to men, which comes down to our time by means of the successions of the bishops (III.iii.2). It behoves us . . . to adhere to those who, as I have already observed, do hold the doctrine of the apostles, and who, together with the order of priesthood (*presbyterii ordine*), display sound speech and blameless conduct for the confirmation and correction of others (IV.xxvi.4).[16]

The above quotations indicate that a fixed designation between two orders of ministry (bishop and presbyter) had not fully developed. Robert M. Grant expresses it in these words: "It is clear that the kind of ministerial succession which Irenaeus upholds is one in which the offices of bishops and presbyters are practically interchangeable."[17]

The Church of Rome. When Paul wrote his epistle to the church in Rome (A.D. 58) he said: "All over the world they are telling the story of your faith" (Rom. 1:8, NEB). We do not know who planted the first seeds. Suggestions have been made that they were planted by Roman Jews present at the first Pentecost in Jerusalem; others think that the Roman Church might have been founded by Antiochene Christians.

Early Christian writers inform us that Peter and Paul (not Peter alone) preached in Rome. The Scriptures do not record that Peter and

Paul died as martyrs in Rome, but from the many historical testimonies it is beyond reasonable doubt. Eusebius asserts that Peter and Paul were both put to death at Rome and their burial places were existing in his own day.[18]

Regarding the development of monarchical episcopacy in Rome it seems that it first appears after the middle of the second century. Clement of Rome and Hermes do not make reference to monepiscopacy. While Ignatius in his letters speaks about a three-fold ministry, we do not find that to be the case in his epistle to the Romans. We have discussed Polycarp's visit with Anicetus in Rome and found that only the title presbyter was used. However, Justin Martyr (d. 165) mentions the president, but no doubt with reference to the "overseer" or presbyter-bishop. However, Eusebius tells us that Dionysius (c. A.D. 170) sent a letter "to Soter who was then bishop."[19]

In A.D. 190 Victor became bishop of Rome and the controversy regarding the date for celebrating Passover was taken up again and this time with the bishop of Ephesus, Polycrates. In the document by Polycrates preserved by Eusebius, and in Eusebius' own comments only the title bishop is used both for the leader of the church in Rome and in the other cities. The growing power of the bishops, not least in the capital city, is obvious in this controversy, which ended by Victor—without any practical result—excommunicating Polycrates and his congregation, and this he did in spite of protest from Irenaeus who exhorted Victor "not to excommunicate whole churches of God for following a tradition of ancient custom."[20] Without going into further details, it suffices to say as one scholar has stated: "If we have rightly understood our sources, it would seem that the region east of the Aegeas had the threefold ministry somewhat earlier than did the Greek and Roman regions to the west."[21] The Paschal controversy between Anicetus and Polycarp, and later between Victor and Polycrates, illustrates, indirectly, the development of the monepiscopacy in Rome and elsewhere as we come to the close of the second century. Regarding Rome, which became the seat of the popes, there is, as we noticed, "strong evidence that the Roman church was ruled, not by a bishop, but by a college of presbyters, until well into the second century."[22]

A CHANGED MINISTRY

Tertullian of Carthage. Early in the third century Tertullian of Carthage, North Africa, wrote a defense against the gnostic heresy similar to that of Irenaeus.[23] His main argument against false teaching is that true doctrines are only found in churches founded by the apostles.

While Irenaeus used "bishop" and "presbyter" interchangeably we find that Tertullian speaks only about a succession of bishops. Philip Schaff writes: "Tertullian was the first who expressly and directly asserts sacerdotal claims on behalf of the Christian ministry, and calls it *'sacerdotium,'* although he also strongly affirms the universal priesthood of all believers. . . . He uniformly and clearly distinguishes bishops and presbyters."[24]

Tertullian had studied and practiced law in Rome prior to his conversion and return to Carthage. He was the first prominent church writer to use Latin and therefore provided, in different ways, a new terminology which led to new concepts that later would become general. He refers to a threefold ministry of bishops, presbyters, and deacons, and calls the bishop the "chief priest."[25]

It is somewhat ironic that Tertullian, who provided the Latin vocabulary to the ecclesiology of the Latin church, became a Montanist. Montanism was first an eschatological revival movement with a renewal of the spiritual gifts, especially prophecy; later the stress was laid upon rigid morality in contrast to a general laxity in the "orthodox" church. Tertullian has been described as an episcopalian in the first part of his life, and in the second a Montanist. His writings from the Montanist period represents a different side to Tertullian's ecclesiology, and we may add, a necessary one. He writes:

> The very Church itself is, properly and principally, the Spirit Himself, in whom is the Trinity of the One Divinity—Father, Son, and Holy Spirit. (The Spirit) combines that Church which the Lord has made to consist in 'three.' And thus, from that time forward, every number (of persons) who may have combined together into this faith is accounted 'a Church,' from the Author and Consecrator (of the Church). And accordingly 'the Church,' it is true, will forgive sins: but (it will be) the Church of the Spirit, by means of a spiritual man; not the Church which consists of a number of bishops.[26]

Tertullian's twofold ecclesiastical view has been described in this way: "Tertullian, then, provides us successively with both an advanced catholic sacerdotal view of the office of the bishop and presbyter and a radical Spiritual doctrine of the priesthood of all believers."[27]

The following balanced view of Tertullian's ecclesiology is worthy of notice: "Tertullian, we may conclude, was protesting not so much against the idea of ministerial order as such as against the failure of bishops, whether by laxity or by officialism, to be what they should have been. Such protests have been needed, and that of Tertullian and the Montanists was the first of many."[28]

Cyprian of Carthage. It is obvious from what we have observed that the way was prepared for Cyprian to whom we will now return. Cyprian was born and lived in Carthage. He became bishop two years after he became a Christian (A.D. 246) and suffered martyrdom in A.D. 258. We will quote from his Epistles.[29]

For Cyprian the basic principle of unity is found in the bishop. Applying to Peter Christ's words, "Upon this rock I will build My church" (Matt. 16:18) and "describing the honour of a bishop and the order of His Church," Cyprian writes: "Thence, through the changes of times and successions, the ordering of bishops and the plan of the Church flow onwards; so that the Church is founded upon the bishops, and every act of the Church is controlled by these same rulers" (xxvi.1). Accordingly, as previously noticed, Cyprian could say: "You ought to know that the bishop is in the Church, and the Church in the bishop; and if any one be not with the bishop, that he is not in the Church" (lxvii.8).

The church which previously was a brotherhood of the priesthood of believers became a community centered in the bishop who has the "sublime and divine power of governing the Church" (liv.2).

As a priest the bishop is a representative of Christ, especially at the Lord's Supper, which is considered as a sacrifice; thus the priest is identified with the priesthood of Aaron. As a consequence the ministry has become a sacerdotal mediatory function and the priesthood of believers is a contradiction. In a lengthy discussion Cyprian says that the bishop does "that which Jesus Christ, our Lord and God, the founder and teacher of this sacrifice, did and taught." Accordingly, the "priest truly discharges the office of Christ" and "offers a true and full sacrifice" (lxii.1, 14).

The Birth of the Christian Priest. It must be re-emphasized that the term priest is not used in the New Testament with reference to a ministerial office; it only applied collectively to the total body of believers. In Israel, as among the heathen nations around them, priests formed a distinct class (Gen. 41:45; 47:22; 1 Sam. 6:2; Acts 14:13).

Their task was to "appease" the gods by offering sacrifices. Among the Israelites the priesthood was hereditary and belonged to the tribe of Aaron. But among the heathen nations it was granted by the state; neither procedure was acceptable by the early church.

Beginning with Tertullian, Hyppolytus and Cyprian the word "priest" came into vogue. Two factors, especially, came together to accomplish this. The Lord's Supper became a sacrifice and from the analogy of the Hebrew and pagan religions, he who administrated the sacraments became a priest (*sacerdos*); accordingly, we speak about sacerdotalism. In this connection it should be noticed that in the apocryphal Acts of John (c. A.D. 160-170) the table for the Lord's Supper is referred to as an altar; likewise, Polycrates of Ephesus (c. A.D. 190) spoke about the Apostle John as a "priest wearing the breastplate."[30] At the same time the presbyter-bishop of a presbytery developed into an order above the presbyter. Hans Lietzmann writes: "About A.D. 200, there are passages comparing the bishop with the high-priest, and the presbyters with the priests; shortly afterwards, the deacons are equated with the Levites."[31] George H. Williams points out: "Presbyters were becoming priests at the very same time they were relinquishing their corporate judicial and disciplinary authority in the bishop's church, while the bishop had become the chief judge; and the law itself was being codified in canons at councils at which bishops alone decreed."[32]

Monarchical Episcopacy. When the council of presbyters with a presbyter bishop as its head developed into a monarchical episcopacy, the one-man autocracy in a local church found easy support on a larger scale until it reached its apex in the pope. The brotherhood of "the saints and the faithful brethren in Christ" (Col. 1:2) gradually disappeared, likewise the charismatic ministry, and gave place to an institutional and hierarchical church. The early church councils, between A.D. 314 and 451, completed the development of the episcopate by enacting canons (laws) regarding its authority. The first universal council was that of Nicaea, A.D. 325, and its significance for our topic has been summarized in these words: "As early as the Council of Nicaea bishops had taken upon themselves the full responsibility for the authoritative definition of dogma in their corporate capacity as the organ of the Holy Spirit. To this doctrinal function had been added the disciplinary and legislative powers to bind and loose by canons deemed superior in authority to locally received traditions and the consensus of local churches in which the laity and the presbyters had customarily voiced their assent in adjudications and in doctrinal formulations."[33]

Apostolic Succession. Up to the time of Cyprian the bishops who presided over the churches founded by the apostles were in succession from the apostles, but now all bishops are considered successors of apostles, also representing Christ by having sacerdotal power like the priesthood of the Old Testament. Theologically and ecclesiologically the two go together and influence the ministry; the stage was set for the medieval church.

The Civil Administrative Structure of the Roman Empire. The Christian ministry and offices were not established in a vacuum. We have observed roots and antecedents in the Old Testament and in Judaism. In the second and third centuries the church expanded into the various parts of the empire and the structure of the appointed ministry began, to a large degree, to be organized as the civil administrative structure of the empire. For the sake of brevity we will quote Arnold Ehrhardt:

> It seems to be well established that the constitution of the early Christian churches was similar in form to the constitution of the *municipia* in the early Roman Empire; this is affirmed by modern historians and even by some early Fathers of the Church. The *municipia* were colonies of Roman veterans in the provinces of the Roman Empire, and their administration was roughly similar to that of the city of Rome itself. The magistracies were always held by more than one person; there was a council of elders, consisting of persons eligible for office, which prepared by its deliberations courses of action to be effected by the executive; there was on the other hand the popular assembly, called in the East the *ecclesia*, and officers called *adparitores*, or in the East deacons, who were the connecting link between the council and the assembly.[34]

This historical observation speaks for itself; however, we wish to make a few comments. There was a council of elders, and the assembly was called the *ecclesia*, which is the common word for assembly and also used in the New Testament for the assembly of believers, the church. The officers are called *adparitores,* which is the Latin for "servants," as "deacons" is in the Greek.

The *municipium* (a Roman town, borough, or colony) had as the head of the administration two or more magistrates; they were named quastors and functioned as prosecutors or judges; or treasury-officials. Paul speaks about overseers (bishops) in the plural together with deacons (Phil. 1:1; Acts 20:28). It is first in the second century with the beginnings of the monepiscopacy, or monarchical episcopacy, that we find only one head in the administration of the local church. Without going into further discussion of a possible Roman influence at this time, we will once more quote Ehrhardt:

> It is here that we may outline the origin of the title *episcopus* so far as concerns the choice between the various non-ecclesiastical meanings of the word. Two facts stand out. The one is that the term was chosen prior to the introduction of mon-episcopacy, but preserved after its introduction. The other is that very rarely in pagan writers is the term used for the description of a supreme or a sacred position, even if describing the function of a heathen god. An *episcopus* is a functionary of an organization, political or non-political. The bursars of Hellenistic clubs were sometimes called *episcopoi*, and for this reason E. Hatch suggested that the bishops had originally adopted the name as treasurers of a Christian congregation. But Church-organization never followed the model of private societies, and it seems more likely that the royal inspectors of Hellenistic times who had become town officials afforded the pattern from which the title came into use.[35]

In this connection it should be noticed that Justin Martyr, in the middle of the second century, speaks about the president (the local elder or bishop) as the one responsible for dispensing the collections in the church. He writes: "What is collected is deposited with the president, who succours the orphans and widows, and those who, through sickness or any other cause, are in want, and those who are in bonds, and the strangers sojourning among us, and in a word takes care of all who are in need."[36]

One hundred years later, about A.D. 251, Cornelius of Rome tells in a letter how the "master" (bishop) was the administrative dispenser in the work of charity. The letter tells us that in the church were "forty-six presbyters, seven deacons, seven sub-deacons, forty-two acolytes, fifty-two exorcists, readers and door-keepers, above fifteen hundred widows and persons in distress, all of whom are supported by the grace and lovingkindness of the Master."[37]

The Constantinian Church and its Sequel. Constantine's recognition of the church in the fourth century and its association with the Roman state was a determining factor in the practical organization of the church and the ministry. The church took shape from the civil organization of the empire. As Christianity spread, there had come to be generally a bishop for each city, together with the territory attached to it. Bishoprics were grouped into provinces, as the districts already were for civil purposes, and its president was the metropolitan or archbishop.

> The power and prestige of the clergy—the Christian *ordo*— increased as those of the civil *ordo*—the municipal magistracy—declined, until the bishop became the most important figure in the life of the city and the representative of the whole community. . . . He wielded almost unlimited power in his diocese, he was surrounded by an aura of supernatural prestige. . . . Moreover, in addition to his religious authority and his prestige as a representative of the people, he possessed recognised powers of jurisdiction not only over his clergy and the property of the Church, but as a judge and arbitrator in all cases in which his decision was invoked, even though the case had already been brought before a secular court.[38]

After the state had placed a positive value on the church and it next became a part of the structure of the empire, lawgiving showed favor toward the clergy and the church with the result that the church was bound together by political ties and the clergy became officials of the state. Even judicial duties were assigned to the bishops "by the new Christianized State. . . . Even in the period of imperial patronage, when the ordinary courts themselves came to reflect Christian principles, bishops continued to enlarge the judicial aspect of their office. All Christians, at the beginning of the Constantinian era, were directed . . . to the courts spiritual presided over by bishops."[39]

When the masses entered the church it was followed by an influx of ideas from pagan temples and worship, which were Christianized. This especially had a bearing on the sacerdotal concept of the priesthood. We have already observed that the priest and bishop, in celebrating the Lord's Supper, were compared to the Aaronic priesthood; now the same could be compared to the pagan priests. The sacramental concept of a mediatory ministry, more than anything, further changed the ministry during the middle ages both theologically and structurally, as reflected in the development of the seven sacraments: Baptism, Confirmation, the Eucharist, Penance, Extreme Unction, Order, and Matrimony. The believer lived his religious life from birth to death within the parameters of the sacraments, believing that through them the priests were dispensing God's grace.

The priest himself had by the sacrament of order been given an indestructible mark (*character indelebilis*). This indelible mark or character the priest could not loose. With the stroke of the pen the pope could place a single person, group of persons, a city, district, and a county under an interdict, which meant that the priests were not permitted to administer the sacraments, and therefore spiritual death for those under interdict. Further, the distinction between clergy and laity was complete.

Reformation Attempts. The structure of the church and its ministry, as it developed in the fourth century, prevailed for more than a thousand years. We have previously observed the growing monepiscopacy of the papacy. We have likewise noticed that men and movements arose to challenge medieval ecclesiology—such as the Albigensians, Waldensians, John Eckhart (d. 1327), Marsilius of Padua (d. 1342), William of Occam (d. 1349), John Wyclif (d. 1386), and John Hus (d. 1415). However, it was first through the Protestant Reformation of the sixteenth century that fruitful attempts succeeded in restoring or coming closer to the ecclesiology of the New Testament and the early church.

LUTHER AND THE MINISTRY

Luther's Reaction. It is significant to notice that the Protestant Reformation was a reaction against the medieval concept of the ministry. The final break with Rome came when Luther, in 1520, wrote, *A Prelude on the Babylonian Captivity of the Church,* in which he criticized the Roman sacramental system, which he believed brought the faithful into bondage to the priestly hierarchy. He asserted that, tried by Scripture, there are only two sacraments, baptism and the Lord's Supper. He also criticized the denial of the cup to the laity.

In his opposition to papal supremacy and the sacramental system he attacked the very foundation and structure of Roman Catholicism and its ministry. His appeal to a general council as the highest authority was contrary to the concept of papal supremacy. Soon after completing *The Babylonian Captivity* Luther received the pope's bull, *Exsurge Domine*. In it Pope Leo X speaks as an infallible and supreme judge, condemning twenty-one propositions selected from Luther's writings as heretical. Among these are Luther's attack on papal supremacy and the seven sacraments.

Luther's Faith Experience. The Lutheran Reformation grew out of Luther's own religious experience in which he found justification by "faith alone" and "grace alone" through "Christ alone" and "the Bible alone." From this experience stems his ecclesiology: negatively as a reaction against sacerdotalism and positively in the doctrine of the priesthood of all believers. This we have observed in our previous discussions.

A Delegated and Representative Ministry. Belonging to the priesthood of believers all Christians are ministers or priests, but for the sake of order some must occupy the office of ministry (*diakonia*). "We are all priests insofar as we are Christians, but those whom we call priests are ministers selected from our midst to act in our name, and their priesthood is our ministry." Further from the pen of Luther:

> Where the Word of God is preached and believed, there is true faith, that (certain) immovable rock; and where faith is, there is the Church; where the Church is, there is the bride of Christ; and where the bride of Christ is, there is also everything that belongs to the Bridegroom. Thus faith has everything in its train that is implied in it, keys, sacraments, power, and everything else. . . . Every Christian has the power the pope, bishops, priests and monks have, namely, to forgive or not to forgive sins. . . . We all have this power, to be sure, but none shall dare exercise it publicly except he be elected to do so by the congregation. In private, however, he may use it.[40]

The essential distinction between "clergy" and "laity" was clearly removed, and the word priest made obsolete. In view of the centrality of the Word the minister was generally called preacher and later pastor ("shepherd").

This new concept of the ministry was to influence the whole

history of Protestant Christianity. However, a complete vision and thereby a total realization of the priesthood of believers did not take place. One scholar writes about this doctrine: "This is a great idea, and a very true one, which the Church is seeking to recover today. Yet it never really took hold even in Luther's day."[41] One basic reason was that at the time of the Protestant Reformation the nature of the church was mainly defined by two marks: The gospel rightly preached, and the sacraments rightly administered. This emphasis is understandable in the tremendous task the reformers had to counteract the seven sacraments, which was foundational for the nature of the Roman Catholic Church.

It is only fitting that the appointed minister preach in the pulpit and serve at the Lord's Supper, but when the impression is left that only they are truly the ministry, then a wrong concept is given of the nature of the church. The result has been expressed in this way: "The laymen can listen to the preaching and receive the sacraments, but their own priesthood is not evident. Furthermore, the old stratification between a religious calling and the demands of daily life is reinstated."[42]

In this present study we have, on a number of occasions, defined the "church" in relationship to the "witness" by all believers. It is therefore of interest to notice that the writer just quoted also says:

> If the emphasis had then been placed not so exclusively on preaching and the sacraments but *on witness and service in and to the world* as marks of the true Church, the laity could have found their place of priesthood. The emphasis was not thus placed, however, and the stratification continued. It still continues, and the same barriers persist. Even before the present emphasis on the laity, occasional attempts have been made to revive the idea in various movements stemming from the Reformation, but in general one may say that the priesthood of all believers was stillborn.[43]

Without minimizing the influence of an appointed ministry it may be proper, at this junction of our study, to note the following appeal:

> The time is ripe for renewal and reconstruction of the idea of the priesthood of all believers, a projection of the Christian gospel into the whole of life through the witness and ser-

vice of every Christian. . . . What is to be deplored is the layman's seeing his Christian duty is limited to being a handyman in the institutional structure of the Church, with no awareness that in his daily occupation, his political responsibilities, and his community contacts he *is* the Church within the world.[44]

Luther's Congregational Church Concept. According to Luther, the power of the church is limited to the ministry of the Word. For some time Luther expressed his concept of the church as rather congregational in its form of organization, built up as a voluntary group of committed Christians. In Luther's answer to a book by his Catholic opponent, Jerome Emser, a secretary to Duke George of Saxony, he writes: "Priest and bishop are one and the same thing in Scripture." Accordingly, the church structure at the time was "not founded on Scripture."[45]

Luther changed his concept of the church and also that of church-state relationships. For political reasons, Luther placed the church under the general supervision of the state, which then to a very large degree dominated the church. On account of their alliance with the state and its magistrates the Protestant reformers are also called Magisterial Reformers. The price which Luther paid for the help of the territorial prince was too high. Even Karl Holl, a defender of Luther, has to admit this, and adds, "The best energies of the Reformation were kept down through this development or they were forced to develop alongside and apart from the Church." An outstanding American Lutheran scholar, the late Professor J. L. Neve, has said that "the establishment of Lutheran territorial churches laid the foundation for a continuing injury to Lutheranism from which Germany is suffering to this present day."[46] Accordingly, Luther's original and ideal ecclesiology is more perfectly carried into effect by Lutheranism in America, where church and state are separated.

CALVIN AND THE MINISTRY

Calvin's Institutes of the Christian Religion. Calvin's major work first appeared as a small edition in 1536, but was, after several editions, completed in 1559 and divided into four books. It has profoundly influenced the development of the Reformed tradition of Protestantism. Book Four, which is the last and by far the longest of the *Institutes*, deals with the doctrine of the church. Chapters one and two deal to a large degree with the value and marks of the church and chapter three with its ministry. In the following sixteen chapters he discusses the history and ecclesiology of the primitive and ancient church. Then, at length, he deals with the papacy and its sacramental system, and explains the true meaning of baptism (he sharply opposes rebaptism) and the Lord's Supper. Book Four closes with a chapter on civil government.[47]

The Church and the Magistrates. Calvin aimed at making the government of Geneva Christian. By having a Christian magistracy it was hoped that church and state would mutually support one another, while the church at the same time would maintain independence in spiritual matters. Sometimes the church-state relationship in Geneva has been referred to as a theocracy and bibliocracy, thereby expressing the influence the Bible had upon the magistracy. The influence upon the administration of the secular society has also characterized the Reformed Churches and English Puritanism both in Europe and America.

In Geneva the governmental power resided in three councils: The Council of the Sixty, who were members of the Council of the Two Hundred; the Council of the Twenty-five were made up of members from the other two councils. The interrelationship between these civil councils and the church will be observed in several connections.

New Testament Ministry. Calvin strongly emphasizes a structured ministry and bases his concept especially on Ephesians 4:4-16. Having quoted these verses he makes the following comment: "By these words he shows that the ministry of men, which God employs in governing the Church, is a principal bond by which believers are kept together in one body. He also intimates, that the Church cannot be kept safe, unless supported by those guards to which the Lord has been pleased to commit its safety." Next, Calvin gives a warning: "Whoever, therefore, studies to abolish this order and kind of government of which we speak, or disparages it as of minor importance, plots the devastation, or rather the ruin and destruction, of the Church. For neither are the light and heat of the sun, nor meat and drink, so necessary to sustain and cherish the present life, as is the apostolical and pastoral office to preserve a Church in the earth" (*Inst.* IV.iii.2).

We will notice Calvin's own explanation of the different ministries (*Inst.* IV.iii.4-5), of which he finds five according to Ephesians 4:11: "Those who preside over the government of the Church, according to the institution of Christ, are named by Paul, first, *Apostles;* secondly, *Prophets;* thirdly, *Evangelists;* fourthly, *Pastors;* and lastly, *Teachers* (Eph. iv. 11)."

1. Apostles. "The nature of the apostolic function is clear from the command, 'Go ye into all the world, and preach the Gospel to every creature' (Mark xvi. 15). No fixed limits are given them, but the whole world is assigned to be reduced under the obedience of Christ, that by spreading the Gospel as widely as they could, they might everywhere erect his kingdom." Accordingly, "they were like the first architects of the Church, to lay its foundations throughout the world."

2. Prophets. "By *Prophets,* he means not all interpreters of the divine will, but those who excelled by special revelation; none such now exist, or they are less manifest."

3. Evangelists. "By *Evangelists,* I mean those who, while inferior in rank to the apostles, were next them in office, and even acted as their substitutes. Such were Luke, Timothy, Titus, and the like; perhaps, also, the seventy disciples whom our Saviour appointed in the second place to the apostles (Luke x. 1)."

Calvin next explains that these "three functions were not instituted in the Church to be perpetual, but only to endure so long as churches were to be formed where none previously existed, or at least where churches were to be transferred from Moses to Christ." Calvin further comments: "I deny not, that afterward God occasionally raised up Apostles, or at least Evangelists, in their stead, as has been done in our time. For such were needed to bring back the Church from the revolt of Antichrist. The office I nevertheless call extraordinary, because it has no place in churches duly constituted."

4. Pastors and Teachers. Regarding these we read: "Next come *Pastors* and *Teachers,* with whom the Church never can dispense, and between whom, I think, there is this difference, that teachers preside not over discipline, or the administration of the sacraments, or admonitions, or exhortations, but the interpretation of Scripture only, in order that pure and sound doctrine may be maintained among believers. But all these are embraced in the pastoral office."

Calvin tries to compare the temporary and permanent ministries with the result that he finds two pairs: prophets and apostles, teachers and pastors.

We now understand what offices in the government of the Church were temporary, and what offices were instituted to be of perpetual duration. But if we class evangelists with apostles, we shall have two like offices in a manner corresponding to each other. For the same resemblance which our teachers have to the ancient prophets pastors have to the apostles. The prophetical office was more excellent in respect of the special gift of revelation which accompanied it, but the office of teachers was almost of the same nature, and had altogether the same end.

Calvin states very categorically that "in giving the name of bishops, presbyters, and pastors, indiscriminately to those who govern churches, I have done it on the authority of Scripture, which uses the words as synonymous. To all who discharge the ministry of the word it gives the name of bishops" (*Inst.* IV.iii.8). Here Calvin clearly distinguishes between Presbyterianism and Episcopalianism.

In Presbyterianism the pastor is also referred to as the teaching elder and the local elder as the ruling elder. In the *Institutes* Calvin states "that three classes of ministers are set before us in Scripture, so the early Church distributed all its ministers into three orders. For from the order of presbyters, part were selected as pastors and teachers, while to the remainder was committed the censure of manners and discipline. To the deacons belonged the care of the poor and the dispensing of alms" (Inst. IV.iv.1.).

Local Elders and the Presbytery. Next, Calvin seeks to explain his biblical base for local elders and the presbytery as well as the office of deacons. He writes that of offices "there are two of perpetual duration—viz. government and care of the poor. By these governors I understand seniors selected from the people to unite with the bishops in pronouncing censures and exercising discipline." He further comments: "From the beginning, therefore, each church had its senate, composed of pious, grave, and venerable men, in whom was lodged the power of correcting faults. Of this power we shall afterwards speak. Moreover, experience shows that this arrangement was not confined to one age, and therefore we are to regard the office of government as necessary for all ages" (*Inst.* IV.iii.8).

The Office of Deacons. Calvin's further reasoning and scriptural reference for the office of deacons should be noticed: "The care of the poor was committed to deacons, of whom two classes are mentioned by Paul in the Epistle to the Romans, 'He that giveth, let him do it with simplicity;' 'he that showeth mercy, with cheerfulness' (Rom. xii. 8). As it is certain that he is here speaking of public offices of the Church, there must have been two distinct classes. If I mistake not, he in the former clause designates deacons, who administered alms; in the latter, those who had devoted themselves to the care of the poor and the sick" (Inst. IV.iii.9).

Four Church Offices. Calvin also distinguishes four offices in the church: pastor, teacher, elder, and deacon. When Calvin, after a three-year stay in Strasbourg, returned to Geneva in 1541, he reached an agreement with the city authorities which was expressed in the Ecclesiastical Ordinances of the Church of Geneva. Agreement was reached on the four church offices which became an integral part of the life of the city.

A minister was nominated by his fellow ministers and the name presented to the city council, which gave him certification. The imposition of hands, spoken of in the New Testament and practiced by the ancient church, was not observed, even though it was permissible "providing that it take place without superstition and without offence. But because there has been much superstition in the past and scandal might result, it is better to abstain from it because of the infirmity of the times."

The office of the teacher or doctor was established for the training of pastors and ministers. It was also essential that "a college should be instituted for instructing children to prepare them for the ministry as well as for civil government."

The heart of Calvin's system was its lay-elders—twelve of them—who, together with the ministers, met weekly. Of the elders two were chosen from the Little Council, four from the Council of the Sixty, and six from the Council of the Two Hundred, thus there was a direct link between the city administration and the church. Each elder was given a special section of the city to oversee. Nomination of the elders was made by the Little Council in consultation with the ministers, and the Council of the Two Hundred gave final approval.

As already observed, Calvin advocated two kinds of deacons, chosen by the same method as the elders. Their responsibility is stated as follows: "There were always two kinds in the ancient Church, the one deputed to receive, dispense and hold goods for the poor, not only daily alms, but also possessions, rents and pensions; the other to tend and care for the sick and administer allowances to the poor. This custom we follow again now for we have procurators and hospitallers."[48]

In his presbyterian church organization Calvin came closer to the New Testament than Luther; however, in his biblical reference and reasoning note must be taken of the comment by Eric G. Jay, who in his discussion of Calvin's ecclesiology, writes: "It is not necessary for our purpose to undertake a close examination of the fourfold ministry of pastors, teachers (or doctors), elders, and deacons. It must be said that his attempt to find a scriptural basis for it is not more noticeably successful than that of the papist, episcopalian, or congregationalist endeavouring to provide scriptural justification for the ministry of his own tradition. The evidence is forced, and what does not fit into the preconceived scheme is explained away."[49]

THE RADICAL REFORMATION

A Significant Movement. From the time of the Protestant Reformation church historians have done the grossest injustice in their description (or lack of description) of the Anabaptist movement. The fanatical Zwikau Prophets in Wittenberg and the millennarian enthusiasm of Thomas Müntzer, as well as the Münster revolution with its anarchy, polygamy, and extreme Jewish apocalypticism—which is now admitted as a caricature of the Anabaptist movement—have been made representative of its beliefs and practices. The Anabaptist leaders have been depicted as the diabolical opponents of the great Reformers, and the angels of Satan incarnate.

When the Anabaptist movement is compared with the classical Protestant Reformation it should be remembered that the sober evangelical leaders among the Anabaptists had much in common with the young Luther and Zwingli. However, after 1525, they dealt with a different Luther, who changed after submitting the Reformation church to the protection and support of the civil authorities, and thereby also compromised some of the basic tenets of evangelical Protestantism.

In the past, historians only spoke about the Reformation initiated by the Protestant Reformers and the opposition to it by the Roman Catholics in the Counter-Reformation. Now it is recognized that there was a third and equally important movement: the Radical Reformation. George H. Williams, while at Harvard Divinity School, contributed greatly to the recovery of this fact. He says: "The Radical Reformation was a tremendous movement at the core of Christendom. . . . It was as much an entity as the Reformation itself and the Counter

Reformation."[50] The contributions made by the Anabaptists are signifi- cant and grew out of their doctrine of the church and its ministry. A knowledge of their concepts and influence is of paramount impor- tance for the understanding and evaluation of the ministry since the Protestant Reformation.

Separation of Church and State. The Anabaptists were firm in their rejection of an alliance between church and state in which each uses the other for its own sake. Their concept of the church as a volun- tary congregation opposed the concept that the church was identical with the people at large in a given territory. Further, the Anabaptists refused to let the problem of a possible survival influence their com- mitment to remain separate from the state. This refusal was anchored in their submission to Scripture, specifically, the teaching and prac- tice of Christ Himself and His apostles.

It is understandable that the Anabaptist groups which developed outside the Lutheran and the Reformed Churches felt more and more strongly, as the evil of the alliance between the church and the state became apparent, that outward separation from the state-church is anything but inward liberation from the influence and principles of the theology and unbiblical ecclesiasticism of the Middle Ages.

Priesthood of Believers and Democracy. It has been widely recognized that the Protestant doctrine of the priesthood of all believers, which taught that all are equal in the eyes of God, made the Protes- tant Reformation the religious starting point of modern democratic ideas; but the development of democratic principles is found in that branch of the Protestant movement where the voluntary church prin- ciple is adhered to. Here the religious voluntarism of the Anabaptists is most significant.

Their idea of the church as a fellowship of active believers and a self-governing congregation led them into an experience of working as a small and thoroughly democratic society, which did not use force in bringing into practice its decisions but was guided by a fellowship of discussion that assumed all the members of the fellowship had something whereby to enlighten the others. Their rejection of exter- nal ecclesiastical and political compulsions, and their application of the principle of consensus, became important in the political sphere. The social, political, religious, and theological framework of the Anabaptist movement of the sixteenth century is in many respects dif- ferent from that of the Magisterial Reformers and the Counter- Reformation of Roman Catholicism; that in turn influenced the

Anabaptist's concept of the nature of the church and its ministry, as well as their contributions to society and Christianity at large.

Religious Freedom. The concept of religious toleration was revived during the sixteenth century by the Protestant Reformers who in the early period of the Reformation advocated freedom of conscience as well as obedience to God, as man's primary duty. Belief in the Bible as the sole authority in matters of faith—the truth of justification by faith, the doctrine of the priesthood of all believers, the participation of Christian laity in church government, as well as the Protestant concept of Christ as the sole head of the church—created a platform on which the cause of religious toleration could be furthered. On the other hand, the Reformers' alliance with the state, the doctrine of the sovereignty of God, and the spirit of Protestant orthodoxy and scholasticism led to intolerance. The Reformers required freedom of conscience and religious liberty for themselves, but generally they were not ready to grant this to others. The experience of the Anabaptists is a classic example of the latter. Referring to the Reformation monument in Geneva, which depicts the Protestant Reformers, Roland H. Bainton makes this sad comment, "The paradox of the monument is that it includes men who would have destroyed each other had they met in life."[51]

The Anabaptists and not the classical Protestant Reformers were the people who advanced the cause of religious toleration by adhering to the positive Protestant beliefs mentioned above, and at the same time rejecting those principles which curtailed the cause of toleration. The Anabaptists did not advocate toleration because they were persecuted. For them religious liberty resulted from the gospel teaching of loving one's neighbor and from the example of Christ and His apostles of not compelling people to believe.

The Fall and the Restitution of the Church. One significant difference between the Magisterial Reformers and the Anabaptists is found in the fact that, while both groups believed that an apostasy had taken place in the church, the former aimed at a reformation of the church but the latter spoke about the restitution of the primitive apostolic church. This is again closely tied up with the Reformers' belief in the idea of the *Corpus Christianum*, where church and state form one whole Christian body, while the Anabaptists adhered to the concept of the believers' church or *Corpus Christi*. The former, therefore, considered the beginning of the golden age of the church from the time of Constantine, but the latter fixed the date of the fall of the church from the same period.

Consequently, the Anabaptists and other "radical" groups saw the beginning of the antichrist's rule in the bishop of Rome from the days of Constantine, while the Reformers recognized the power of antichrist in the medieval papacy. The Anabaptists noticed that the church before Constantine was a church of martyrs, and believed that the true church was generally a suffering church. Likewise the primitivism of the apostolic church was to be normative in every age of the church. As man fell in the beginning, likewise the church fell, but as a full restitution was needed for man, so also the church needed a complete restitution. For the individual and the church, which is the voluntary body of believers, the believers' baptism became a realistic symbol of the restitution.[52]

The Discipleship of Christ. The centrality of Anabaptists' belief is often expressed by the words, *Nachfolge-Christi*, conveying the thought: following Christ, imitating Christ, and, as generally translated, the discipleship of Christ. The obedience of Christ and his perfect life was not only a prerequisite for his vicarious atonement for mankind, but became also the criterion for Christian ethics. Accordingly, Christ's perfect obedience to the Father should be exemplified (on the pragmatic level of everyday living) in the regenerated life of the believer. The whole life of the believer should be brought under the Lordship of Jesus Christ and the life and sayings of Christ as found in the four Gospels should be normative for Christian living, and concretely and realistically imitated.

The Christian Brotherhood. Out of the Anabaptist concept that the church is a voluntary congregation of converted and dedicated Christians grew the concept of a Christian brotherhood, in German *Gemeinschaft*. The Anabaptists addressed one another as brothers and sisters. In a realistic way the priesthood of believers was furthered. Their common faith eliminated class distinction and also affected their economic ethic which was characterized by sharing and bearing one another's burdens. In the brotherhood the priesthood of believers and the primitivism of the apostolic church was realized. The covenant-remnant-eschaton motifs of the Old and New Testaments were basic to their ecclesiology. The local churches appointed deacons and elders; and as in the early church, evangelists or missionaries, named apostles and prophets, unified the congregation in faith and mission, and made known synodical recommendations. The priesthood of believers functioned within a strong unity between the charismatic and the appointed ministry. Anabaptists sought, not a mere reformation of the church, but a restitution of the apostolic church.

The Sociological Outlook. In all their human relationships the Anabaptists sought to apply the same principle of love to non-members as to their own. The principle of love functioned not between God and man alone, nor between man and man alone, but both inseparably together. In the Christian attempt to influence or even transform society Roman Catholics and the Reformed Churches have generally been optimistic. Luther was rather pessimistic regarding redeeming society and therefore tended to compromise. The Anabaptists held the same pessimistic view, but they were not ready to sacrifice any of the principles of the kingdom of God in their relationship with society. Since society at large was under the power of Satan, a true Christian social order could only be established within the brotherhood. On account of the great conflict between God and Satan, good and evil, there would always be a tension and very often a conflict between the true church and the world. The church was always the church militant.

For the Anabaptists the ideals of the kingdom of God could not be realized in an ecumenical *Corpus Christianum*, but only in a brotherhood which adhered to the primitivism of the apostolic church. However, even here there was a tension between the present and the eschatological fulfillment in the eternal kingdom. The fulfillment of the great commandment of loving God and one's neighbor was taken most literally, as illustrated in their firm belief in pacifism, which made them abandon all participation in war and violence. While they did not believe that society at large would be transformed, they still maintained that the kingdom of God, as realized within the brotherhood, should be a light and a leaven in the world.

The Gathered Church. The conflict between the Magisterial Reformers and the Anabaptists did not begin with the issue of baptism, but regarding the concept of the church. It has been said that "the reformers aimed to reform the old Church by the Bible;" but the Anabaptists "attempted to build a new Church from the Bible."[53]

For the Anabaptists, apostolicity meant a realistic following or imitation of Christ and a restitution of the apostolic ecclesiology and doctrine; that in turn led to the significance of the believer's baptism, which became the sign of the covenant. The church was the church of the gathered ones ("called out") who had entered into covenant relationship with God. "The idea of a covenantal relation to God and one's fellows became the foundation of the Anabaptist community."[54] The covenant-remnant-eschaton motif was foundational in their ec-clesiology. As the sixteenth century moved on, Protestant theology, in the words of Robert Friedmann, "abandoned the idea of a 'second coming' of Christ, concentrating exclusively on the theme of personal certitude of salvation (*Heilsgewissheit*). There was simply no room left for a meaningful eschatology within the late Lutheran and post-Lutheran theology. The only place where such ideas were kept alive and had a legitimate function was the 'left wing' of the Reformation or, as we now call it, the Radical Reformation: Anabaptism and related movements."[55]

In this branch of the Reformation the advent hope shone bright-ly. To be ready and to be vigilant for the second coming of Christ became the eschatological framework within which great missionary zeal and endeavors were manifested. We are here distinguishing bet-ween those who held extreme chiliastic views and sought to realize them by force, and those who held to a peaceful eschatology.

Church Offices. In the brotherhood, the doctrine of the priesthood of believers was realized. The spiritual gifts were sought, but a struc-tural Christian community was also implemented. A Hutterite leader wrote: "How can there be a Christian Community where no Chris-tian order and command is [maintained], with separation, the ban, discipline, brotherly love and other [practices]; further that one after the other may speak openly, give of his gifts and insights freely before the people at the appointed time?"[56]

The Hutterite communities founded in Moravia by Jacob Hutter (d. 1536), established clearly defined church offices. In one writing the author admonishes

> . . . the brethren to honor one another and especially the *''Dienner'* [servant]. These leaders were laymen, chosen by the congregation on the authority of the New Testament ex-ample of Acts 14:23; Acts 20:17 and 28; Titus 1:5; I Timothy 3, 5:17; I Corinthians 9:14. They were chosen, on the basis of piety and dedication, to shepherd the community—to read, to warn, to teach, to punish. There were other officers. Among the Hutterites the most notable were the 'shepherds' (*Hirten*), the missioners (*Diener des Wortes* [servant of the Word]), the stewards (*Diener der Notdurft* [servant of those in need]).[57]

In Holland, as in many other parts of Europe, Anabaptism spread first as an unorganized movement in which the lay people preached and explained the Word. However, the office of deacon was establishfor in order to take care of the poor. Mention is also made of "those who bear the purse." As time moved on, leaders of congregations were appointed; first they were named bishops but later elders, or the names were used interchangeably. In many cases elders were traveling evangelists who went from congregation to congregation. Such a one was Menno Simons, who became an Anabaptist in 1536 and remained such unto his death in 1561. He did much to organize Anabaptism in Holland, and his followers bear the name Mennonites.[58]

A Mennonite document of 1560 bearing the title, "The Seven Ordinances of the True Church," lists them as follows: "true teaching, correct ministry"; "proper use of the two sacraments, baptism and the Lord's Supper"; "foot-washing"; "evangelical separation"; "brotherly love"; "keeping all His commandments"; and "accepting suffering and persecution."[59]

The Mennonites had a great influence upon English Separatists who had fled to Holland, and on their return brought Anabaptism to their home country. An English Anabaptist leader is referred to as a "missionary and elder," and a report of their meetings tell us that some of the members "are made bishops, elders, and deacons, who call them to one of the disciples' houses."[60]

The itinerant preachers, evangelists, or elders were also named apostles and prophets. Speaking about Austrian Anabaptism, George H. Williams writes: "The consciousness of being prophets or apostles was keenly developed among them."[61] Dealing with Anabaptism in Strasbourg, the same author refers to a certain John Bunderlin as a "visiting apostle"; he also points out that "the Italian Anabaptists readily called their itinerant pastors apostoli." At a certain synod "several participants were designated as 'apostolic bishops' to bring the synodal decisions to the constituent and related congregations." Reference is made to the fact that itinerary preachers "regarded themselves as apostolic emissaries."[62]

In any ecumenical dialogue and study of ecclesiology the Anabaptist vision and view of the nature of the church and its ministry is of great importance and must not be neglected.

WORLD COUNCIL OF CHURCHES

We will close this part of our study with another reference to the

Faith and Order Commission's document on the Ministry.[63] The historical sketch we have made should be helpful in evaluating this document. The document asserts: "The New Testament does not describe a single pattern of ministry which might serve as a blueprint or continuing norm for all future ministry in the Church. In the New Testament there appears rather a variety of forms which existed at different places and times." Next it affirms what we have observed:

> During the second and third centuries, a threefold pattern of bishop, presbyter and deacon became established as the pattern of ordained ministry throughout the Church. In succeeding centuries, the ministry by bishop, presbyter and deacon underwent considerable changes in its practical exercise. At some points of crisis in the history of the Church, the continuing functions of ministry were in some places and communities distributed according to structures other than the predominant threefold pattern. Sometimes appeal was made to the New Testament in justification of these other patterns. In other cases, the restructuring of ministry was held to lie within the competence of the Church as it adapted to changed circumstances (Ministry, Section 19).

In section 22 of the Faith and Order document on the Ministry the World Council of Churches speaks in favor of a threefold ministry as the best structure for an ecumenical unity of the church. We read:

> Although there is no single New Testament pattern, although the Spirit has many times led the Church to adapt its ministries to contextual needs, and although other forms of the ordained ministry have been blessed with the gifts of the Holy Spirit, nevertheless the threefold ministry of bishop, presbyter and deacon may serve today as an expression of the unity we seek and also as a means for achieving it. Historically, it is true to say, the threefold ministry became the generally accepted pattern in the Church of the early centuries and is still retained today by many churches. In the fulfillment of their mission and service the churches need people who in different ways express and perform the tasks of the ordained ministry in its diaconal, presbyteral and episcopal aspects and functions.

The great question is, of course, what threefold pattern will be the model: Ignatius, Cyprian, the Constantinian Church, the medieval church, the Anglican Church, the Orthodox Churches, etc.? The many responses from the churches reveal the different concepts of a threefold pattern. The document no doubt had anticipated this, for it states: "The threefold pattern stands evidently in need of reform. . . . In general, the relation of the presbyterate to the episcopal ministry has been discussed throughout the centuries, and the degree of the presbyter's participation in the episcopal ministry is still for many an unresolved question of far-reaching ecumenical importance. In some cases, churches which have not formally kept the threefold form have, in fact, maintained certain of its original patterns. The traditional threefold pattern thus raises questions for all the churches" (Ministry, Sections 24-25).

Churches without an episcopal church structure, have, in general, concern about the episcopalian tendencies expressed in the World Council of Churches' document. Its threefold foundation for the church and its ministry; namely, Scripture, ancient ecumenical creeds, and later confessions of faith, seems to weaken the priority of Scriptures over tradition in the pragmatic attempt for an ecumenical solution. However, all agree that the concept of the ministry should be rooted in "the calling of the whole people of God." We referred to this in our discussion of the priesthood of believers.

It is hoped that the historical observations we have made and the theological perspectives we have drawn, have not only been helpful in evaluating the nature of the ministry, but also in preparing the way for the subject of ordination. In turn this subject will throw further light upon the Christian ministry. We will now inquire biblically and historically: What is ordination?

5 ORDINATION: A BIBLICAL-HISTORICAL INQUIRY

Ordination, if it is anything at all, is nothing else than a certain rite whereby one is called to the ministry of the church.
—Martin Luther

By divine institution some among the Christian faithful are constituted sacred ministers through the sacrament of orders by means of the indelible character with which they are marked.—Roman Catholic Canon Law

The basic reality of an ordained ministry was present from the beginning. The actual forms of ordination and of the ordained ministry, however, have evolved in complex historical developments. The churches, therefore, need to avoid attributing their particular forms of the ordained ministry directly to the will and institution of Jesus Christ.
—World Council of Churches on the Ministry

ORDINATION DEFINED

The Roman Catholic Concept. The Roman Catholic sacramental concept and sacerdotalism is rooted in the sacrificial functions of the priesthood, who by ordination are endowed with supernatural power to administrate the sacraments, which in turn by the very act—*ex officio*—confers supernatural grace to the recipient. According to the Council of Trent at baptism and ordination to the priesthood "a character is imprinted which can neither be effaced nor taken away." Therefore, they are in error who assert "that those who have once been rightly ordained can again become laymen, if they do not exercise the ministry of the Word of God." Further, the bishops "have succeeded to the place of the Apostles, . . . they are superior to priests" whom they ordain. Accordingly there is "a hierarchy by divine ordination." The bishops assume their position "by authority of the Roman Pontiff." It should further be noticed that in ordination the consent of the people is not required and those who say "that order, or sacred ordination, is not truly and properly a sacrament . . . or, that it is only a kind of rite for choosing ministers of the Word of God and of the sacraments: let him be anathema."[1]

Canon Law of 1917 and 1983 confirm that "the Church is hierarchical in nature and only clerics can obtain jurisdiction," and the "ministry is viewed as fundamentally sacramental and clerical. The role of non-clerics including religious is to assist the cleric in fulfilling the responsibilities of ministry." Defining the nature of the sacrament of order, Canon Law of 1983 (Canon 1008) states: "By divine institution some among the Christian faithful are constituted sacred ministers through the sacrament of orders by means of the indelible character with which they are marked." The hierarchical and papal structure of the ministry is confirmed by the fact that "No bishop is permitted to consecrate anyone a bishop unless it is first evident that there is a pontifical mandate" (Canon 1013). In turn, only the bishop can ordain priests and deacons (Canon 1015). Here, ordination is in conflict with the doctrine of the priesthood of believers; further, ordination distinguishes not only between different kinds of ministries, but establishes degrees, or a hierarchy of ministries.[2]

The Protestant Concept. Among the Protestant churches ordination is commonly defined as the setting apart, the recognition and confirmation of a divine call, the commission, the consecration or the installation to an official ministerial function or public office in the church. However, the functions and offices are not uniformly defined among the different branches of Protestantism; yet, they seek to have an official ministry which ecclesiologically is not to be in conflict with the doctrine of the priesthood of believers. The principle of equality but with functional differences without being hierarchical is attempted (more or less successfully) to be maintained within a spirit-filled organic structure: the body of Christ. For those who hold the sacramental concept of ordination it is the act of ordination which gives significance to the person and ministry, but not so for the one who does not hold that view. Here it is the function, order, office, or service which modifies the act of "ordination," that is, the installation or election. From a biblical perspective a better word may be dedication or consecration. Since there is a variety of ministerial functions, so the installation or consecration must differ in their specific purpose; however, the general purpose of all ministries is to serve the body of Christ in the work of reconciliation.

The Word "Ordain" in the New Testament. The meaning of

ordination or installation must be sought in the Bible, but when one turns to the Bible we find that confusion arises from translation in the various versions. In the English speaking world the King James Version has been the most influential for three centuries. Here, the word "ordain" is translated from more than twenty different Hebrew and Greek words, each having its own connotation.[3] When the English word "ordain" is read with one's pre-conceived idea of ordination then it has tainted the interpretation of the biblical material. We will notice the usage of the word where it relates to appointment to an official ministry.

The only place in the Gospel narratives where one finds the word ordain is in Mark 3:14 (KJV): "And he ordained twelve, that they should be with him, and that he might send them forth to preach." Modern translations have a more correct reading of the Greek *poieo*, when they write that Christ "appointed twelve." The Greek actually says that he "made twelve," indicating that they were a closely united group. The Living Bible says: "He selected twelve."

When it came to replacing Judas among the twelve, the KJV reads: "Beginning from the baptism of John, unto that same day that he was taken up from us, must one be ordained to be a witness with us of his resurrection" (Acts 1:22). Here the Greek *ginomai* is used, meaning "to become." Other translations do not use the word "ordain," but "select," "join us," "become with us," etc.

The Apostle Paul writes about himself: "Whereunto I am ordained a preacher, and an apostle, . . . a teacher of the Gentiles in faith and verity" (1 Tim. 2:7, KJV). Here "ordain" is translated from still another Greek word, *tithemi*, the meaning of which is to "place," "set," "assign," etc. In the text just quoted modern versions, in the main, use the word "appoint." The Living Bible has the word "chosen" and the Jerusalem Bible has "been named." The same Greek word is used in John 15:16 where the KJV reads: "I have chosen you, and ordained you," but, again, newer translations have the word "appointed;" the Jerusalem Bible has the word "commissioned."

The New American Standard Bible has—correctly—not one single place where the word "ordain" is used in the New Testament for the ministry.[4] When the KJV reads that Titus should "ordain elders in every city" (Titus 1:5), newer versions read in the main "appoint," but never "ordain." The Greek word *kathistemi* means "cause to be" or "arrange"; it is also translated "put in charge" (see Matt. 24:45, 47; Luke 12:14).

In Acts 14:23 where the KJV reads: "And when they had ordained them elders in every church" the Greek word means "appointed."
The same Greek word is used in 2 Cor. 8:19, where it is said that
Titus had "been appointed by the churches to travel with" Paul. In
this text the KJV has the word "chosen," but in Acts 14:23 "ordain."

The Greek word in these two texts is *cheirotoneo*. This is composed of the two words: *cheiros*, "hand," and *toneo*, "to stretch," thus
meaning "to stretch out the hand." It is a technical word expressing
appointment or agreement by lifting the hand in voting. The English
word "ordain" has its roots in the Latin *ordinare* meaning "to set in
order," "arrange" or "regulate." The two Greek and Latin words have
different connotations. This is brought out by the World Council of
Churches' document on the Ministry when dealing with the question
of ordination. We read:

> It is evident that there is a certain difference between the
> unspoken cultural setting of the Greek *cheirotonein* and that
> of the Latin ordo or *ordinare*. The New Testament use of the
> former term borrows its basic secular meaning of "appoint-
> ment" (Acts 14:23; II Cor. 8:19), which is, in turn, derived
> from the original meaning of extending the hand, either to
> designate a person or to cast a vote. . . . *Ordo* and *ordinare*,
> on the other hand, are terms derived from Roman law where
> they convey the notion of the special status of a group distinct
> from the plebs, as in the term *ordo clarissimus* for the Roman
> senate."[5]

In the West, Latin became the language of the church at the time
the monarchical episcopacy was consolidated, the bishop became a
"highpriest," the presbyter a "priest," and the organizational structure of the church gradually followed that of the empire. It is obvious
that the words *ordo* ("order," "ordinance") and *ordinare*, as understood within the Roman society, enhanced the power of the church
hierarchy with the result that the priesthood of believers and the
spiritual gifts became obsolete.

Having different connotations, usage of the Greek or Latin words
has ecclesiological consequences. Accordingly, the World Council of
Churches document (quoted above) makes the following closing
remark: "The starting point of any conceptual construction using these
terms will strongly influence what is taken for granted in both the

thought and action which result."[6]

The apparent confusion, lack of clarity, and fluid character of foundation for ordination by the use of the word "ordain," is made apparent in other areas. In Romans 12, 1 Corinthians 12, and Ephesians 4 are listed the special gifts given to the church "for the work of the ministry" (Eph. 4:12, KJV). In none of these three chapters is ordination mentioned. There seems to be no relationship between the possession of these gifts, their exercise, and ordination. Paul lists apostles, prophets, evangelists, pastors, and teachers (Eph. 4:11), but no reference is made to ordination.

LAYING ON OF HANDS IN THE OLD TESTAMENT

In the church rite of ordination the laying on of hands has become so significant that it seems unthinkable to have ordination without the laying on of hands, leaving the impression that ordination is the laying on of hands. Before we look to the New Testament for an answer to this question we will turn to the Old Testament for a possible background and antecendent.

The Symbolic Meaning of Hands. From ancient time the hand has had a most significant symbolic meaning, which is richly illustrated in the Old Testament and in secular history.[7] We will merely attempt to summarize. Hands were considered the principal organ of feelings, the instrument of power. Hands were the symbols of human action; just hands were pure action and unjust hands were deeds of injustice. Washing of the hands was the symbol of innocence. Prayer was accompanied with lifting up the hands. The elevation of the right hand was the method of voting in assemblies. To give the right hand was a pledge of fidelity and was considered as confirming a promise.

Hands in general were the symbol of power and strength, the right hand particularly. To hold by the right hand was the symbol of protection and favor. To stand or be at one's right hand was to assist or aid someone. The right hand of fellowship signifies a communication of the same power and authority. To lean upon the hand of another was a mark of familiarity and superiority. To give the hand, as to a master, was the token of submission and future obedience. To kiss the hand was an act of homage.

In the Bible the hand of God is spoken of as the instrument of power, and to it is also ascribed that which strictly belongs to God Himself. As the symbolism of the hand goes back to antiquity, so also the imposition or laying on of hands, which takes place in various settings.

The Laying on of Hands by Jacob. The first biblical reference regarding the laying on of hands goes back just prior to the death of Jacob, when Joseph came with his two sons, Manasseh and Ephraim, to visit his father. When it came to the moment of blessing Joseph's two sons, Jacob "stretched out his right hand and laid it on the head of Ephraim, who was the younger, and his left hand on Manasseh's head, crossing his hands, although Manasseh was the first born" (Gen. 48:14). Joseph had placed the two sons before Jacob so his right hand could be placed on Manasseh, the first born. Joseph objected, but the father said that Ephraim was going to be the father of a greater people than Manasseh. Here the imposition of the hands represented the transmission of a special blessing.

The Appointment of Joshua. Prior to his death God told Moses to appoint Joshua as his successor. Regarding the installation and consecration of Joshua we read that Moses "laid his hands on him and commissioned him, just as the Lord had spoken through Moses" (Num. 27:23).

Several points should be noticed. Joshua's experience made him an obvious choice. A very close relationship had existed between the two. He was richly endowed by the Holy Spirit. His call was from God and confirmed by the Urim and Thummin placed on the breastplate of the high priest. He should be commissioned in the sight of the congregation, who were convinced that his call was from God. Moses placed his hands on him indicating that Moses' authority and responsibility rested in Joshua. It was a once-and-for-all installation for a specific and unique historical event—the entrance into the promised land—by "the congregation in the wilderness" (Acts 7:38). The uniqueness of the laying on of hands in the case of Joshua may also be seen by the fact that it was not repeated, and in the installation of priest, king, and prophet no imposition of hands took place.

Hands Placed on the Sacrifice. The laying on of hands played a significant part in the sacrificial system. When a person offered a burnt-offering (Lev. 1:4), a peace-offering (Lev. 3:2), and a sin-offering (Lev. 4:4) he placed his hand on the head of the animal. In the case that a person had blasphemed and cursed he should be brought "outside the camp, and let all who heard him lay their hands on his head; then let all the congregation stone him. And you shall speak to the sons of Israel, saying, 'If anyone curses his God, then he shall bear his sin' " (Lev. 24:14-15).

The services in the temple reached an annual high-point on the Day of Atonement. The climactic event of that day, and thus of the church calendar, took place in the ritual of the scapegoat. God had commanded: "Aaron shall lay both of his hands on the head of the live goat, and confess over it all the iniquities of the sons of Israel, and all their transgressions in regard to all their sins; and he shall lay them on the head of the goat. . . . And the goat shall bear on itself all their iniquities" (Lev. 16:21-22).

In connection with the sacrificial system the laying on of hands meant that guilt, sin, and punishment were transferred.

Hands Placed on the Levites. The priestly functions in the sanctuary were performed by Aaron and his descendants, who belonged to the tribe of Levi. They acted as mediators between God and the people; the rest of the Levites assisted the priests in various ways (Num. 1:50-53; 3:6-9, 25-27; 4:1-33; 1 Sam. 6:15; 2 Sam. 15:24; 1 Chron. 24-26). It should also be noticed that the Levites represented the first-born among the Israelites (Num.3:12, 41, 45; 8:14, 16; 18:6), and thereby the people. Their consecration or installation is described in Numbers, chapter eight. After purification, offering, and sacrifice Moses was asked to "present the Levites before the tent of meeting. You shall also assemble the whole congregation of the sons of Israel and present the Levites before the Lord; and the sons of Israel shall lay their hands on the Levites" (Num. 8:9-10). The Levites' role as representatives of the people is confirmed by the act of hands being laid upon them by people (probably represented by the firstborn or elders). The service of the Levites was now representative in nature, and their consecration was the people's consecration. We read that after hands were laid upon the Levites, Aaron should "present the Levites before the Lord as a wave offering from the sons of Israel, that they may qualify to perform the service of the Lord" (Num. 8:11).

God concludes his instructions about the consecration of Levites with these words: "And I have given the Levites as a gift to Aaron and to his sons from among the sons of Israel, to perform the service of the sons of Israel at the tent of meeting, and to make atonement on behalf of the sons of Israel, that there may be no plague among the sons of Israel by their coming near to the sanctuary" (Num. 8:19). As in the case of the priests and high priests the Levites' functions were by birth and the laying on of hands was not repeated.

The Meaning of three Hebrew Words. Before we leave these examples of the laying on of hands it should be noticed that "laying on" is translated from three different Hebrew words.[8] Where we deal with a special blessing the words *s'im* or *shith* (synonymous) are used as in the story of Jacob and the sons of Joseph; the act of healing, for example, would fall into this category. In the case of consecration and offering the Hebrew makes use of the word *samak*. This Hebrew word was used of Moses laying his hands on Joshua, and of the people placing their hands on the Levites. The first two Hebrew words are expressed by a light touch, but the latter by a heavy touch—as in the sense of "to lean upon." The examples we have observed illustrate that when *samak* was used, the person transfers "something" (conditioned by the particulars of the event) to another person (or sacrificial animal) who/which then became his substitute or representative. A joining of responsibility takes place. Much confusion could be avoided if the different meanings and usages of the Hebrew words are kept in mind. They can also illuminate the various usages of "the laying on of hands" in the New Testament. When it comes to the lifting of hands in priestly blessing the Hebrew word *nasa* is used, as when "Aaron lifted up his hands toward the people and blessed them" (Lev. 9:22).

THE INSTALLATION OF PRIEST, KING, AND PROPHET

Consecration of the Priest. We have previously observed that Israel in their covenant relationship with God became a kingdom of priests, and thus occupied a unique role among the nations. In the early history of Israel the first-born son gave leadership to the life of the family and thus also served as priest, as in connection with the Passover ceremonies and rites. At the time of Moses Aaron and his sons were installed as priests. A detailed description is found in Exodus 28 and 29, and Leviticus 8. After having described "the vestments for the consecration of Aaron as my priest," God said to Moses: "With these invest your brother Aaron and his sons, anoint them, install them and consecrate them; so shall they serve me as priests" (Ex. 28:41, NEB).

Only Aaron the high priest was anointed—"the anointed one." His anointing no doubt embraced his sons.

The word "consecrate" (in NEB and NASB) is from the word for "sanctify" (KJV), meaning "separate" or "set apart."

The word rendered "install" (NEB) is the most difficult to

translate. The KJV has "consecrate" and the NASB, "ordain." The Hebrew word means "to fill the hands." The most likely meaning is that the hands should be filled with those objects they were to offer up in the temple as part of the sacrifice. "In Eastern lands installation into office was usually accomplished by putting into the hand of the official the insignia marking his functions. Here certain portions of the offerings were used for that purpose."[9]

The words "fill the hands" (Hebrew *mille' yadh*) clearly emphasize that the installation is to a service totally connected with the sacrificial system and rites of the temple (see Ex. 29:20-28).

All the rituals connected with the installation of Aaron and his sons refer to *mille' yadh*, which is translated "install" or "consecrate." It should be noticed that the NASB does not once use the word "ordain" in connection with installation, in the New Testament, but uses it constantly in connection with the installation of Aaron and his sons. We have the "ram of ordination," "the flesh of ordination," "the ordination offering," "the period of your ordination is fulfilled" (see Ex. 29:22, 26, 27, 31, 33, 34; Lev. 7:37; 8:22, 29, 31, 33).

Anointing the King. In the inauguration of a king the anointing was of central significance and symbolized the endowment of "the Spirit of the Lord" (see 1 Sam. 10:1; 16:13). The king, as custodian of the Book of the Law, was supposed to copy it with his own hand (Deut. 17:18-20). The covenant was renewed as a covenant between God, the king, and the people. While the high priest's hands were filled with oblations, the king's hands were "filled" with the Law. He was also crowned and enthroned (see 1 Kings 1:33 ff; 2 Kings 11:12; 1 Chron. 29:22 ff).

Anointing the Prophet. Regarding the consecration of the prophet, we know Elijah anointed Elisha and transferred to him the prophetic mantle (1 Kings 19:16, 19). It appears that the "anointed ones" and the "prophets" in Psalm 105:15 are the same. The Lord's servant (Isa. 61:1) speaks of himself as anointed "to bring good news." This was fulfilled in Christ (Luke 4:18).

Christ: Priest, King, and Prophet. The installation, or consecration, to the office of high priest, king, and prophet was fulfilled in Christ, who renewed the covenant relationship with God. Christology and soteriology must always be seen in light of this threefold office of Christ. Calvin writes: "Therefore, that faith may find in Christ a solid ground of salvation, and so rest in him, we must set out with this principle, that the office which he received from the Father consists of three parts. For he was appointed both Prophet, King, and Priest; though little were gained by holding the names unaccompanied by a knowledge of the end and use" (*Inst.* II.xv.1).

RABBINICAL ORDINATION[10]

Before we turn to the subject of the laying on of hands as it relates to the ministry in the New Testament, we will inquire about rabbinical ordination and its relationship, if any, to the primitive church. We have previously observed the growing importance of rabbis for the religious life of Judaism, so that after the destruction of the temple in A.D. 70 they were ready to be the "new priests."

The Judaic Tradition. According to tradition Moses ordained Joshua and the 70 elders, who in turn ordained others, with the result that there was an unbroken succession down to the time when rabbis came into vogue.

The steps of succession descended "in a direct line from Moses to Joshua, from Joshua to the elders, from the elders to the prophets, from the prophets to the men of the Great Assembly [Ezra, Nehemiah, and the Sanhedrin created after the return from captivity] and so on, until it reached the patriarchs [the heads of the Sanhedrin after the destruction of Jerusalem, A.D. 70] and the other heads of the Rabbinical schools."[11] Thus the rabbi became a final link in an unbroken chain reaching back to Moses, who spoke face to face with God "just as a man speaks to his friend" (Ex. 33:11).

The Codified Tradition. The oral tradition developed during the intertestamental period. First, however, at the close of the second century of the Christian era the material was codified in the Mishnah by Rabbi Judah, the patriarch of the court (Sanhedrin) at Jamnia. The Mishnah was considered authoritative and interpreted in the Talmud. There are two versions of the Talmud—the Palestinian and the Babylonian. The two editions were completed about A.D. 400 and A.D. 500, respectively. The Mishnaic and Talmudic literature is the source for a discussion of ordination within Judaism.

Mishnah and Talmud became representative of Judaism after A.D. 70 "Thus it comes about that while Judaism and Christianity alike venerate the Old Testament as canonical Scripture, the Mishnah marks the passage to Judaism as definitely as the New Testament marks the passage to Christianity."[12] While the material in the Mishnah is oral tradition codified, it may supply us with information from the first century. At the same time care must be taken in evaluating the historical material, for the rabbis often read their own theological concepts into the biblical texts and the historical material, as did the Christian theologians. In this respect there is a parallel between the Christian arguments for apostolic succession of the monarchical bishop and the pope as the successor of Peter, and the Talmudic "proof" for rabbinical succession from the time of Moses. This also includes the subject of ordination.

The Scriptural Exposition. The key texts under consideration deal with the laying of hands on Joshua by Moses (Num. 27:22-23; Deut. 34:9) and the act of choosing the seventy elders (Num. 11:16-17, 24-25). In the case of the seventy elders, who in the Greek Old Testament are referred to as "scribes" (as previously noticed), we read that God said to Moses: "I will take of the Spirit who is upon you, and will put Him upon them" (Num. 11:17). However, there is no indication that hands were laid upon them.

Regarding Joshua it is said that Moses "laid his hands on him and commissioned him, just as the Lord had spoken through Moses" (Num. 27:23). As previously observed the laying on of hands is translated from the Hebrew *samak*, but it is not stated that the Spirit was given by the laying on of hands. Before the latter took place God said to Moses: "Take Joshua the son of Nun, a man in whom is the Spirit, and lay your hand on him" (Num. 27:18). However, we read in Deut. 34:9 that Joshua "was filled with the spirit of wisdom, for Moses had laid his hands on him." The "spirit of wisdom" no doubt refers to the skill the one commissioned to succeed Moses would require.

In rabbinic exegesis these two events are basic for ordination, and are considered analoguous. According to the hermeneutical principles of the rabbis, "in two analogous texts, a particular consideration in one may be extended to the other as a general principle."[13] Thus it is taken for granted that hands were placed on the seventy elders, even though it is not mentioned in the text. However, the fact still remains that the laying of hands on Joshua was a once-and-for-all event. There is no reference in the Old Testament indicating that it was repeated in other cases. The laying on of hands in connection with an appointment was first mentioned again in the oral tradition and written down in the Mishnah.

Mishnaic Ordination. Based on the Mishnah the *Encyclopaedia Judaica* asserts that "ordination was required both for membership in the Great Sanhedrin, and the smaller Sanhedrins and regular colleges of judges empowered to decide legal cases." We are further told that the "lowest degree of ordination entitled the rabbi to decide only religious questions, while the highest degree entitled him to inspect firstlings, in addition to deciding religious questions and judging criminal cases."[14] Accordingly, this made the "ordained person" of importance not only in the religious but also the civil life of the people.

In light of the latter it would be understandable that the emperor Hadrian, during the Jewish revolt led by Bar Kokhba (A.D. 132-135), sought to curtail the influence of the new Sanhedrin established in Jamnia, by forbidding ordination. The Talmudic record reads that "whoever performed an ordination should be put to death, and whoever received ordination should be put to death, the city in which the ordination took place demolished, and the boundaries wherein it had been performed uprooted."[15] How far, if at all, this declaration was implemented is a great question; however, during the third century the laying on of hands ceased, and the rabbi was appointed and dedicated by his name being pronounced. The authority for the appointment rested with the patriarch and not, as earlier, when a teacher would place his hand on his pupil; further, any ceremony of installment performed by the council or college of judges "without the consent of the patriarch was invalid, while the patriarch received the privilege of performing the ceremony without the consent of the college."[16]

The historical sequel of rabbinic ordination until it ceased in the third century has been stated concisely by David Daube. He writes:

> From the latter half of the 2nd cent. A.D., far-reaching reforms were introduced into the institution of Rabbinic ordination. Above all, whereas before that time any scholar himself authorized could confer authority on others, now the right to ordain became the exclusive right of the Patriarch and his court. About the middle of the 3rd cent. at the latest the ceremony of *samakh* itself was abandoned. The centralization of ordination at the Patriarch's court may have contributed to this result. For one thing, it was certainly a factor making for the ordination of absent candidates, in which case the rite was physically impossible; for another, once it was no longer the teacher who ordained his own disciple, the notion of the

creation of a second self would naturally lose ground. Again, the practices of the Patriarch Judah II, who seems on occasion to have sold the Rabbinic authority for money, doubtless helped to diminish the importance of the ceremony: a *samakh* performed by such a man cannot have been regarded as a sacred act. Another reason for giving it up probably was the increasing role played by the imposition of hands in the Christian religion.[17]

The fact of "the increasing role played by the imposition of hands in the Christian religion" is also given in *The Jewish Encyclopedia* as a reason why the Jews ceased to lay on the hands. The name of the ordination service was also changed from " 'semikah' or 'semikuta,' which had been derived from the practise of laying on of hands." A new name was chosen; namely, "minnuy," meaning appointment.[18]

We have previously observed that the monarchical episcopacy was consolidated in the third century. In our discussion of ordination in the ancient church we will see that the earliest historical record of a Christian ordination service with the laying on of hands is from this period.

Returning to the Mishnah, the most important statement regarding the laying on of hands is in the section, "The Sanhedrin." A description is given of its meeting: "The Sanhedrin was arranged like the half of a round threshing-floor so that they all might see one another. Before them stood the two scribes of the judges, one to the right and one to the left, and they wrote down the words of them that favoured acquittal and the words of them that favoured conviction."[19]

An account then follows of how a new member was chosen. It is significant to notice that in the account where the English translation has "to appoint" the original has the Hebrew word *samak* (the laying on of hands). We read that before the Sanhedrin "sat three rows of disciples of the Sages, and each knew his proper place. If they needed to appoint [another as a judge], they appointed him from the first row, and one from the second row came into the first row, and one from the third row came into the second; and they chose yet another from the congregation and set him in the third row. He did not sit in the place of the former, but he sat in the place that was proper for him."[20]

As already pointed out, it is not easy to evaluate the Mishnah and the Talmud, but in order to obtain possible clues we will bring together some perspectives and opinions from scholars who have examined the material and studied the historical and theological situations.

Scholars' Evaluation. In the article on Jewish ordination in the *Encyclopaedia of Religion and Ethics* we read: "Behind this institution there lies a chapter of Jewish history which has not yet been sufficiently elucidated, viz. the appointment of judges, of those who would have to administer the law, both temporal and spiritual."[21]

This question was taken up by Hugo Mantel of Bar-Ilan University, Israel, in an article in *The Harvard Theological Review.*[22] He is of the opinion that during the Second Temple period there were two separate judiciary institutions: "(a) the appointment of official urban judges—particularly for cases involving fines and capital punishment; (b) manual ordination authorising an advanced student to teach in public, to decide matters of a legal and ritual nature, and perhaps also to judge financial cases not involving fines. This latter ordination was not an official government appointment, but under the supervision of the Pharisees."[23]

Regarding the relationship between a teacher and a student Hugo Mantel finds "that even in Temple times it was forbidden for a student to teach without obtaining his master's permission;" accordingly, "during the period of the Temple a teacher would customarily lay his hand on his student's head in granting him permission to teach and expound the Torah in public." Further, "the laying on of hands was a blessing that the student should prove successful in his teaching."[24] Mantel also asks the question: "Who was empowered to ordain students?" His answer reads: "Obviously, the student's own teacher. During the lifetime of the teacher, no student could request permission from anyone else. After his death, however, the city elders, the head of the synagogue, the heads of the Pharisaic sect or any other sect, were entitled to ordain the student and to permit him to teach publicly and decide legal matters."[25]

We closed our previous section with reference to ordination as described in the Mishnah. We will now turn to Mantel's comment on this specific account. He writes:

> We still have to explain the Mishnah which states that in the Temple period it was customary in the High Court to "ordain" students from the front row seated before them. But we have already argued that the ordaining of students was entirely distinct from the appointment of judges. It would be logical to assume that students were not appointed until they

had received ordination and been entitled "sages" with the consequent right to teach publicly. And that is precisely what we find. Judges were not appointed unless they were already qualified "sages," that is, ordained teachers. Thus the Mishnah describes here two stages: first, they ordained the student (the scholar sitting at the top of the front row was given the official title of *Hakam* [sage]), and then they appointed him judge and sat him in the High Court.[26]

We will close our references to Mantel by noting his comment on how Mishnaic ordination may relate to the primitive church of the New Testament:

> It is well known that the early Jewish Christians, especially in Jerusalem, borrowed their customs from Judaism. They regarded themselves as a Jewish sect separated from the Pharisees only by their belief in Jesus. It is clear that the early Christians did not invent this laying on of hands, nor could they have borrowed it from the Hellenistic world. And since we find this institution, or one similar to it, in Judaism of the post-Destruction period, there is again no room for doubt that it existed during Temple times.[27]

F. Gavin (General Theological Seminary, New York) seems to concur (in *Jewish Antecedents of the Christian Sacraments*) with Mantel's interpretation of the Mishnah.[28]

Reference has already been made to *The New Testament and Rabbinic Judaism* by David Daube of Oxford. His emphasis is that the laying on of hands in the New Testament, for any appointment, should be seen in the light of the meaning of the Hebrew *samak*. He asserts that within Judaism *samak* was only used in connection with the sacrifices and "rabbinic ordination in the New Testament era."[29]

Burton Scott Easton (also of the General Theological Seminary, New York) deals with the same subject but with a different interpretation.[30] He summarizes his contention in the following statement:

> The only ordained religious officials who were certainly recognized in Judaism before A.D. 70 were the elders. These elders, in collegiate organization, were at the head of every Jewish community, great or small, in Palestine or out of it. And the collegiate organizations were known as "sanhedrins."

. . . In non-Palestinian localities such bodies had a recognized president, the gerousiarch, but in the Holy Land there is no evidence for presiding officers except in Jerusalem, where the high priest was *ex officio* the head. These sanhedrins administered all the affairs of their communities on the basis of the Law of God, as written in the Old Testament and interpreted (and expanded) in the later tradition.[31]

It is Easton's opinion that the members of the Sanhedrin were installed by the laying on of hands (*samak*) and were the "elders." They were the trustees of the synagogue and "they appointed the 'ruler of the synagogue,' who chose the readers and speaker, etc., and the 'chazan' or sexton, who assisted the ruler at service time and was custodian of the building. Neither ruler nor chazan was ordained."[30]

It is suggested that after A.D. 70 "the scribes replaced the elders," and then were ordained. Easton writes: "Whether scribes were ordained before A.D. 70, however, is uncertain. No concrete evidence exists either way and a priori considerations are hazardous. Perhaps the scribes took up the rite only after they replaced the elders. Perhaps their sense of their own importance led them at an earlier time to inaugurate members with as much solemnity as an elder was inaugurated."[33]

The great and uncertain question regarding the views noticed so far, is whether or not the installment or ordination service described in the Mishnah refers to the Sanhedrin in Jerusalem before A.D. 70 or to the court of the patriarch in Jamnia after A.D. 70.

Another view other than that represented by Mantel, Gavin, and Easton (with their variances) is advocated in the article, "Jewish and Christian Ordination" by Arnold Ehrhardt.[34] His opinion is that the Mishnah is not historically reliable and does not prove rabbinical ordination in New Testament times.

Regarding the title "rabbi" for an ordained Jewish scholar, Ehrhardt states: "There can be no question that in Talmudic times it was 'Rabbi', but in the period before A.D. 70 this title was freely given to non-ordained Jewish scholars—a fact which is borne out by the evidence of the New Testament."[35]

Ehrhardt points out that the title given to the members of the Sanhedrin was "presbyter," and that was not synonymous with "scribe" or "rabbi." In the New Testament "the elders and scribes are mentioned side by side as separate groups in Mat. xxvi. 57 and Acts vi.

12, which suggests that the elders were not necessarily scribes." Further, "all our research so far has pointed to the fact that the earliest Jewish ordination was bound up with admission to this body." If, therefore, Jewish ordination, prior to the destruction of the Temple, bestowed the title presbyter "it would strongly argue in favour of the assumption that Jewish ordination before A.D. 70 was by no means a hole-and-corner affair, to be administered by any rabbi to his disciples at will, but the solemn ritual of admission to one of the seats in the Jerusalem Sanhedrin."[36]

From his study Ehrhardt draws these conclusions:

> The first and best founded is that the development of Jewish ordination confirms our assertion that the Christian description of ministers as presbyters was derived from the title of the members of the Jerusalem Sanhedrin. The second is that in the matter of ordination the Church and the Synagogue appear not in the relation of son and mother, but as half-brothers, like Isaac and Ishmael (Gal. iv. 22 f.) both in their way appropriating the Old Testament example. The third is that it may be wise, especially with regard to the rites of imposition of hands and enthronement of bishops, to allow for a period of development extending right down to the middle of the second century. Neither the witness of Acts nor that of the Pastors will in itself be sufficient to enlighten us on the conditions—or even the existence—of an ordination rite in the Primitive Church. When they are unsupported by other sources their witness is valid only with regard to second-century conditions.[37]

We will now turn to a third and different view regarding the origin of Christian ordination. Everett Ferguson proposes an origin which is purely Christian, that is, a distinct New Testamental invention.[38]

In an article, "Laying on of Hands: Its Significance in Ordination," Ferguson associates the laying on of hands, not with the Hebrew *samak* but *s'im*, which expressed the transfer of a blessing. He agrees that "on the surface there appears to be good reason to connect Christian usage with *samakh*. It was used for appointment to office in the Old Testament and became the technical term for ordination in Judaism. However much a crossfertilization of ideas may have occurred, it will be argued here that the background of Christian usage is to be found in the associations with *s'im*."³⁹

The deciding issue for Ferguson is "the question of the category to which Christian ordination belongs." He explains:

> The basic idea in early Christian ordination was not creating a substitute or transferring authority, but conferring a blessing and petitioning for the divine favour. Blessing, of course, in ancient thought was more than a kindly wish; it was thought of as imparting something very definite (as in the patriarchal blessings of the Old Testament). "Hand" in biblical usage was symbolic of power. The laying-on of hands accompanied prayer in Christian usage. It was essentially an enacted prayer, and the prayer spelled out the grace which God was asked to bestow. As an act of blessing, it was considered to effect that for which the prayer was uttered.⁴⁰

In his article on "Jewish and Christian Ordination" Ferguson emphasizes that a "confirmation that Christian ordination is rooted in *s'im* and not in *samakh* is the fact that laying on of hands in the church occurs only as an accompaniment to prayer. There is no indication that prayer was a part of Jewish ordinations."⁴¹ He points out some other features which differentiate rabbinic and Christian ordination: "Rabbinic ordination conferred an equal status and had a legal rather than spiritual significance in that it conferred judicial functions. That these features were absent or not prominent in Christian ordination further supports a separation of the Christian rite from a background in *samakh*."⁴²

Ferguson finds it doubtful that "private ordination of a Rabbi by his teacher by imposition of hands did not originate, or at least did not come into prominence, until the troubled years between A.D. 70 and 135."⁴³ In this connection it should be mentioned that while H. Mantel believes that the Mishnah describes an ordination service in the Sanhedrin prior to A.D. 70 others feel that this is questionable. Edward J. Kilmartin (University of Notre Dame) asserts (in his essay "Ministry and Ordination in Early Christianity against a Jewish Background") that "it is not altogether clear whether the Sanhedrin in Jamnia or an old Jerusalem Sanhedrin is being discussed."⁴⁴

THE HAND OF GOD IN THE NEW TESTAMENT

We have observed that in the Old Testament the hand of God (mentioned about 200 times) is spoken of as the instrument of power, and to it is also ascribed that which strictly belongs to God Himself.

When Israel (Jacob) prophesied and blessed his sons he spoke about the "hands of the Mighty One of Jacob" (Gen. 49:24). Moses reminded the people and told them to teach their children, that "the Lord brought us from Egypt with a mighty hand" (Deut. 6:21; cf. Ex. 13:9). Moses was God's spokesman, and we often read that revelation and instruction came from the hand of Moses: "Aaron and his sons did all things which the Lord commanded by the hand of Moses" (Lev. 8:36, KJV).

Old Testament Motif Fulfilled in Christ. Throughout the history of Israel the metaphor of the hand of God and the hand of his servants was specifically used within the covenant-remnant-eschaton motif. When we, therefore, come to the fulfillment of this motif in Christ as the Messiah it is not surprising that we find the hand of God used anew as an instrument of power and to confirm the covenant relationship. It is most significant that it was said about John the Baptist: "The hand of the Lord was certainly with him" (Luke 1:66), and when he baptized Christ he said: "The Father loves the Son, and has given all things into His hand" (John 3:35). The stories of blessings and healings by the hands of Jesus are well-known, they attest that God's mighty hand was with Jesus Christ as the expected Messiah. In Christ the covenant relationship was renewed.

The Hand of God in the Early Church. In the founding of the church and in the life of the apostles and the early church the mighty hand of God was likewise of significance. We read (Acts 4) that five thousand men had accepted the gospel and the apostles were brought before the Council. Peter "filled with the Holy Spirit" gave a short speech, the Council conferred and decided to let them go but denied them to preach again. Peter and John replied: "Whether it is right in the sight of God to give heed to you rather than to God, you be the judge; for we cannot stop speaking what we have seen and heard" (Acts 4:19-20).

Returning from the Council to "their own companions" they reported the event and in unison they all expressed their belief that God's hand was with the New Israel as a fulfillment of the covenant-remnant-eschaton motif (see Acts 4:23-33).

Next we read that "at the hands of the apostles many signs and wonders were taking place among the people; and they were all with one accord" (Acts 5:12).

Stephen in his speech of defense before the Council clearly compares the New Israel with the old covenant-remnant-eschaton motif and speaks about God's active hand (see Acts 7:25, 35, 50; KJV has "hand," as in the Greek).

The Samaritans who had only been baptized by the baptism of John the Baptist received the Holy Spirit when the apostles laid their hands upon them (Acts 8:17).

When Ananias came to Paul he laid his hands upon him; Paul regained his sight, was filled with the Holy Spirit, and was baptized (Acts 9:17, 18).

Luke records that the persecution after the stoning of Stephen became a blessing by the fact that the believers scattered and witnessed wherever they went. In this connection he mentions that some "men of Cyprus and Cyrene" began to preach to the Greeks in Antioch "And the hand of the Lord was with them, and a large number who believed turned to the Lord" (Acts 11:20-21).

We read that when Paul and his companions came to Iconium "they spent a long time there speaking boldly with reliance upon the Lord, who was bearing witness to the word of His grace, granting that signs and wonders be done by their hands" (Acts 14:3).

Also in Ephesus we find a group of people who had been baptized "into John's baptism" and had "not even heard whether there is a Holy Spirit." They were then "baptized in the name of the Lord Jesus. And when Paul had laid his hands upon them, the Holy Spirit came on them, and they began speaking with tongues and prophesying" (Acts 19:1-6). It is further stated that "God was performing extraordinary miracles by the hands of Paul" (Acts 19:11). One of these is mentioned in Acts 28, where it is recorded that on the Island of Malta the father of Publius "was lying in bed afflicted with recurrent fever and dysentery; and Paul went in to see him and after he had prayed, he laid his hands on him and healed him" (Acts 28:7-8).

THE LAYING ON OF HANDS AND THE MINISTRY

Of the numerous texts in the New Testament which deal with the laying on of hands, only two in the Acts of the Apostles (6:6; 13:3) are related to the ministry, and only one case is described in the

Epistles—that of Timothy.

Terminology: the Hebrew Background and the Covenant. The laying on of hands we have referred to so far in the New Testament brought a special blessing and was, in the Old Testament, expressed by the two Hebrew words *s'im* or *shith*. We now turn to the laying on of hands which may illustrate the added significance expressed by the Hebrew *samak*, the meaning of which we have studied in detail.

We have observed that the references in Acts to the laying on of hands were an integral part of salvation history demonstrating God's mighty hand in renewing the covenant relationship and creating a new Israel, with the old Israel as an analogy. Likewise, we find that the two accounts in Acts (6:1-6; 13:1-3) regarding the laying on of hands for an appointment is found within the same context. According to Marjorie Warkentin (*Ordination: A Biblical-Historical View*) the significance of the two events are found in the evidence that God has renewed His covenant. The Moses-Joshua and people-Levites *samak* experiences are now repeated. Accordingly, in Acts 6:6 it is the apostles who laid their hands on the Seven, as Moses laid his on Joshua, while in Acts 13:3 it is the people who laid their hands on Paul and Barnabas, as in the case of the Levites. Warkentin underscores the once-and-for-all significance and rests the case here.[45]

The Laying of Hands Upon the Seven. We have previously referred to the unique position of the Seven in Acts 6. In this section we will ask the question: Who placed their hands upon the Seven and why? The first question may seem unnecessary for it is generally conceived that it was the apostles, as expressed in the New English Bible: "These they presented to the apostles, who prayed and laid their hands on them" (Acts 6:6).

In the Greek text the construction is such that those who "laid their hands on" could equally well be the ones who presented them. The only Greek manuscript that has a reading which makes it definite that it was the apostles is Codex Bezae, also named Codex D. It is a late manuscript from the fifth or sixth century, and according to scholars "marked by great variation from all others in what seem to be bold modifications and interpolations or additions." In this connection Ira Maurice Price (in *The Ancestry of Our English Bible*) points out that "an interesting example of addition is the Sabbath saying attributed to Jesus by Luke 6:4-5: 'On the same day, seeing someone working on the Sabbath, he said to him, Man, if you really know what you are doing, you are blessed, but if you do not know, you are cursed, and a transgressor of the law.' "[46]

The change in Acts 6:6 of Codex Bezae reflects a historical development beginning in the third century, when only the bishop in apostolic succession could ordain, followed by the assertion that bishops are the vicars of Christ—a claim later applied to the pope.[47] This does not necessarily mean that the apostles could not have placed their hands on the Seven, for the text can be interpreted both ways. Reference has already been made to Majorie Warkentin, who believes that hands were laid on by the apostles. Eduard Schweizer likewise thinks it is the apostles, but acknowledges that it is not clearly expressed. He further asserts that the laying on of hands, both on Paul and Barnabas (Acts 13:1-3) and on the Seven, was for special service and "blessing." He therefore states: "Thus it is plain that it is not a matter of ordination, as both already belonged to the company of 'prophets and teachers'. It is therefore an 'installation', i.e., a placing in a particular sphere of service which differs in some respects from that previously occupied."[48]

David Daube emphasizes the meaning of *samak* and responsibility of representation; accordingly, the appointment of the Seven was modeled on "Seven of a City," who "are as if they were the city itself." Daube acknowledges that the "Seven of a City" were "installed without any *samak*," but since hands were laid upon the Seven in Acts and they represented the people it would be *samak*. For Daube the analogy to Old Testament use of *samak* seems obvious.[49]

The well-known Scottish theologian, T. F. Torrance, thinks that the Early Church did not take "over the rite of laying on of hands from Judaism so much as from the OT directly." He believes that "hands were laid on the seven by the congregation, not by the Apostles (except according to Codex Bezae), but they were set before the Apostles, to indicate that the Apostles had part in the act. It was, however, an act of lay-ordination like that of the Levites in the OT." He also acknowledges that in the story of the Seven the language also reflects the Moses-Joshua *samak*, and "the appointment of the seventy elders in Num. 11.6, when, without any laying on of hands, God put His Spirit upon them, to enable them to fulfil their appointment to the Presbytery of Israel."

T. F. Torrance brings out still another point: "The fact that the Apostles did not lay hands on them suggests that they were not being appointed as their deputies, but only as their assistants, i.e. Levites! Hence it was natural to describe these 'elders' as 'deacons' in distinction from the others."[50] This argument is based on the understanding that "the Seven of a city" were elders. As a footnote it should be mentioned (as previously pointed out), that while they could—in a certain sense—be described as "deacons" (which they are not called), in actuality the function of the Seven and the structure or framework for their work was different from the deacon in the Pastoral Epistles. T. F. Torrance, accordingly, refers to the Seven as elder-deacons.

The Commission of Paul and Barnabas. The record of the laying on of hands upon Paul and Barnabas (Acts 13:1-3) is clearly a consecration service for a special missionary task. They were themselves among the group of prophets and teachers in Antioch, but while the group was praying and fasting the Holy Spirit impressed them to set apart Barnabas and Paul for a missionary work. In our discussion of the Christian ministry we observed that the word apostle was used in the secondary sense for others than the Twelve. Both the Roman Empire and Judaism made use of emissaries who bore special messages and represented the sender. They were called apostles (Greek *apostoloi*; Hebrew *shaliach*).

The extension of the local church in Antioch into a world-wide church is expressed by the laying on of hands—and "they sent them away" (Acts 13:3). Their work for Christ was extended through their two representatives who became apostles (messengers, emissaries, agents). The language used in the laying on of the hands upon Paul and Barnabas corresponds to the consecration of the Levites (who by the *samak* represented the people), to which there is indirect reference. God told Moses: "Take the Levites from among the sons of Israel. . . . You shall separate the Levites from among the sons of Israel" (Num. 8:6, 14).

In Acts the directive of the Holy Spirit was: "Set apart for Me Barnabas and Saul for the work to which I have called them" (Acts 13:2). The Levites were also set apart to the work (Num. 8:11, 15) to which God had called them (the Greek Septuagint has the same word for work—*ergon*—as the New Testament). Also in the event of Acts 13:1-3 we find the basic concept of the rite of *samak* (representation) persevered (with indirect allusions to Old Testament antecedence) but given a New Testament circumstantial role and significance.

David Daube states that the language of Acts 13 "echoes that of the Old Testament in the chapter dealing with the consecration of the Levites." T. F. Torrance suggests: "They were not ordained as 'rabbinic' pupils or disciples, but rather sent out as 'apostles' or authorised messengers of the community on a limited mission. . . . It does not seem to refer to ordination in the proper sense."[51]

What we have said seems to be confirmed by the sequel. After Paul and Barnabas' missionary journey they returned "to Antioch, from which they had been commended to the grace of God for the work that they had accomplished. And when they had arrived and gathered the church together, they began to report all things that God had done with them and how He had opened a door of faith to the Gentiles" (Acts 14:26-27).

It should also be remembered (as we will notice later) that prior to Acts 13 Paul already had a decade of evangelistic activity.

The Laying of Hands Upon Timothy. In the two Epistles to Timothy we find three references to the laying on of hands. They read as follows: "Do not neglect the spiritual gift within you, which was bestowed upon you through prophetic utterance with the laying on of hands by the presbytery" (1 Tim. 4:14).

"Do not lay hands upon anyone too hastily and thus share responsibility for the sins of others; keep yourself free from sin" (1 Tim. 5:22).

"I remind you to kindle afresh the gift of God which is in you through the laying on of my hands" (2 Tim. 1:6).

These passages have caused exegetes some difficulty. The obvious meaning of the first is that the presbytery placed their hands upon Timothy; in the third it was Paul. If Paul ordained Timothy (2 Tim. 1:6) and Timothy in turn ordained others (1 Tim. 5:22), then—it is said—we have the earliest example of a bishop ordaining another to become bishop, in other words apostolic succession. Since apostolic succession first began to appear in the second century, many scholars conclude that Paul was not the author of the two epistles but that they were written in the second century.

The Paul-Timothy Relationship. A common and plausible explanation is that the presbytery ordained Timothy, but that Paul presided at the occasion. During most of Paul's ministry we find a close relationship between him and Timothy. In the evaluation of the texts under discussion a few chronological facts on the relationship between the two men may be helpful.

Paul calls Timothy "my true child in the faith" (1 Tim. 1:2), "Timothy, my son" (1 Tim. 1:18), "my beloved son" (2 Tim. 1:2), and "my beloved and faithful child in the Lord" (1 Cor. 4:17). He and his family may have been converted during Paul's first visit to Lystra, during his first missionary journey (A.D. 45-47). During his second journey Paul again visited Lystra, and Timothy is mentioned by name as one "well spoken of by the brethren" (Acts 16:1-2). Timothy accompanied Paul on his second missionary journey (A.D. 49-52) through Asia Minor and Greece. When Paul left for Jerusalem Timothy may have stayed in Greece. During his third journey (A.D. 53-58) Paul stayed three years in Ephesus, and from there sent Timothy on a special mission to Corinth (1 Cor. 4:17) and Macedonia (Acts 19:21-22). Later, Paul joined Timothy in Corinth (Rom. 16:21) and, together with others, they traveled to Jerusalem (A.D. 58).

Paul was imprisoned in Rome (A.D. 61-63) for the first time for two years (Acts 28:30). During some of the time Timothy was with him (Col. 1:1, Phil. 1:1). In the letter to the Philippians he says that he hopes "to send Timothy to you shortly" (Phil. 2:19).

Paul was released from prison for a period of about three years (A.D. 63-66) and probably wrote the first letter to Timothy about A.D. 64. Prior to that Paul and Timothy must have been together, for he wrote: "As I urged you upon my departure for Macedonia, remain on at Ephesus, in order that you may instruct certain men not to teach strange doctrines" (1 Tim. 1:3). Ephesus had become a center for the work in Asia Minor during Paul's time, and the Apostle John lived there prior to his exile to Patmos.

Again Paul was arrested and taken a second time as prisoner to Rome (c. A.D. 66), where he wrote his second letter to Timothy urging him to come quickly (2 Tim. 4:9). Timothy, no doubt, fulfilled this request.

Timothy, the Apostle. Timothy's nearly two decades of association with Paul is clear evidence of his close relationship with Paul and his service as an emissary (*apostolos*). Timothy's position was similar to that of Titus, about whom Paul writes: "He has also been appointed by the churches to travel with us in this gracious work." In the same connection Paul also speaks about the "messengers [*apostoloi*] of the churches" (2 Cor. 8:19, 23). That Paul should have ordained Timothy, as a bishop in later centuries would ordain another to become bishop in apostolic succession, is not true to the historical situation. The act of laying the hands on Timothy no doubt took place early in his service for the church. His career followed that of Paul and was not that of a local elder or overseer (bishop). We are told that the latter was "appointed"; no mention is made of hands being placed upon him.

Paul himself experienced the laying on of hands twice. The first time was when Ananias laid hands on him, and he regained his sight and was "filled with the Holy Spirit." The result was that "immediately he began to proclaim Jesus in the synagogues . . . and confounding the Jews who lived at Damascus by proving that this Jesus is the Christ" (Acts 9:17, 20, 22).

The second time was when the brethren in Antioch were instructed by the Holy Spirit to set apart Barnabas and Paul: "When they had fasted and prayed and laid their hands on them, they sent them away" (Acts 13:3). By that time Paul had already been engaged in evangelistic activities for ten years.

In the unique historical situation and task of Paul in the early church, to which Timothy was closely related and often represented Paul personally, Paul may have laid his hands upon Timothy as Ananias had placed his on Paul—and as a rabbi on his pupil (if that was the custom in Paul's time). One thing is certain: Timothy represented Paul and the church universal; the presbytery as a whole had placed their hands upon him, and with Paul no doubt among them and possibly presiding over the rite (1 Tim. 4:14); 2 Tim. 1:6 may refer to the same event.

Whether there were one or two occasions of the laying on of hands is of minor importance; the significant fact is that Timothy was chosen by the Holy Spirit, commissioned by Paul (who had, like the twelve, a unique and once-for-all apostolate) and by the people, as an emissary (apostle). What has just been stated was fully recognized in Paul's writings to the different churches at different times. "Timothy my fellow worker greets you" (Rom. 16:21); "I exhort you therefore, be imitators of me. For this reason I have sent to you Timothy, who is my beloved and faithful child in the Lord, and he will remind you of my ways which are in Christ, just as I teach everywhere in every church" (1 Cor. 4:16-17); "But I hope in the Lord Jesus to send Timothy to you shortly, so that I also may be encouraged when I learn of your condition. For I have no one else of kindred spirit who will genuinely be concerned for your welfare. For they all seek after their own interests, not those of Christ Jesus. But you know of his proven worth that he served with me in the furtherance of the gospel like a child serving his father" (Phil. 2:19-22). The following epistles were sent not only in the name of Paul but jointly in the name of Timothy (2 Cor. 1:1; 1, 2 Thess. 1:1; Phil. 1:1; Col. 1:1; and Philem. 1:1).

The Injunction of 1 Timothy 5:22. Among a number of injunctions which Paul writes to Timothy is the following: "Do not lay hands upon anyone too hastily and thus share responsibility for the sins of others; keep yourself free from sin" (1 Tim. 5:22). In the light of the meaning of the two texts dealing with the laying on of hands on Timothy it is obvious that he was not ordained to be a local bishop, who then in turn could ordain another bishop, priest or deacon (which is a late second and third century phenomenon). But this is the way it has often been interpreted. Acts 6:6 and 13:3, 1 Tim. 4:14; 5:22, and 2 Tim. 1:6 have been brought together and given the sense of ordination, as the church later conceived ordination. At the same time Timothy is considered a bishop of Ephesus.

The confusion is expressed in various translations of the New Testament. The KJV, RSV, JB, NIV, and NASB have a literal translation of the text. But the NEB reads: "Do not be over-hasty in laying on hands in ordination"; the LB: "Never be in a hurry about choosing a pastor; you may overlook his sins and it will look as if you approve of them"; and PME: "Never be in a hurry to ordain a man by laying your hands upon him."

The context itself seems to favor that Paul speaks about a person who has been under church discipline, specifically an elder. Paul therefore also admonishes Timothy that he himself be sure to live "free from sin," that is a pure, chaste, blameless, and upright life. Kenneth S. Wuest in his Greek word studies writes:

> The words, "Lay hands suddenly," have to do with the restoration of a sinning church member back into the fellowship of the local church. . . . In verse 19, we see the accusation, in verse 20, the conviction and sentence, and in verse 22, the restoration to church fellowship. Expositors say: "Timothy is bidden to restrain by deliberate prudence, the impulses of mere pity. A hasty reconciliation tempts the offender to suppose that his offence cannot have been so very serious after all; and smooths the way to a repetition of the sin; 'good-natured easy men' cannot escape responsibility for the disastrous consequences of their lax administration of the law. They have a share in the sins of those whom they have encouraged to sin. Those who give letters of recommendation with too great facility, fall under the apostolic condemnation."[52]

Further Comments and Evaluation. The three texts in the Epistles to Timothy do not deal with church-ordination as generally perceived. The two key texts tell us about Timothy's calling and commission as an associate of Paul, which is similar to that of Paul and Barnabas (Acts 13:3). They functioned as envoys or missionary-apostles (as previously described) and represented the church at large. The two texts in Acts and the three in the Epistles to Timothy do not set a precedent for a third century concept of a local monarchical bishop and his role in performing the rite of ordination.

For most people ordination by the laying on of hands is taken for granted, and it is therefore a surprise to find that the rite is not so clearly and directly defined in the New Testament as expected. We have earlier pointed out that the word "ordain" does not appear in the Greek New Testament at all for the ministry, and in most recent standard translations the word "appoint" is most commonly used (Mark 3:14, 16; Luke 10:1; John 15:16; Acts 14:23; 1 Cor. 12:28; 1 Tim. 2:7; 2 Tim. 1:11). The words "set apart" also appear (Acts 13:2).

Appointment is not synonymous with the "laying on of hands." It cannot be taken for granted that "to be appointed" automatically means "the laying on of hands." Further, elders and deacons were appointed in local churches, and their work was administrative in nature. The ministries (services) growing out of the "gifts of the Spirit" (charismatic ministries) nurtured the church. We have also observed that the laying on of hands for a certain ministry (service, *diakonia* as for example Acts 6:1-6; 13:1-3) may not necessarily mean "ordination" as it was conceived later, but represents a dedication and blessing for a special task.

In a collection of articles in honor of the Finnish theologian Toivo Harjunpaa, Birger A. Pearson writes concerning the "Ministry and Ordination in the Early Church": "The ecclesiological situation in Paul's churches, therefore, seems to be one of free, charismatic expression, and we find no concrete evidence of hierarchical organization, nor anything at all about 'ordination' to church offices. It should be observed, too, that despite the variety of terminology for church leadership found in Paul's letters, no mention is made of any system of church elders (presbyters), a situation which marks the Pauline churches off against the 'Jewish-Christian' churches."[53]

Professor Kilmartin (to whom reference has been made) writes about his own study in these words: "This brief overview of the literature on early Christian ordination rites may serve to indicate that almost every issue related to the subject remains unresolved."[54]

Having examined the texts under discussion in *Jesus and His Church* Professor R. Newton Flew of Cambridge says: "As the New Testament says so little about 'ordination', we may rest content with the conclusion of Hort [the renowned Cambridge theologian, in *The Christian Ecclesia*]: 'It can hardly be likely that any essential principle was held to be involved in it. It was enough that an Ecclesia should in modern phrase be organized, or in the really clearer Apostolic phrase be treated as a body made up of members with a diversity of functions; and that all things should be done decently and in order.' " Flew himself asks: "Was ordination necessary for any or all of these ministries? We do not even know whether ordination was practised for the chief of the offices which survived, that of presbyters." Pointing out the uniqueness of the primitive church, he further states: "There is nothing in that Greco-Roman world comparable to this community, conscious of a universal mission, governed and indwelt by an inner Life, guided by the active divine Spirit to develop these ministries for the expression of its message to mankind. All the ministries are based on the principle of the universal ministry of all believers."[55]

This statement brings into focus what we have said about the priesthood of believers and the nature of the church as constituted in the New Testament; likewise, it underscores that the significance and meaning of "ordination" or "appointment" must be evaluated within that framework.

EARLY HISTORICAL SEQUEL

We have observed that the word "ordain" is not used in the Apostolic period; nor is the laying on of hands as a rite of installment to the ministry definitely defined. From the post-Apostolic period we have no historical account of the rite of ordination being administrated. The earliest description of an ordination service is from the third century, but accounts become common in the fourth century.

Hippolytus of Rome. The oldest Christian record of an ordination rite is found in *The Apostolic Tradition* by Hippolytus, who was a presbyter in the church of Rome in the early part of the third century (d. 236 A.D.). The writings of Hippolytus bridge the periods of Tertullian and Cyprian. His description of ordination confirms the changed concept of the ministry which took place in the third century and expressed (as already observed) in the writing of Tertullian and Cyprian.

A distinction between the bishop and the presbyter is clearly drawn. A new bishop can only be ordained by other bishops, who alone "lay their hands on him, and the presbytery shall stand by in silence." In the ordination prayer the bishop is called God's "high priest"; the ordination granted him "the Spirit of high-priesthood" by which he had "authority to remit sins."

The distinction between the bishop and the presbyter was further widened by the fact that only the bishop could ordain the latter. "But when a presbyter is ordained, the bishop shall lay his hand upon his head, while the presbyters touch him." The latter indicates "the common and like Spirit of the clergy. Yet the presbyter has only the power to receive; but he has no power to give. For this reason a presbyter does not ordain the clergy; but at the ordination of a presbyter he seals while the bishop ordains."[56]

In the case of the ordination of a deacon, only the bishop places his hand upon him for "he is not ordained to the priesthood but to serve the bishop and to carry out the bishop's commands. He does not take part in the council of the clergy; he is to attend to his own duties and to make known to the bishop such things as are needful. He does not receive that Spirit that is possessed by the presbytery, in which the presbyters share; he receives only what is confided in him under the bishop's authority. For this cause the bishop alone shall make a deacon."[57]

We have previously sketched the development of the episcopal authority from the Apostolic age to the third century. We have also observed that the first historical record of the mode of ordination sealed that authority. The significance of this is expressed by Eric G. Jay in *The Church: Its Changing Image Through Twenty Centuries*. He writes:

> The authority to exercise a bishop's office must officially be imparted by those who already hold that office. This is the first clear evidence for this procedure, which rapidly became universal. As we have seen, evidence is lacking about the mode of appointment of the monarchical bishop up to this time. Whatever the previous practice had been, Hippolytus insists that only a bishop possesses the authority to consecrate another bishop. Indeed, Hippolytus sees the bishop as alone

having authority to ordain presbyters and deacons.[58]

Constitutions of the Holy Apostles. From the fourth century we have a church manual, the Constitutions of the Holy Apostles[59], which purports to tell us what the apostles supposedly said and did. Regarding a threefold ministry and the mode of ordination it follows in the main what we observed in *The Apostolic Tradition*. We read: "But being taught by the Lord the series of things, we distributed the functions of the high-priesthood to the bishops, those of the priesthood to the presbyters, and the ministration under them both to the deacons; that the divine worship might be performed in purity. For it is not lawful for a deacon to offer the sacrifice, or to baptize, or to give either the greater or the lesser blessing. Nor may a presbyter perform ordination" (VIII.v.xlvi).

The distinction between the laity and the priesthood is emphasized. Taking up the question, "How the governed are to obey the bishops who are set over them," it is stated: "Let the lay person honour him, love him, reverence him as his lord, as his master, as the high priest of God, as a teacher of piety. For he that heareth him, heareth Christ; and he that rejecteth him, rejecteth Christ" (II.iii.xx). Further, the bishop is "the mediator between God and you in the several parts of your divine worship. He is the teacher of piety; and, next after God, he is your father, who has begotten you again to the adoption of sons by water and the Spirit. He is your ruler and governor; he is your king and potentate; he is, next after God, your earthly god, who has a right to be honoured by you. . . . For let the bishop preside over you as one honoured with the authority of God, which he is to exercise over the clergy, and by which he is to govern all the people" (II.iv.xxvi).

The bishop is ordained "by three bishops" in the presence of presbyters, deacons, and the people, who "give their consent." When it comes to a presbyter and deacon, then they are "ordained by one bishop" (III.ii.xx; VIII.ii.iv). Provision is also made for ordination of deaconesses. The deacon and deaconess serve the bishop (II.iv.xxvi, xxix-xxxi; VIII.iii.xvi-xx).

Augustine of Hippo. In considering the concept of the Christian priest and the rite of ordination as it developed in the ancient church, it is significant to notice that Augustine (bishop in North Africa, A.D. 396-430) followed the main tenets of Cyprian's ecclesiology, but furthered the development of the so-called Christian priesthood by "his sacramental concept of the ministry whereby the validity of a cleric's sacramental action was seen to be independent of his personal character." Roman Catholics adhere to this principle when asserting that by the sacrament of ordination the priest is marked by an indelible character. Regarding ordination, Augustine made it "wholly a permanent possession of the individual apart from the community in which and through which it was conferred."[60]

Having stated this, George H. Williams, in his essay on "The Ministry in the Later Patristic Period (314-451)," makes the following pertinent observation:

> In thus individualizing ordination Augustine witnesses indirectly to the extinction in the West c. 400 of the older catholic feeling for the corporate ministry of the local church. Within four centuries the hereditary priesthood of Israel had been replaced by the indelible priesthood of Christendom, valid not by inheritance and birth but through a kind of rebirth in the solemn rededication of ordination in the descent of the Holy Spirit, an action which also represented a tactile succession going back to the apostles.[61]

The sacerdotal aspect of the new Christian high priest changed the New Testament concept of the ministry and appointment to it. It has been well expressed by Eric G. Jay in the following statement:

> This was to introduce a new idea of the Christian ministry, and one which endangered the teaching of the N.T. that the sacrifice of Christ alone is the sufficient redemptive act on man's behalf. This view of the ministry, as it gained acceptance, doubtless aided by the common use of sacerdotal terminology, inevitably led to a new ecclesiology which sees the Church as essentially a hierarchical body. The concept of the Church as the whole people of God lost ground, and the distinction between clergy and laity was highly sharpened as the latter were relegated to the role of passive dependants. This ecclesiology was to come under formidable attack in the sixteenth century.[62]

We will now briefly turn to Luther and Calvin in order to ascertain their concepts of ordination, the Protestant Reformation being the Western watershed between medieval and modern Christendom.

LUTHER AND CALVIN'S CONCEPT OF ORDINATION

Ordination is Not a Sacrament. Luther's early attack on the Roman sacramental system in *A Prelude on the Babylonian Captivity of the Church* (1520), includes his criticism of ordination as a sacrament and opens up some of his concepts of ordination. Concerning ordination, the sixth of the seven sacraments, "the church of Christ knows nothing; it is an invention of the church of the pope. Not only is there nowhere any promise of grace attached to it, but there is not a single word said about it in the whole New Testament. Now it is ridiculous to put forth as a sacrament of God something that cannot be proved to have been instituted by God" (*LW* 36:106-107). Accordingly, for Luther "ordination, if it is anything at all, is nothing else than a certain rite whereby one is called to the ministry of the church" (*LW* 36:116). Luther closes his discussion of the ministry as a sacrament by pointing out that the "indelible character" which the sacrament is supposed to give a person is a "fiction," and ministers can either be "suspended temporarily, or permanently deprived of their office" (*LW* 36:117).

Calvin likewise attacks the Roman Catholic sacramental idea of ordination, which is supposed to confer upon the recipient the power of "offering sacrifice to appease God." Accordingly "all are injurious to Christ who call themselves priests in the sense of offering expiatory victims" (Inst. IV.xix.28).

Ordination and the Priesthood of Believers. The call to the ministry is connected with the doctrine of the priesthood of believers. Through baptism and faith "every Christian possesses the word of God and is taught and anointed by God to be priest" (*LW* 39:309) wrote Luther in 1523, and that concept he never changed. Ceremonial ordination was first instituted in Wittenberg in 1535, but even after that he wrote (1539): "It is enough that you are consecrated and anointed with the sublime and holy chrism of God, with the word of God, with baptism, . . . then you are anointed highly and gloriously enough and sufficiently vested with priestly garments" (*LW* 41:152).

Writing to the senate and the people of Prague (1523) concerning the ministry, Luther points out that "a Priest is not identical with Presbyter or Minister—for one is born to be priest, one becomes a minister." He further writes:

First, regard as an unmovable rock that the New Testament knows of no priest who is or can be anointed externally. If there are such, they are imitators and idols. There is neither example nor command nor a simple word in Gospels or Epistles of the apostles in support of this vanity. They are established and brought in only by the kind of human invention of which Jeroboam once was guilty in Israel's history [I Kings 12:32f.]. For a priest, especially in the New Testament, was not made but was born. He was created, not ordained. He was born not indeed of flesh, but through a birth of the Spirit, by water and Spirit in the washing of regeneration [John 3:6f.; Titus 3:5f.]. Indeed, all Christians are priests, and all priests are Christians. Worthy of anathema is any assertion that a priest is anything else than a Christian. For such an assertion has no support in the Word of God and is based only on human opinions, on ancient usage, or on the opinions of the majority, any one of which is ineffectual to establish an article of faith without sacrilege and offense, as I have sufficiently shown elsewhere (*LW* 40:18, 19).

Having emphasized "that all of us that have been baptized are equally priests" and "we are all priests, as many of us as are Christians," Luther points out that those who are priests so-called "are ministers chosen from among us" and the ministry is "committed to them, yet with our common consent, they would then know that they have no right to rule over us except insofar as we freely concede it. . . . All that they do is done in our name; the priesthood is nothing but a ministry" (*LW* 36:112-113).

While every Christian through baptism is "assured of this, that we are all equally priests, that is to say, we have the same power in respect to the Word and the sacraments"; yet, that "power" no one should use on his own initiative for "what is the common property of all, no individual may arrogate to himself, unless he is called" (*LW* 36:116). Here is Luther's bridge to an official or public ministry.

In *An Open Letter to the Christian Nobility Concerning the Reform of the Christian Estate* (1520) Luther challenged the older system of emphasizing the responsibility of the laity in church affairs. Here he writes:

For whoever comes out of the water of baptism can boast that he is already a consecrated priest, bishop, and pope, although of course it is not seemly that just anybody should exercise such office. Because we are all priests of equal standing, no one must push himself forward and take it upon himself, without our consent and election, to do that for which we all have equal authority. For no one dare take upon himself what is common to all without the authority and consent of the community (*LW* 44:129).

Luther's concept of the priesthood of believers grew out of his Christology and soteriology: "Because we all have one baptism, one gospel, one faith, and are all Christians alike; for baptism, gospel, and faith alone make us spiritual and a Christian people" (*LW* 44:127). In turn, because of the *ekklesia* being the priesthood of believers, the official ministry is a representative ministry, also referred to as the delegated or transferral ministry.

The Protestant Reformers' common view of the priesthood of believers was in a special way brought into practice by Calvin in his presbyterian form of church organization. Calvin emphasized that as believers in Christ "we are all priests" (*Inst.* IV.xix. 28), and from the point of view of conducting church affairs this was illustrated in the work of the Presbytery. Here the pastors and the elders (who outnumbered the pastors) exercised paternal criticism, counsel, and discipline. The members of the Presbytery or Consistory met every Thursday.

The appointment of a new minister came from a suggestion of the ministers who had their own council, the Venerable Company, but consent had to be obtained from the body of believers and finally from the city authorities. The pastor was installed or commissioned by the people, their church councils and the civil government.[63]

Importance of the Call and the Commission. We have observed that Luther refers to ordination as a ritual (and not as a sacrament) because the call, rather than the ceremony of laying on of hands, is decisive and confers the role of ministry. In a detailed study of this subject R. W. Schoenleber comes to the following conclusion:

Luther denied the idea that ritual ordination at the hands of a bishop is a necessary prerequisite for holding and exercising the office of the ministry. A call, not ritual ordination, is the only theological prerequisite for holding the office of the ministry. A ceremony using prayer and the imposition of hands may be used to install ministers in their congregations (as a public affirmation of their call), but it is optional and repeatable each time the ministers change congregations.

In his polemics against the Enthusiasts and self-appointed preachers Luther emphasized the necessity of a proper call but he did not stress ordination. Luther's theology of ordination did not change from 1525 to 1535 even though he increasingly found himself in the role of being a representative of the religious establishment.[64]

It is also pointed out that "in the final analysis, neither having ceremonial ordination nor lacking it made any difference to Luther. The real issue for Luther was always the nature of the office rather than the presence or absence of ordination." Further, "the emphasis was entirely on the 'call and commission' to the office of the ministry."[65] This point coincides with the observation previously made in this study, that it is not ordination which creates or validates the office, but the appointment.

For Calvin, too, the call is important, not the rite of ordination. Having discussed the various offices in the church Calvin writes: "Therefore, if any one would be deemed a true minister of the Church, he must *first* be duly called." Together with "the external and formal call which relates to the public order of the Church," we also have "that secret call of which every minister is conscious before God" that is "the good testimony of our heart, that we undertake the offered office neither from ambition nor avarice, nor any other selfish feeling, but a sincere fear of God and desire to edify the Church. This, as I have said, is indeed necessary for every one of us, if we would approve our ministry to God" (*Inst.* IV.iii.10, 11).

Having discussed "whether a minister should be chosen *by the whole Church,* or only by *colleagues* and *elders*, who have the charge of discipline; or whether they may be appointed by the authority of one individual," Calvin writes: "We see, then, that ministers are legitimately called according to the word of God, when those who may have seemed fit are elected on the consent and approbation of the people. Other pastors, however, ought to preside over the election, lest any error should be committed by the general body either through levity, or bad passion, or tumult" (*Inst.* IV.iii.15). The call of the church and a service of commission were the essential elements in the installment to a church office. The laying on of hands was not always practiced in Geneva.

Ritual Ordination Not Necessary. It should be noticed that in Luther's endeavors to establish an evangelical church prior to 1535 "ritual ordination was not required for holding the office of ministry, and no regular method of ordination for the new Church was introduced until 1535."[66] Even when that happened there "is no evidence to indicate that before 1535 Luther either tried to persuade the Elector to authorize ordinations or ever claimed that ordination is necessary for holding the office of the ministry."[67] In this connection it is of interest to notice that Philip Melanchthon, who was the founder and systematizer of Protestant theology, and recognized by Luther as his superior in scholarship, was a lay theologian.

Calvin found biblical support for the laying on of hands in connection with the installation ceremony of a minister. Luther did the same. However, Calvin, like Luther, looked at it as a mere rite or ceremony, "agreeing unto order and comeliness," but having "of itself no force or power."[68]

As already observed, it is the call which is important and not the rite of ordination. The call is recommended by the church. "It is asked, 'Was grace given by the outward sign?' To this question I answer, whenever ministers were ordained, they were recommended to God by the prayers of the whole Church, and in this manner grace from God was obtained for them by prayer, and was not given to them by virtue of the sign, although the sign was not uselessly or unprofitably employed, but was a sure pledge of that grace which they received from God's own hand."[69] "In sum, this is the end why they laid their hands upon Barnabas and Paul, that the Church might offer them to God, and that they might with their consent declare that this office was enjoined them by God; for the calling was properly God's alone, but the external ordaining did belong to the Church, and that according to the heavenly oracle."[70]

Speaking about a candidate for the ministry, Calvin writes: "As to the manner of introducing him, it is good to use the imposition of hands, which ceremony was observed by the apostles and then in the ancient Church, providing that it take place without superstition and without offence. But because there has been much superstition in the past, and scandal might result, it is better to abstain from it because of the infirmity of the times."[71]

Formal Ordination Required. In the spring of 1535 the Elector John of Saxony mandated that formal ordination was to be a prerequisite for holding ministerial office in his territory. Candidates for the ministry were in the future to be examined and ordained by the theological faculty in Wittenberg. "It seems that the Elector doubted that unordained people were truly able to hold and exercise the office of the ministry. He evidently saw a theological necessity for ritual ordination and so finally mandated ritual ordination as a legal precondition for holding the office of the ministry."[72]

The pastor of the city church in Wittenberg, Johann Bugenhagen, "was initially opposed to the new practice. He did not like the separation of the confirmation of the call from the actual installation of the new pastor in the calling congregation. He felt that at most the lay elders of a calling congregation should consecrate their new pastor."[73]

Luther accepted Elector John's mandate without changing his theological concept of ritual ordination as long as the preaching of the Word could be enhanced. He seems to have been motivated pragmatically; he saw the mandate as an opportunity by which a needed ministry could be developed with higher morality, better education, and reasonable salary, and a recognized and respected professional and social status in society; a worthy goal but to be achieved with the assistance of the secular powers. In the autumn of 1535 Luther delivered an ordination sermon in which he further explained the reason and result of the new ordination arrangement. Referring to this sermon the following comment is made:

> The ordination mandate was in accord with the practice of the early Christian Church since the early Church, too, found it necessary to adopt centralized rather than local ordinations lest disunity in doctrine develop. Luther noted that Saxony faced a major threat from false teaching in its parishes and that the ordination mandate was a proper step towards rooting out false teaching since it gave Wittenberg control over the quality of new pastors. By 1535 the ordination mandate was possible in a practical sense because there was by then a well-established mechanism of ecclesiastical authority that could enforce sound doctrine in Saxony.[74]

In other words, Luther recognized advantages "in a governmentally enforced necessity of ordination for holding the office of the ministry in Saxony. Yet he did not modify his theology of ordination in order to justify the new governmental policy of 1535."[75] This involves a churchstate relationship dilemma and a theological-pragmatic dilemma and contradiction, which have remained with European Lutheranism and other branches of Protestantism and are seen up to the present time.

We will now return to the situation in Geneva, where Calvin found it best to abstain from the laying on of hands. When Calvin returned to Geneva from Strasbourg in 1541 the city council had promised to cooperate with him, but as Calvin scholar Francois Wendel has pointed out, only "on condition that this did not infringe any of the prerogatives of the civil power, or affect certain customs that the Genevan Church observed in common with the Bernese Churches, and which had to be maintained for political reasons." As an example Wendel refers to different practices regarding how often the Lord's Supper should be celebrated; "Thus it was that Calvin was not able to obtain the celebration of Holy Communion every month as he desired, but only once a quarter." Regarding not laying on the hands at the time of the installation service we read: "Similarly, the installation of new pastors could not be accompanied by the laying on of hands according to the example of Strasbourg; they had to be inducted simply by a prayer, and with a sermon upon the pastoral functions. These were, after all, details of minor importance, and Calvin gave way."[76]

It is of interest to observe that Luther introduced the rite of laying on of hands under the influence of the Duke of Saxony, while Calvin withheld it because of the civil authorities, according to Wendel.

Robert G. Bolt, in a study on ordination in the writings of Calvin, confirms what seems to be the conclusion from the various statements we have quoted from Calvin. He writes: "Calvin feared the misunderstanding of the people. Laying on of hands might appear to be a rejection of the priesthood of all believers, and an artificial elevation of the minister. It also might give to the ordained too much of the rejected notion of the absolutism and indelibility of the Roman ordination. For the time Calvin laid aside the imposition of hands. The practice could be resumed when the Church had a clearer understanding of its purpose."[77]

So far the present writer has not been able to pinpoint a special date when the rite of laying on of hands began in Geneva. However, note should be taken of two references. Between his first and second (and final) stay in Geneva Calvin spent three years in Strasbourg as minister for its congregation (1539-1541). There, he was greatly influenced by Martin Bucer.

Bucer was later invited to England (1549) and became professor of divinity at Cambridge. He was highly regarded by the young Protestant king, Edward VI, and to him Bucer dedicated his major work, *De Regno Christi*, 1550. Here Bucer makes reference to the practice of laying on of hands, and the Reformers in general would no doubt agree with his statement:

> We have spoken above about the laying on of hands for those who are consecrated to the sacred ministry of the Church; although we have no express command of the Lord, we have nevertheless the examples of the apostles (Acts 6:6; 13:3) and also a precept to Timothy (I Tim. 4:14; 5:22), so that it is entirely likely that the apostles used that sign for the ordination of ministers of the Church at the command of the Lord. On this account, this ceremony was observed in the early churches quite religiously, and in the Reformed churches it has now been devoutly recalled into use.[78]

The question is, did Bucer, in the last sentence, include the church in Geneva? That Calvin agreed with Bucer theologically there is no doubt. In the last edition of the *Institutes* (Latin, 1559 and French, 1560) Calvin in a positive way endorsed the ritual of laying on of hands by referring to the common texts in the New Testament. He takes it for granted that pastors, teachers, and deacons were consecrated in this way. He admits that "there is no fixed precept concerning the laying on of hands," but he considered it a useful symbol by which "the dignity of the ministry should be commended to the people, and he who is ordained, reminded that he is no longer his own, but is bound in service to God and the Church. Besides, it will not prove an empty sign, if it be restored to its genuine origin. For if the Spirit of God has not instituted anything in the Church in vain, this ceremony of his appointment we shall feel not to be useless, provided it be not superstitiously abused" (*Inst.* IV.iii.16). Here Calvin seems to plead for a proper, not superstitious, use of the rite.

Early Development in the Reformed Churches. Martin Bucer's statement that among the Reformed Churches the rite of laying on of hands "has now been devoutly recalled into use" needs further explanation. J. L. Ainslie, in his extensive study of the ministry in the Reformed Churches of the sixteenth and seventeenth centuries,[79] takes up the question of "the rite or ceremony of the imposition of hands in the service of admission to the Ministerial Order of the Reformed Churches." He makes this comprehensive statement: "It may be said at the outset that opinions have differed in most of the Churches, both Reformed and others, as to the rite being essential in ordination or otherwise. Some have held it to be an absolute essential, while others have considered it better omitted, or, at the most, not essential, but only to be used as a helpful outward indication of ordination."[80]

A number of examples, which J. L. Ainslie gives, illustrate the different concepts. However, it is also pointed out that the rite eventually found acceptance by all. For example, the Scottish First Book of Discipline speaks against the imposition of hands. "The rite continued to be regarded as unnecessary from thirty to forty years after the Church had been instituted, even though it might come to be practised more and more, and though there were those latterly who laid more stress on it as the years ran on towards the seventeenth century."[81] In 1581 the Second Book of Discipline "definitely authorised the rite, though this is to be noted, the wording does not indicate any enforcing of it in ordinations. And it was not enforced. Ministers were admitted freely, in what proportions one cannot say, without the use of the rite, and without their ordination being thought irregular."[82]

The Reformed Church in Holland also found the rite unnecessary. In its Canons of 1577 "the omission of laying on of hands in ordinations" was decreed, but at the Synod of Dort, in 1619, the imposition of hands was stipulated.[83]

Where the imposition of hands was practiced there were variations regarding who should lay on the hands. "The chief differences in the agents of ordination will be that sometimes the act of ordination will be performed by one minister, in other cases by several ministers, and in other cases by ministers and laymen."[84] The different arrangements reflect the different interpretations of the meaning of the laying on of hands (and by whom) in the Old and New Testaments; a topic with which we dealt earlier.

In our discussion of ordination in the Lutheran Reformation we observed that Philip Melanchthon was not ordained. In the case of Calvin "no formal ceremonial ordination" took place. "He was invited by the Genevan authorities to be a minister in their city. He had been recognised and accepted as such by the people. That would be sufficient to constitute his induction to the Reformed Church of Geneva." The same was the case with Guillaume Farel (1485-1565), a close colleague of Calvin in Geneva and a reformer of the City of Neuchatel.

When we turn to Scotland we are told that Andrew Melville (1545-1622), "although occupying some of the highest positions in the Church, yet apparently had never been ordained with the imposition of hands." We are also informed that Robert Bruce, "the leading minister in Edinburgh, . . . had been admitted to the Ministry without the rite, and without any question, indeed with the Assembly concurring and joining in his appointment, and not requiring any ceremonial of imposition of hands. That was about 1587. He continued as an honored minister in Edinburgh for over ten years, and occupied the highest places in the Ministry. He was twice Moderator of the Assembly."[85]

These examples may tell us two things: First, that the call and the appointment are of basic significance, and not any formal ceremonial rite. Second, that God, under specific circumstances, calls people to unique tasks; the call—through the Holy Spirit—being obvious to the persons them selves and all concerned. In our previous discussion of Calvin's comments on apostles, prophets, evangelists, pastors, and teachers (Eph. 4:11) Calvin wrote that "of these, only the two last have an ordinary office in the Church. The Lord raised up the other three at the beginning of His kingdom, and still occasionally raises them up when the necessity of the times requires" (*Inst.* IV.iii.4). It was no doubt perceived that the leaders of the Protestant Reformation belonged to this latter group.

Through the writings of Bucer and Zwingli, Peter Martyr (1500-62), an Italian member of the Augustinian order, sympathized with the Protestant Reformation. He had to flee his home country and went to Zurich, Basel, and then Strasbourg, where Bucer appointed him professor of theology (1542). Two years later he came to England and was made professor at Oxford. When Mary came to the throne in England he fled to Strasbourg, where he took up teaching again, but from 1556 to his death he was a professor in Zurich. From here he was in correspondence with future reformers during the Elizabethan period. From this highly respected and well-known man we have the following statement, which has bearing upon the point under discussion:

> Since the Ministry, alike under the ancient Law as according to the Gospel, has been fulfilled without imposition of hands, this imposition is not absolutely necessary. . . . One does not need to be astonished, if, amidst the vices and corruptions of the Church, God, in order to restore it, has caused to arise vocations out of the ordinary. . . . The Holy Spirit is not bound to external ceremonies.[86]

In our discussion of the requirement of formal ordination we noticed, especially in Wittenberg and Geneva, how in different ways church and civil administrations took part in nominating and electing the candidate. For this reason some pertinent observations regarding church-state relationship are in order.

Ordination and Church-State Relations. Not only theology, Christology, and soteriology have influenced ecclesiology, but also church-state issues. Here there is a reciprocal influence, which in turn has a bearing upon the concept of ministerial appointment and the rite of installment (ordination).

The Protestant Reformation of the sixteenth century resulted ecclesiologically in the establishment of territorial and national churches. At the Peace of Augsburg, 1555, it was decided that each ruler should determine the faith within his territory according to the principle *cuius regio, eius religio* ("each region, his—the ruler's—religion"). The pragmatic application of this principle and its bearing on ecclesiology and ordination was already illustrated twenty years earlier in Saxony and Wittenberg. The different types of ecclesiology: Roman Catholic, Eastern Orthodox, Anglican, Classical and Radical Protestantism have been influenced by their respective church-state philosophies, which have theoretical and pragmatic consequences on the concept of the ministry. The moral, spiritual, and educational preparedness for an appointed ministry is part of the process of leading to a "call" confirmed by an official appointment, installment or dedication; but it must be theologically motivated, rooted, and originated, for only then can the appointed person be a true guardian of the unity and the very nature and characteristics of church.

The question must be asked: Are there any church-state concepts attached to the ministry and its appointment which are not in full accord with the biblical marks of the church? In this connection the truth of the dictum that "in a relative sense the history of the church is a progressive judgment of the church" becomes of special significance. Luther was justifiably criticized by the leaders of the Radical Reformation. Luther's pragmatic, apparently plausible and progressive actions and his well-meaning mistakes, may serve as an excuse for church leaders who fall for the temptation to deal with ecclesiological precepts and concepts pragmatically, but isolated from the constitutional marks of the church. However, the judgment of history will unavoidably and with depressing consequences invalidate such compromising methods.

History tells us that in close church-state relations energies which should be used for spiritual pursuits are diverted or diluted in cooperation with secular powers, whose goals and methodologies are not spiritually motivated. Likewise, ecclesiology cannot help but be tarnished, and the spiritually representative status of the appointed minister is compromised. The rite of ordination has been performed with diverse concepts of church-state relationships in mind. Marjorie Warkentin writes: "The church of Jesus Christ has continued to seek its patterns for church office in the society in which it is placed, in spite of our Lord's warnings that he is initiating a new society with its own unique authority structure." Further, "if we are convinced that the individual believer can be or is being transformed by the Spirit of God, then the church too must demonstrate to the world that it is the community of the redeemed. Its political structures must reflect the transformed character of the community as a whole if the world is to take its gospel seriously."[87]

EPILOGUE

Just as you cannot say "citizen" without implying the State, so, the New Testament teaches, you cannot say "Christian" without in turn implying the Church.—H. R. Mackintosh

If the revelation of God in Christ is of supreme moment for mankind, the Christian community is also supremely signifi-cant. For the revelation occurred only within the life of that community. God did not manifest himself in Jesus alone, but in the life of the group which was formed about him and in whose creation he was himself the decisive factor. It was in Jesus as known in the Church *that the fresh activity of God among men, which we call the revelation in Christ, occur-red. And that revelation is not merely remembered in the Church; it is constantly present wherever there is genuine Christian fellowship.—Prof. John Knox*

The ministry and ordination are not autonomous subjects, and neither is ecclesiology, to which they belong; the overarching subject is theology.

The Bible depicts God as Creator and Lawgiver. Man, created as a moral being, has personal freedom and was placed in covenant relationship with God. Life was to be fulfilled by being in harmony with the will of God; thus human beings were the children of God.

After the Fall it was possible to restore the relationship with God by entering the covenant of redemption; doing so, the family of God was renewed and became the people of God, which historically became the church. Accordingly, the church has its origin in the covenant con-cept and antedates New Testament times.

The people of God were those—like Noah, Abraham, Isaac, Jacob—who entered into covenant with God. During the course of history God repeatedly renewed His covenant with "a remnant."

The Old Testament places the people of God, the church, in the center of a great cosmic drama which began back in eternity, with the final scenes taking place at the coming of Messiah.

The New Testament church came into existence as an eschatological community, a remnant, and should always remain such. The realism of biblical eschatology must have its rightful place. The church ought continually to be on guard against the trend to humanize and naturalize biblical eschatology, and then with an uneschatological gospel seek to transform the present world into the "celestial city" of God.

At His first advent the people and their leaders rejected Jesus because they were looking exclusively for a Messiah who would give them political freedom from Rome and establish their nation as the kingdom of God. It has always been difficult for sinful man to distinguish between spiritual realities and temporal goals. In His great discourse on watching for the signs of the times Christ compared the time of the end with the destruction of Jerusalem, where incompatible religio-political ambitions and goals were buried under the ruins of the city.

The early Christians were conscious of living through the turning point of the great controversy between good and evil. Christ's birth, life, crucifixion, resurrection, and ascension had already set in motion a change in the order of this world. Through the opened door the Holy Spirit descended and empowered the early Christians with a new life they could not have obtained by themselves, and that power was to remain with them until the end. Though they felt certain that the transition was already well under way, they also realized that it would not reach completion this side of the second advent.

The Apostle John said: "Beloved, now we are children of God, and it has not appeared as yet what we shall be. We know that, when He appears, we shall be like Him, because we shall see Him just as He is" (1 John 3:2). To the Christian the time between the two advents is one of a certain tension between "now we are children of God" and "it has not appeared as yet what we shall be." This tension cannot be eliminated, and Christian historical realism advises us that the present and the future must be seen and lived in the light of this polarity.

Church history tells us that, to a large degree, Christian doctrines and practices have focused upon either the first advent or the second advent. The former has been the inclination by established churches, the latter by apocalyptic movements. Each advent is a distinct event, to be sure, but the message or truth of each should be seen in totality, both in doctrinal teaching and in the pragmatic life of the individual and the church. The two advents should also serve as a helpful guide, or tuning fork, in understanding the church's activities and its relation to society and the world at large. The Christian lives in the world but is "not of the world" (John 17:14). His Christian realism regarding a sinful world tells him not to hope for a lasting peace apart from the second advent. Only in the correlation of the two advents can the Christian hope, promises, and redemptive activities be fulfilled, partly in this present life and completely in the everlasting kingdom of God. The first advent made the second advent possible; but what the first advent gained, can only be realized fully at the second advent.

In man's view of the future the pendulum has generally swung between optimism and pessimism. The first has its source in the original divine design for man and is renewed in the belief in the kingdom of God; the latter originated in the fall of man and continued because of his sinfulness. The Christian view of the future is one of biblical realism. Having experienced the power of the Holy Spirit, the Christian is not a hopeless pessimist. But also realizing the demonic power of sin in the "present" age the Christian is not unduly or naively optimistic either. Christ said, "My kingdom is not of this world" (John 18:36). Christian optimism is anchored in the inseparability of the two advents of Christ. The closing words of the Bible: "Come, Lord Jesus" (Rev. 22:20), echo the prayer of both the Old and the New Testament.

The New Testament maintains that one's Christian profession is only Christian in proportion to its correct theological and experiential understanding of Jesus Christ as a person, and the practical application of this understanding. The only valid evaluation of the church, with its doctrines, structures, functions, and life, is the Christ-evaluation. The Christ-evaluation asks whether or not all the components making up the church are Christ-originated, Christ-founded, Christ-motivated, Christ-oriented, Christ-spirited, Christ-approved, Christ-centered, and Christ-like. If we remove the Christ of Scripture from the church we will be left with an empty shell, or a house built on sand and not on the rock (Matt. 7:24-27).

To this must be added that the "Christ," and thereby true ecclesiology, can only be realized by a congregation made up of members being filled with the Holy Spirit. Here is the key to solve any ecclesiological problem and the source for fulfilling the church's glorious mission. The endowments of the Holy Spirit given to the church at its inauguration include methodology and motivation as well as power of actualization, and are constitutive for the church at any time and place.

The ancient church listed the characteristics of the church as oneness, holiness, catholicity (universality), and apostolicity. In their conflict with the Church of Rome, the Protestant Reformers emphasized that the marks of the true church are that the gospel is rightly taught, and the sacraments rightly administered. These two notes of the church were undergirded with four theological principles: "The Bible alone," "Christ alone," "grace alone," and "faith alone" (*sola Scriptura, solus Christus, sola gratia, sola fide*).

Whatever aspect of the church we have considered, it has been noticeable that each is centered and founded in Christ as its source for realization. It should be emphasized that what we have said regarding the motifs inherited from the Old Testament, and the principles foundational for the nature of the church as well as its identifying characteristics—one, holy, catholic, apostolic—should serve as the framework, control factors, and guideposts for any evaluation and structuring of the church, including its ministry.

There is no doubt that the reconciling mission of the church is a mission to the whole world by the whole people of God. This is illustrated by an experience of a colleague of mine who had a lecture appointment in a small country in Central America with a population similar to that of his home country in Europe. However, he found that while his church in his home country had 3,000 members, in this Central American country the membership was 45,000. Yet both countries had about the same number of ordained ministers. But the one in Central America had several hundred lay preachers and church leaders. While there are cultural, social, and economic differences between the two countries that have a bearing upon different church situations, one fact still remains: where the priesthood of believers are active, church growth takes place and the church in its totality is consolidated. No doubt when we look at church growth universally we will find it to be in proportion to the involvement of the total body of believers.

The covenant promise to Abraham: "In you all the families of the earth shall be blessed" (Gen. 12:3), and that Israel should "be called the priests of the Lord; . . . ministers of our God" (Isa. 61:6), will be fulfilled by the total body of Christ as a priesthood of believers. (See Matt. 24:14; 28:19; Mark 16:20; Acts 1:8). The Apostle Paul writes: "Now the promises were spoken to Abraham and to his seed. He does not say, 'And to seeds,' as referring to many, but rather to one, 'And to your seed,' that is, Christ. . . . For you are all sons of

God through faith in Christ Jesus. For all of you who were baptized into Christ have clothed yourselves with Christ. There is neither Jew nor Greek, there is neither slave nor free man, there is neither male nor female; for you are all one in Christ Jesus. And if you belong to Christ, then you are Abraham's offspring, heirs according to promise" (Gal. 3:16, 26-29).

In order to fulfill the glorious, world-wide mission of the church, its structure must be a mission structure. This means that the local church board is a mission board and the church at large a mission body. The body of Christ must manifest a sensitivity to the guidance of the Holy Spirit and be centered in the spiritual life and mission of the total priesthood of believers.

Roy Coad in his book *A History of the Brethren Movement* makes the following pertinent observation:

> When it is understood that "gift" extends to every necessary task within the church's life and witness, and that the ideal is that every member of the church should have his or her function within that life and witness made plain, then recognition becomes the open acknowledgement by the congregation of the formal place of each of its members. In this way the churches can be revolutionized by a partnership of grace in which every member has his or her own function to fulfil, without jealousy or frustration, and where the Holy Spirit will weld the individual gifts of the many into a united testimony to His power. . . . In the present haphazard state of things, very much true gift finds no opportunity for expression, and runs to waste, simply because of natural diffidence on the part of the sensitive. It is the most forceful who tend to be heard, rather than the most gifted. An ordering of ministry provides both an incentive and an outlet for gifts which often remain unused today.[1]

Reference has been made to the spiritual, moral, and social effects of the concept of the priesthood of believers on the countries where Protestantism has been influential. Having examined the doctrine of the priesthood of believers since the beginning of the Protestant Reformation in the sixteenth century, Cyril Eastwood makes the following significant statement: "The History of the Reformation, the History of Puritanism, and the History of the Evangelical Revival, are the story of the extent to which Christians have understood and applied the doctrine of the priesthood of all believers."[2]

Appropriately the question could be asked: Should the spiritual and moral decline, with all its social consequences, in the Protestant West in this century be attributed to the churches' clericalism? Have most of the Christians been told only to function as citizens, and not as a priesthood of believers? We should remind ourselves what Pietism did for Germany in the seventeenth century and its subsequent influence on John Wesley, who in eighteenth century England founded the Methodist movement with its many chapels and lay preachers. We should also keep in mind the Great Awakening in eighteenth century America as well as the Second Great Awakening in the nineteenth century. To this should be added the lay people's involvement in the rise of foreign missions, establishment of Bible Societies and other Christian voluntary associations for religious and social renewal.

The early believers did not have a speculative abstraction, a vague idea, or an undefined concept of the church, but one that was most realistic and concrete. They demonstrated the covenant truth of "a kingdom of priests" (Ex. 19:6) and the fulfillment of "priests of the Lord" (Isa. 61:6). Christ had said to the believers: "You are the salt of the earth You are the light of the world" (Matt. 5:13, 14). In their burning love for Christ, the early Christians were aflame for Him, confirming the saying, "The church exists by mission just as fire exists by burning." They saw it as their mission to manifest Christ. They found an immense satisfaction in being Christ's representatives and taking part in transforming the lives of others. Since they themselves had been changed by Jesus Christ, and energized by His Spirit they were able to change the lives of men and women. They exclaimed, "But thanks be to God, who always leads us in His triumph in Christ, and manifests through us the sweet aroma of the knowledge of Him in every place" (2 Cor. 2:14).

The nature and the essence of any church ministry is that of service in the spirit and pattern of Christ. Every structural and vocational aspect of the ministry must have as its soul the covenant of redemption. If the church—congregations and institutions (such as schools and hospitals)—loses that sense of Christ-ministry it ceases to be "church"; it forfeits the right to be Christ's unique community and becomes secular, united in many inconspicuous ways with the business, finances, and methods of the kingdom of this world. Church history tells us that here lies the constant danger for the church;

therefore, the church must continually be called to the renewal and reformation of the soul of its ministry, for the structure of any church ministry is dead without the soul: the being a bond-servant of Jesus Christ in the saving work of reconciliation. This includes the total priesthood of believers.

The Apostle Peter writes: "As each one has received a special gift, employ it in serving one another, as good stewards of the manifold grace of God. Whoever speaks, let him speak, as it were, the utterances of God; whoever serves, let him do so as by the strength which God supplies; so that in all things God may be glorified through Jesus Christ, to whom belongs the glory and dominion forever and ever. Amen" (1 Peter 4:10-11).

We have observed that in the New Testament the nature of the ministry is expressed by the words "servant," "to serve" and "service," also translated "minister," "to minister" and "ministry." The King James Version rather consistently does this. But such usage demands that one keep in mind that when we speak about a minister and a ministry we are speaking about a servant (*diakonos*) and a service (*diakonia*). No ministerial office represents status or rank in a political or social sense; its influence is measured by its Christ-likeness and the extent to which it is a medium for the working of the Holy Spirit. The office holder is elected and commissioned by the collective priesthood of believers, who in turn regard the office holder as called and uniquely equipped by the Holy Spirit. He has given the person the discernment and spiritual gifts needed to serve and represent their collective concerns. The ministry is placed within the congregation and not above it.

Any appointed ministry must be evaluated and must function within the total framework of the church as the body of Christ, of which He Himself is the Head. The members "should work together as a whole with all the members in sympathetic relationship with one another" (1 Cor. 12:25, PME). The relatedness of the body of Christ is constituted in the divine relatedness as both its source and model.

God is a triune God. Unity and harmony between personalities is central to the way God operates. The Godhead in its total being and acting can best be defined in terms of relatedness; accordingly, we speak about the triune God. In the divine plurality is found the fullness of divinity, and within the triune God are personalities in absolute harmony and in complete unanimity of intention, plan, and action. True relatedness lies in the center of divine reality. The creative and sustaining power of the universe flows from the divine relational oneness; likewise, the possibility and reality of redemption is rooted in it.

The unity of the triune God—that is, the coexistence of the Father, the Son, and the Holy Ghost, or the One God existing in Three Persons but of one indivisible essence—is a foundational belief in Christianity and is theologically referred to by the term Trinity. While there is no formal teaching on the Trinity in the Bible, the relationship of God the Father to Christ and to the Holy Spirit, and of Christ to God the Father and to the Holy Spirit, are spoken of or referred to throughout the New Testament.

Although the unity of the Godhead exists in oneness of essence, nature, will, etc.—implying absolute equality—complementary and different functions are exercised in complete harmony or unison, as noted in the covenant of redemption and clearly spelled out in the biblical description of the functions of the three Persons in the work of redemption. These functions are well-known to the student of the Bible. With the divine oneness in mind—a unity of complementary functions—Christ prayed that the believers "may be one, just as We are one" (John 17:22). There is a complete harmony between the being and acting of the triune God; and so it should be between the members of the body of Christ.

On account of the very nature of the divine oneness and equality, identified in all aspects of existence within the Trinity (none of the three would think or act differently from the other two), there can never be domination in functional activities, different as they are of necessity even within the divine realm. There is no need for authority in order to enforce conformity or unity. Yet, there seems to be an apparent "hierarchy": Father, Son, and Holy Spirit.

Because of equality the divine headship is not authoritative, but represents a responsibility created by love (*agape*) and manifested in giving and serving (*diakonia*), as expressed in the word: "For God so loved the world, that He gave His only begotten Son" (John 3:16). It is illustrated also in the headship of Christ as expressed by the Apostle Paul when he writes: "Have this attitude in yourselves which was also in Christ Jesus, who, although He existed in the form of God, did not regard equality with God a thing to be grasped, but emptied Himself, taking the form of a bondservant, and being made in the likeness of men. And being found in appearance as a man, He humbled Himself by becoming obedient to the point of death, even death on a cross. Therefore also God highly exalted Him, and bestowed on Him the name which is above every name" (Phil. 2:5-9).

In other words, Christ did not find equality antithetical with headship (or a certain hierarchy) and functional differences. Christ exemplified, as man, the divine relatedness and renewed the order of creation by a life of *agape*. His very being was in full harmony with the divine will, therefore His actions were, likewise.

Humanly speaking, even within the Trinity, headship resembles the role of a chairman, the first among equals, who are in complete accord; any directive given is rooted in a delegated or representative authority (the words "representative responsibility" are more correct than "authority") reflecting order, oneness, and harmony (John 14-17). Headship within the Trinity—one of representativeness, responsibility, and love (agape)—does not create the categories of superiority and subordination. In human terms this is a contradiction. The distorted relational principles of the Fall (as authoritative domination and subservience) cannot be used when evaluating the divine relatedness and headship. The church as a new creation—the body of Christ and the temple of the Holy Spirit—is asked to mirror the divine principles of relatedness in functions and relationships.

In the New Testament the development of a church structure and an official ministry is obvious, even though all details are not clear or uniform. Christ appointed "twelve" and "seventy"; He also said that He would send "prophets and apostles" as well as "wise men and scribes" (Luke 9:1; 10:1; 11:49; Matt. 23:34). We have observed that these and other ministries functioned in New Testament times.

A council of Seven was established among the Hellenistic Jewish Christians. Paul and Barnabas were commissioned by the church in Antioch. James, the brother of Jesus, was chairman of a council of the apostles and elders in Jerusalem. Consultation was essential for the growing church in its missionary outreach in order to avoid disruptions and disunity. The procedure of the decision-making process is reflected in the closing words of one council session: "Then it seemed good to the apostles and the elders, with the whole church" (Acts 15:22).

Outside Jerusalem local elders (*presbyteroi*) were appointed; they were also named "overseers" (*episcopoi*). We find only two references to the office of deacons; their work is not spelled out.

The ecclesiology of the New Testament has its own unique features. However, there are certain analogies to the Old Testament and Judaism, indicating that the primitive church was structured so it could become the people of God: a new Israel. Analogy is found between the twelve apostles and the twelve tribes, the seventy appointed by Christ and by Moses (the Jersualem Sanhedrin had seventy members), the Seven in Acts 6, and "the seven of the city," the wider use of the word "apostle" and the Jewish *shaliach* (messenger), the local elders and deacons and the board of elders, ruler and custodian of the synagogue.

When Luke wrote that the first Christian community was "of about one hundred and twenty persons" (Acts 1:15), did he make a point of the fact that in Judaism 120 could organize themselves as a community? Did Christ follow the Jewish pattern of sending messengers (*shaliach*) in pairs, when He sent the disciples "two and two" (Luke 10:1)? Jerusalem had not only the Sanhedrin of seventy members (71 with the high priest), but also a threemember consultative council. It would be tempting to ask if there is any analogy between this and the three-member inner circle of Christ (Peter, James, and John).

The New Testament church was developed within its own adopted structure; however, the structure was not alien nor created in a vacuum, but was understood and was appropriate to the times. It should also be mentioned (as previously quoted) that " 'church' is not originally an abstract theological term, but one that denotes an actual happening. . . . The Church is spoken of as something that really 'takes place'." Karl Barth made the same point by referring to the congregation as "event."[3] In the New Testament we have specific statements and hints of emergence of the adaptable structures that are different from the congregational structure. In today's church we have the congregation, but also youth societies, service agencies, radio and television programs, relief operations, church schools, and many other agencies. These are also "church," being one in spirit and practice with the nature and marks of the church. If the latter is not the case these agencies cease, of course, to be "church" and become a mere secular phenomenon, and will eventually lose the spiritual and reconciling power of "church."

The story of the formation of the structure of the apostolic church reveals two aspects: a charismatic and an appointed ministry, unified in a Christ-centered and spirit-filled *diakonia*. In such a setting the charismatic ministry did not create confusion or disorder; on the other hand the appointed ministry preserved order and unity so necessary for any "society," but without transforming the local community of faith into an institutional and hierarchical organization. The total *diakonia* preserved the apostolic church as "the body of Christ."

It must also be acknowledged that the main difficulty—for the first century church and ever since—is the proper relationship and interaction between the spiritual gifts (freely exercised) and the appointed, organized ministerial offices. Accordingly, it must continually be recognized that the two aspects of structure are not separate entities, for *ecclesia* is a body of which Christ is the Head. Here lies the uniqueness of the Christian community.

Each member is "born again" into a new life experience with Christ. The individual spiritual experience becomes the common and energizing experience, and thus makes "church" possible. Further, the total community is collectively under the testimony of Scripture. When the church moved into the post-apostolic period many influences were felt—for better or worse—but fortunately one significant thing was accomplished: the acceptance of the apostolic writings as the New Testament.

The New Testament church, which was a brotherhood of the priesthood of believers, became, by the third century, a community centered in the bishop. The latter had developed as a separate office above the presbyter. The bishops were considered successors of the apostles, and represented Christ by having sacerdotal power like the priesthood of the Old Testament. The bishop is compared with the high priest, the presbyter with the priest, and the deacon with the Levites. At the same time the charismatic ministry began to disappear and gave place to an hierarchical and institutional church. As the church expanded into various parts of the empire, the Roman judicial system and governmental structure were taken over into the organization and governance of the church. The stage was set for the medieval church and the contours took shape: pagan Rome grew into papal Rome. The pope claimed to be the successor of Peter and the vicar of Christ.

The structure of the church and its ministry, as it developed in the third and fourth centuries, prevailed for more than a thousand years. While men and movements challenged medieval ecclesiology, it was the Protestant Reformation that brought churches closer to the pattern of the New Testament and the early church.

In the reconstruction of the Reformation church there were four options.[4] An episcopal system could be maintained but without the papacy. This was the option followed in the Scandinavian countries and in England. Second, since government was ordained by God and in the Christian community was part of the priesthood of believers, Luther taught that the Christian magistracy could represent the church and might therefore organize and supervise it. This was the pattern for the Lutheran churches in Germany. A third possibility was a presbyterian system "on the basis of the parity of ministers, congregational lay-elders, and deacons, and a representative synodical government, with strict discipline, and a distinction between nominal and communicant membership." Luther did not favor this, but it was realized by Calvin in Geneva. Finally, there is congregationalism, which is based on the autonomy of the individual congregation but in a free association with other similar churches. The doctrine of the priesthood of believers would favor the last two forms. Luther's early writings point in this direction, but this was changed by Luther's alliance with the civil government after the Peasant Revolt of 1525.

The evangelical leaders of the Anabaptist movement had much in common with the young Luther and Zwingli, but on account of different ecclesiological concepts they broke with the classical Protestant Reformation.

The Anabaptists came to the conviction that because of the alliance with the state the Protestant Reformers had only been half-way reformers. They became advocates of the principle of separation of church and state. Their religious voluntarism and concept of the church as a fellowship of active believers and self-governing congregations is most significant. The Anabaptist idea of freedom of conscience and toleration stems to a large degree from their concept of the church as a voluntary and free society. The apostolic church was to be normative in every age of the church; accordingly, the aim was not a mere reformation of the church but a restitution of the New Testament church as a Christian brotherhood in which the ideals of the kingdom of God would be realized. The covenant-remnant-eschaton motifs of the Old and New Testaments were basic to Anbaptist ecclesiology.

From the beginning the matter of ordination was never a cardinal doctrine of the church, not one of the fundamentals. Ministry (service) is what the church is all about. Ordination to office is another matter and secondary in the minds of the apostles and the Protestant Reformers. However, the way the church interprets the biblical and historical material related to ordination reflects its ecclesiology and, in turn, its theology.

In older versions of the Bible such as the King James the word "ordain" is translated from various Hebrew and Greek words, none of which mean "ordain" in our modern sense of the word. Modern translations are more correct as they express the original meaning by the use of words such as "assign," "choose," "select," "appoint."

Paul makes no reference to ordination when he lists the special gifts given to the church "for the work of the ministry" (Rom. 12; 1 Cor. 12; Eph. 4), nor when he lists apostles, prophets, evangelists, pastors, and teachers. We are not told that elders were "ordained;" the text reads "appointed" or "chosen."

The rite of ordination leaves the impression that the significance of ordination is the laying on of hands. This leads to the question: What is the New Testament practice and injunction? The laying on of hands has a significant symbolic meaning. Hands were laid on baptized believers and they received the Holy Spirit; others were healed by the same act. In only three instances were hands laid on people for an official service in the church: The Seven in Acts 6, Paul and Barnabas, and Timothy. Each of these instances has been studied.

Some pertinent questions need to be asked regarding ordination. First, has the rite and practice of ordination in one's church come down by the way of tradition from the third century (we have dealt in some detail with significant ecclesiological changes in that century), or is it rooted in Scripture by precept and example, and/or deduction? Could it even be a blend of both tradition and Scripture? The most common interpretation is that the Seven of Acts 6 were deacons, and since hands were laid on them, hands must also have been laid on the deacons mentioned by Paul. The mistake is that the Seven were not deacons like those mentioned by Paul; the latter were not ordained but appointed.

Hands were laid on Paul, Barnabas, and Timothy, but it had no relationship to an office as local elder or pastor. The New Testament does not tell us that hands were laid on elders. Further, it was the people (the elders) who laid their hands on the three persons mentioned, and the same may have been the case with the Seven.

The word "ordain" (Latin *ordinare* "to set in order," "arrange," "regulate") came into use in the third century when the monarchical episcopacy was consolidated and the bishop played the significant role in the appointment of deacons, presbyters, and bishops. The third century concept of priesthood and ordination was perpetuated by use of the word "ordain" in the Latin and later versions of the Bible.

The result was that preconceived ideas of ordination (appointment and laying on of hands) tainted the interpretation of the biblical material and the translations of the Greek New Testament.

Laying the tradition aside and turning to the biblical material, some further questions should be asked. Does the laying on of hands in the three instances observed in the New Testament represent a special blessing (as in the story of Jacob and the sons of Joseph) or does it express a transfer of representative responsibility or substitution (as when Moses laid his hands on Joshua, the people on the Levites, and the rabbis on their pupils)? The answer or interpretation will determine or reflect the structure of one's church and the nature of its ministry.

A cardinal question is: For what ministries or offices should the laying on of hands be practiced? We have observed the Seven and the three emissaries on whom hands were laid. Elders and deacons were appointed to minister in local churches, and others functioned in the strength of spiritual gifts. Through a historical development a threefold ministry of bishops, presbyters, and deacons developed, and by the third century they had become the ordained ministry. This development has been considered. Its outcome cannot be accepted by those who deny a sacramental and sacerdotal priesthood. If ordination is for the preaching ministry, then there still remains an unsolved problem: To what degree is a deacon a part of the preaching ministry?

The Protestant Reformation replaced the altar with the pulpit, and the priest with the preacher. Because of *ecclesia* being the priesthood of believers, the official ministry is a representative ministry, also referred to as a delegated or transferral ministry. Here the appointment is of basic significance, the laying on of hands is a ritual, and not necessary; but it was thought to be meaningful if done within a true theological and ecclesiological framework. Yet, within the Protestant churches there are variances in the sphere of influence, responsibility, and loyalty for the ordained person, all depending upon church structure. In some cases ordination is valid for a local church, in other cases for a territorial, national, or universal church.

In our study we have observed what was expressed in the World Council of Churches document, that "the actual forms of ordination and of the ordained ministry . . . have evolved in complex historical developments."

From the known developments in the New Testament we find structural principles and concepts emerging from the doctrine of the priesthood of believers and from the biblical teaching about the nature and marks of the church and its ministry (*diakonia*). When the body of Christ faithfully operates within this framework it should, at any time and place through the aid of the Holy Spirit, be able to ascertain what is biblically normative for the ministry and the structure of the *ecclesia*. It is the principles and concepts which are of paramount significance; they must serve as underlying presuppositions, and church polity should be derived from them. It is within the framework growing out of Scriptural perspectives of ecclesiology that the question of male and female ministries should be explored.

To a large degree history is a judgment over the church's (or churches') lack of adopting normative biblical principles and concepts which should undergird and constitute the structure and life of the church and its ministry, and thus in turn mirror the relatedness of the triune God in the ministry (*diakonia*) of reconciliation and redemption. All too often theologians and church leaders have taken an *a priori* approach to the New Testament in their study of ecclesiology, with the result that the biblical text has been tarnished and its principles and concepts blurred.

The World Council of Churches document on the ministry and the many replies from churches clearly indicate the significance of the quest for a better understanding of ecclesiology. As an example, the Seventh-day Adventist Church acknowledged in its official response that "the ministry statement raises several questions in the area of belief and practice that the Seventh-day Adventist Church can hardly ignore. This includes questions on the involvement of the whole people of God in the church's life and witness; on the extent to which the corporate priesthood of all believers is practised personally and collectively; on how ordination is understood and practised; on how the principle of collegiality in church life should be applied in church elections; and how Seventh-day Adventists can best affirm a multiplicity of ministries in the church. These and other questions confront Seventh-day Adventists as they respond to the Lima statement thus allowing themselves to be questioned by it."[5] This statement no doubt gives expression to the challenge which faces the Christian churches as a whole.

We repeat what was stated in the introduction. This study is not intended as a closing of the subject of ecclesiology, but rather as a new opening of the theme, keeping in mind the maxim: *Ecclesia reformata semper reformanda* ("the church reformed, always in need of reform"). In the spirit and prayer of the Pauline doxology for the church

(Eph. 3:14-21) we bring this present study to a close.

DOXOLOGY

"I bow my knees before the Father, from whom every family in heaven and on earth derives its name, that He would grant you, according to the riches of His glory, to be strengthened with power through His Spirit in the inner man; so that Christ may dwell in your hearts through faith; and that you, being rooted and grounded in love, may be able to comprehend with all the saints what is the breadth and length and height and depth, and to know the love of Christ which surpasses knowledge, that you may be filled up to all the fulness of God. Now to Him who is able to do exceeding abundantly beyond all that we ask or think, according to the power that works within us, to Him be the glory in the church and in Christ Jesus to all generations forever and ever. Amen."

REFERENCE NOTES

INTRODUCTION

1. *Baptism, Eucharist and Ministry,* Faith and Order Paper No. 111 (Geneva: World Council of Churches, 1982), pp. 20-21. Hereafter referred to as *BEM.*

2. Max Thurian, ed., *Churches respond to BEM: Official responses to the "Baptism, Eucharist and Ministry"* text, vol. III, Faith and Order Paper 135 (Geneva: World Council of Churches, 1987), p. 49.

3. Karl Ludwig Schmidt, "The Church," p. vi, book II of *Bible Key Words* from Gerhard Kittel's *Theologisches Worterbuch Zum Neuen Testament,* trans. & ed. J. R. Coates (New York: Harper & Brothers, Publishers, 1951).

4. Richard Hanson, *Christian Priesthood Examined* (Guildford and London: Lutterworth Press, 1979), pp. 32, 8.

5. *BEM,* p. 20.

6. Hans-Ruedi Weber, "The Rediscovery of the Laity in the Ecumenical Movement," in *The Layman in Christian History,* eds. Stephen Charles Neill and Hans-Ruedi Weber (Philadelphia: The Westminster Press, 1962), p. 377.

Part One

1. See V. Norskov Olsen, *John Foxe and the Elizabethan Church* (Berkely: University of California Press, 1973), pp. 51-100; Belgic Confession, art. xxvii, in *Creeds of Christendom,* ed. Philip Schaff, 3 vols. (New York: Harper & Brothers, 1919), vol. III, p. 417; Scotch Confession, art. v, in *ibid.,* p. 442; J. Overall, *Bishop Overall's Convocation Book of 1606* (London, 1960), pp. 151-152.

2. Jaroslav Pelikan and Helmut T. Lehmann, gen. eds., *Luther's Works,* 55 vols. (Saint Louis: Concordia Publishing House; Philadelphia: Fortress Press and Muhlenberg Press, 1955-   ), vol. 13, p. 88. Hereafter referred to as *LW.*

3. Westminster Confession of Faith, VII.v, in Schaff, *Creeds of Christendom,* vol. III, pp. 617-618.

4. Anthony Tyrrell Hanson, *The Pioneer Ministry* (London: SCM Press Ltd., 1961), pp. 44, 45.

5. T. W. Manson, *The Church's Ministry* (Philadelphia: The Westminster Press, 1948), pp. 35, 17.

6. *Ibid.,* p. 35.

7. John Oman, *The Church and the Divine Order* (London: Hodder & Stoughton, 1911), p. 17.

8. John D. Zizioulas, "Episkope and Episkopos in the Early Church—A Brief Survey of the Evidence," *Episkope and Episcopate in Ecumenical Perspective,* Faith and Order Paper 102 (Geneva, 1979), p. 42, quoted by Emmanuel Clapsis, "The Sacramentality of Ordination and Apostolic Succession: An Orthodox-Ecumenical View," *Greek Orthodox Theological Review,* vol. 30, no. 4 (1985), p. 432.

9. Paul S. Minear, *Images of the Church in the New Testament* (Philadephia: Westminster Press, 1960), p. 28.

10. Scotch Confession of Faith, art. xviii (1560); Belgic Confession, art. xxix (1561); Heidelberg Catechism, quest. 83 (1563).

11. Jaroslav Pelikan, *The Riddle of Roman Catholicism* (New York: Abingdon Press, 1959), pp. 50, 46.

12. Edward C. Fendt, ed., *What Lutherans Are Thinking* (Columbus, Ohio: The Wartburg Press, 1947), p. 22.

13. Pelikan, *Riddle of Roman Catholicism*, pp. 50-51.
14. John T. McNeill, *Unitive Protestantism* (Richmond, Virginia: John Knox Press, 1964), pp. 86-87.
15. Nehemiah Curnock, ed., *The Journal of John Wesley* (New York: Capricorn Books, 1963), p. 51.

Part Two

1. "The Necessity of Priesthood," *Evangelical Dictionary of Theology* (Grand Rapids, Michigan: Baker Book House, 1984), p. 875.
2. Roland de Vaux, *Ancient Israel: Its Life and Institutions* (New York: McGraw-Hill Book Company, Inc., 1961), p. 346
3. Oscar Cullmann, *The Christology of the New Testament* (London: SCM Press Ltd., 1963), p. 89.
4. *Ibid.*, pp. 104, 107.
5. *Ibid.*, pp. 137, 145.
6. A. Glasser, personal correspondence with the author, June 1989.
7. John Hall Elliott, *The Elect and the Holy: An Exegetical Examination of I Peter 2:4-10* (Leiden: E. J. Brill, 1966), pp. 221-222.
8. Eduard Schweizer, *Church Order in the New Testament* (London: SCM Press Ltd., 1961), pp. 188-189.
9. Karl Barth, "The Church—The Living Congregation of the Living Lord Jesus Christ," in *Man's Disorder and God's Design,* The Amsterdam Assembly Series (New York: Harper & Brothers, 1949), pp. 68, 69, 72.
10. George Huntston Williams, "The Ancient Church AD 30-313," in *The Layman in Christian History,* eds. Neill and Weber, pp. 31, 34.
11. Tertullian, On Baptism in *Ante-Nicene Fathers,* eds. Alexander Roberts and James Donaldson, 10 vols. (Grand Rapids, Michigan: Wm. B. Eerdmans Publishing Company, 1951-1956), vol. III, ch. VII, p. 672. Herein referred to as ANF.
12. Quoted by Charles Gore, *The Ministry of the Christian Church* (New York: James Pott & Co., 1889), p. 91; see also Cyril Eastwood, *The Priesthood of all Believers* (Minneapolis, Minnesota: Augsburg Publishing House, 1962), p. 20.
13. *LW,* vol. 44, p. 127; vol. 36, p. 113.
14. *LW,* vol. 41, p. 152; vol. 38, p. 188.
15. *LW,* vol. 44, p. 127.
16. Williams, "The Ancient Church," in *The Layman in Christian History,* eds. Neill and Weber, p. 32.
17. Cyprian, Epistles, lxii.17; lxviii.8, in *ANF,* vol. V, pp. 363, 374-375.
18. Williston Walker, *A History of the Christian Church* (New York: Charles Scribner's Sons, 1959), p. 84.
19. Thomas M. Lindsay, *The Church and the Ministry in the Early Centuries* (New York: George H. Doran Company, n.d.), p. 286.
20. *Ibid.,* pp. 203-204.
21. Philip Schaff, *History of the Christian Church,* 8 vols. (Grand Rapids, Michigan: Wm. B. Eerdmans Publishing Company, 1910), vol. VII, p. 25.
22. Quoted by Gustaf Wingren, *Luther on Vocation* (Philadephia: Muhlenberg Press, 1957), pp. 73, 72.
23. F. W. Kampschulte, *Johann Calvin, seine Kirche und sein Staat,* 2 vols. (Leipzig: Dunker & Humblot, 1869-1899), p. 268, quoted in William A. Mueller, *Church and State in Luther and Calvin: A Comparative Study* (Nashville, Tennessee: Broadman Press, 1954), pp. 115-116.

24. August Bernhard Hasler, *How the Pope Became Infallible* (Garden City, New York: Doubleday & Company, Inc., 1981), p. 34. For further study of this section, see V. Norskov Olsen, *Papal Supremacy and American Democracy* (Riverside, California: Loma Linda University Press, 1987), pp. 11-17, 120-122.

25. *Ibid.*, p. 35.

26. *Ibid.*

27. J. W. C. Wand, *A History of the Early Church to A.D. 500* (London: Methuen & Co., Ltd., 1949), p. 237.

28. Philip Schaff and Henry Wace, eds., *A Select Library of Nicene and Post-Nicene Fathers of the Christian Church*, vol. XII (Grand Rapids, Michigan: Wm. B. Eerdmans Publishing Company, 1956), p. 117.

29. *Ibid.*

30. Schaff, *History of the Christian Church*, vol. IV, p. 212.

31. Alexander Clarence Flick, *The Rise of the Mediaeval Church* (New York: Burt Franklin, 1909), p. 191.

32. Ernest F. Henderson, trans. and ed., *Select Historical Documents of the Middle Ages* (London: George Bell and Sons, 1905), pp. 366-367.

33. H. Burn-Murdoch, *The Development of the Papacy* (London: Faber & Faber Limited, 1954), p. 76-77.

34. Shaff, *History of the Christian Church*, vol. V, p. 157.

35. Oliver J. Thatcher and Edgar H. McNeal, *A Source Book for Mediaeval History* (New York: Charles Scribner's Sons, 1905), p. 315. 36. Ibid., pp. 316-317.

37. Schaff, *History of the Christian Church*, vol. V, p. 674.

38. Thomas Aquinas, *Commentum in IV Libros Sententiarum*, in Ewart Lewis, *Medieval Political Ideas*, vol. II (London: Routledge & Kegan Paul, 1954), p. 567.

39. Reinhold Seeberg, *Textbook of the History of Doctrines*, vol. II (Grand Rapids, Michigan: Baker Book House, 1958), p. 146.

40. Schaff, *History of the Christian Church*, vol. V, p. 590.

41. J. M. Parker, *Christianity and the State in the Light of History* (New York: Harper and Brothers, 1955), p. 133. For further study of this section, see V. Norskov Olsen, *Papal Supremacy and American Democracy*, pp. 108-120, 122-124.

42. A. P. D'Entreves, *The Medieval Contribution to Political Thought* (Oxford: Oxford University Press, 1939), p. 44.

43. Reginald Lane Poole, *Illustrations of the History of Medieval Thought and Learning* (London: Society for Promoting Christian Knowledge, 1920), p. 238.

44. Ephraim Emerton, "The Defensor Pacis of Marsiglio of Padua," in *Harvard Theological Studies, vol. VIII* (Cambridge: Harvard University Press, 1920), p. 1.

45. Marsilius of Padua, *Defensor pacis*, in *Marsilius of Padua: The Defender of Peace*, vol. II, *The Defensor pacis*, trans. Alan Gewirth (New York: Columbia University Press, 1956), p. 431.

46. *Ibid.*, p. 425.

47. *Ibid.*, pp. 51, 52, 53.

48. *Ibid.*, p. 103.

49. *Ibid.*, p. 103.

50. *Ibid.*, p. 323.

51. George H. Sabine, *A History of Political Theory* (New York: Holt, Rinehart and Winston, Inc., 1950), pp. 300-301.

52. Alan Gewirth, *Marsilius of Padua: The Defender of Peace*, vol. I, *Marsilius of Padua and Medieval Political Philosophy* (New York: Columbia University Press, 1951), pp. 262-263.

53. Marsilius of Padua, *Defensor pacis,* in *Marsilius of Padua,* trans. Gewirth, vol. II, p. 301.

54. *Ibid.,* p. 143.

55. Gewirth, p. 9.

56. F. Sander, "Marsilius of Padua," in *The New Schaff-Herzog Encyclopedia of Religious Knowledge,* vol. VII, ch. 7, p. 209.

57. Charles Augustine, *A Commentary on the New Code of Canon Law,* vol. II, *Clergy and Hierarchy* (St. Louis: B. Herder Book Co., 1918), 208-209.

58. Sander, "Marsilius of Padua," *Shaff-Herzog Enc.,* p. 209.

59. J. P. Mayer, Political Thought: *The European Tradition* (New York: The Viking Press, 1939), p. 102.

60. Stephen Chak Tornay, *Ockham: Studies and Selections* (LaSalle, Illinois: The Open Court Publishing Company, 1938), p. 81.

61. William of Occam, *De Imperatorum et Pontificum Potestate,* in Lewis, *Medieval Political Ideas,* p. 607.

62. *Ibid.,* p. 611.

63. *Ibid.,* pp. 606-607.

64. R. Seeberg, "William of Occam", *The New Schaff-Herzog Encyclopedia of Religious Knowledge,* vol. VIII, pp. 219-220.

65. Schaff, *History of the Christian Church,* vol. VII, p. 24.

66. Hans Küng, *The Church* (Garden City, New York: Image Books, 1976), p. 465.

67. *Ibid.,* p. 473.

68. Walter M. Abbott, gen. ed., *The Documents of Vatican II* (London: Geoffrey Chapman, 1967), p. 489, note 2.

69. *Ibid.,* p. 489.

70. *Ibid.,* p. 490.

71. *Ibid.,* p. 486.

72. *Ibid.,* p. 43.

73. *Ibid.,* p. 56.

Part Three

1. Küng, *The Church,* p. 496; Marjorie Warkentin, *Ordination: A Biblical-Historical View* (Grand Rapids, Michigan: William B. Eerdmans Publishing Company, 1982), pp. 186-187; Robert S. Paul, *The Church in Search of Its Self* (Grand Rapids, Michigan: William B. Eerdmans Publishing Company, 1972), p. 265.

2. See *Apostolos* in *Theological Dictionary of the New Testament,* eds. Gerhard Kittle and Gerhard Friedrich, trans. and ed. Geoffrey W. Bromily, 10 vols. (Grand Rapids, Michigan: Wm. B. Eerdmans Publishing Company, 1964-1974), vol. I, pp. 414, 415, 417. Also in *Evangelical Dictionary of Theology,* ed. Walter A. Elwell (Grand Rapids, Michigan: Baker Book House, 1984), p. 71; *Encyclopaedia Judaica,* vol. III (Jerusalem: The Macmillan Company, 1971), p. 216.

3. Manson, *The Church's Ministry,* pp. 43-45.

4. *Ibid.,* p. 58.

5. The Didache, Or Teaching Of The Twelve Apostles, xi.8, in Kirsopp Lake, *The Apostolic Fathers,* 2 vols. (Cambridge, Massachusetts: Harvard University Press, 1959-1965), vol. I, p. 327.

6. The First Epistle of Clement to the Corinthians, xlii.4, in *ibid.,* p. 81.

7. The Epistle of Barnabas, viii.3, in *ibid.,* p. 368.

8. The Didache, xi.4-6, in *ibid.,* p. 327.

9. The Shepherd of Hermas, Similie IX.xv.4, in *ibid.,* vol. II, p. 261.

10. The Epistle of Barnabas, iv.9, in *ibid.,* vol. I, p. 351.

11. Didache, xii; xiii; xv.2, in *ibid.*, pp. 329, 331.

12. Eusebius, *The Ecclesiastical History*, VII.xxiv.6-9, in *Eusebius: The Ecclesiastical History*, trans. Kirsopp Lake and J. E. L. Oulton, 2 vols. *(Cambridge, Massachusetts: Harvard University Press, 1953-1965), vol. II, p. 195.*

13. C. W. Dugmore, *The Influence of the Synagogue Upon the Divine Office*, (Westminster: The Faith Press Ltd., 1964), p. 111.

14. Henry Kendall Booth, *The Bridge Between The Testaments* (New York: Charles Scribner's Sons, 1929), p. 95.

15. *Ibid.*, p. 89.

16. *Theological Dictionary of the New Testament*, eds. Kittel and Friedrich, vol. VI, p. 660.

17. Burton Scott Easton, "Jewish and Early Christian Ordination," *Anglican Theological Review*, vol. 5, p. 313.

18. *Ibid.*, p. 312.

19. *The First Book of Maccabees*, trans. Sidney Tedesche (New York: Harper & Brothers, 1950), p. 229.

20. Jacob Neusner, *Between Time and Eternity* (Encino, CA: Dickenson, 1975), p. 29, quoted by Warkentin in *Ordination*, p. 23.

21. See various Commentaries on Acts 6:1-6; for example, *The Interpreter's Bible*, vol. IX (New York: Abingdon Press, 1954), p. 90.

22. W. Robertson Nicoll, ed., *The Expositor's Greek Testament*, vol. II (Grand Rapids, Michigan: Wm. B. Eerdmans Publishing Company, 1961), p. 168.

23. Flavius Josephus, *Antiquities of the Jews*, IV.viii.14, 38, in *The Life and Works of Flavius Josephus*, trans. William Whiston (Philadelphia: The John C. Winston Company, n.d.), pp. 131, 132; see also Lindsay, *Church and Ministry in Early Centuries*, p. 117.

24. Quoted by J. Rawson Lumby, *The Acts of the Apostles* (Cambridge: At the University Press, 1912), p. 153.

25. See T. F. Torrance, "Consecration and Ordination," *Scottish Journal of Theology*, vol. II (1958), p. 237, note 1; also *The Mishnah*, trans. Herbert Danby (Oxford University Press, 1933), p. 383.

26. Quoted by C. S. C. Williams, *A Commentary on the Acts of the Apostles* (New York: Harper & Brothers, 1957), p. 97.

27. *New Catholic Encyclopedia*, vol. IV (1967), p. 667.

28. Küng, *The Church*, p. 534; also *Documents of Vatican II*, ed. Abbott, p. 55; Lumby, *Acts of Apostles*, pp. 150-155.

29. *Theological Dictionary of the New Testament*, eds. Kittel and Friedrich, vol. II, p. 91; also *The Interpreter's Dictionary of the Bible* (New York: Abingdon Press, 1962), pp. 489-490, sec. 8.

30. For a study of the word "helper" see *The Analytical Greek Lexicon* (London: Samuel Bagster and Sons Limited, 1794), p. 344; James Hope Moulton and George Mulligan, *The Vocabulary of the Greek Testament* (Grand Rapids, Michigan: Wm. B. Eerdmans Publishing Company, 1963), pp. 541, 551; William F. Arndt and F. Wilbur Gingrich, *A Greek-English Lexicon of the New Testament* (Chicago, Illinois: The University of Chicago Press, 1957), pp. 713-714, 726; Henry George Liddell and Robert Scott, comps., *A Greek-English Lexicon* (Oxford: At the Clarendon Press, 1940), pp. 1482-1483, 1526; S. Scott Bartchey, "Power, Submission, and Sexual Identity Among the Early Christians," in *Essays on New Testament Christianity*, ed. C. Robert Wetzel (Standard Publishing, 1978), pp. 64-65.

Part Four

1. Schaff, *History of the Christian Church*, vol. III, p. 95.

2. Wand, *A History of the Early Church to A.D. 500*, p. 118.

3. *Ibid.*, p. 27

4. In Lake, *The Apostolic Fathers,* vol. I, pp. 8-121.

5. In *ibid.*, pp. 172-277.

6. See Kenneth Strand, "The Rise of the Monarchical Episcopate," *Andrews University Seminary Studies,* vol. IV (January 1966), pp. 65-88.

7. Lindsay, *Church and Ministry in Early Centuries,* p. 198.

8. In Lake, *The Apostolic Fathers,* vol. I, pp. 282-301.

9. Eusebius, *Eccl. Hist.,* V.xx.7, in *Eusebius: Eccl. Hist.,* trans. Lake and Oulton, vol. I, p. 499.

10. *Ibid.*, V.xxiv.14, 16, in *ibid.*, pp. 511-513.

11. George H. Williams, "The Ministry of the Ante-Nicene Church (c. 125-315)," in *The Ministry in Historical Perspectives,* eds. H. Richard Niebuhr and Daniel D. Williams (New York: Harper & Brothers, 1956), p. 33.

12. Justin Martyr, The First Apology of Justin, in *ANF,* vol. I, p. 185.

13. In Lake, *The Apostolic Fathers,* vol. II, pp. 6-305.

14. In *Ibid.*, vol. I, pp. 305-333.

15. Eusebius, *Eccl. Hist.,* V.v.1, in *Eusebius: Eccl. Hist.,* trans. Lake and Oulton, vol. I, p. 445.

16. Irenaeus, Against Heresies, in *ANF,* vol. I, pp. 415-506. Further quotations from Irenaeus: "It is within the power of all, therefore, in every Church, who may wish to see the truth, to contemplate clearly the tradition of the apostles manifested throughout the whole world; and we are in a position to reckon up those who were by the apostles instituted bishops in the Churches, and [to demonstrate] the succession of these men to our own times" (III.iii.1.). "Wherefore it is incumbent to obey the presbyters who are in the Church,—those who, as I have shown, possess the succession from the apostles; those who, together with the succession of the episcopate, have received the certain gift of truth, according to the good pleasure of the Father. But [it is also incumbent] to hold in suspicion others who depart from the primitive succession, and assemble themselves together in any place whatsoever" (IV.xxvi.2.). "Such presbyters does the Church nourish, of whom the prophet says: 'I will give thy rulers in peace, and thy bishops in righteousness.' . . . Where, therefore, the gifts of the Lord have been placed, there it behoves us to learn the truth, [namely,] from those who possess that succession of the Church which is from the apostles (IV.xxvi.5). "As I have heard from a certain presbyter, who had heard it from those who had seen the apostles, and from those who had been their disciples (IV.xxvii.1).

17. Robert M. Grant, *Augustus to Constantine* (New York: Harper & Row, 1970), p. 153.

18. Eusebius, *Eccl. Hist.,* II.xxv.6-8, in *Eusebius: Eccl. Hist.,* trans. Lake and Oulton, vol. I, p. 183.

19. *Ibid.*, IV.xxiii.9, in ibid., p. 381.

20. *Ibid.*, V.xxiv.11, in ibid., p. 509.

21. Strand, "The Rise of the Monarchical Episcopate," *Andrews Univ. Seminary Studies,* pp. 74-75.

22. Manson, *The Church's Ministry,* p. 67.

23. Tertullian, The Prescription Against Heretics, in *ANF,* vol. III, pp. 243-265.

24. Schaff, *History of the Christian Church,* vol. II, pp. 126, 150.

25. Tertullian, On Baptism, in *ANF,* vol. III, p. 677.

26. Tertullian, On Modesty, in *ANF,* vol. IV, pp. 99-100.

27. Williams, "Ministry of Ante-Nicene Church," in *Ministry in Historical Perspectives,* eds. Niebuhr and Williams, p. 42.

28. Eric G. Jay, *The Church: Its Changing Image Through Twenty Centuries* (Atlanta: John Knox Press, 1978), p. 55.

29. Cyprian, Epistles, in *ANF,* vol. V, pp. 275-408.

30. Eusebius, *Eccl. Hist.,* V.xxiv.4, in *Eusebius: Eccl. Hist.,* trans. Lake and Oulton, vol. I, p. 507; also Williams, "Ministry of Ante-Nicene Church," in *Ministry in Historical Perspectives,* eds. Niebuhr and Williams, p. 37.

31. Hans Lietzmann, *The Founding of the Church Universal* (London: Lutterworth Press, 1953), pp. 129-130.

32. George H. Williams, "The Ministry in the Later Patristic Period (314-451)," in *Ministry in Historical Perspectives,* eds. Niebuhr and Williams, pp. 60-61.

33. *Ibid.,* p. 63.

34. Arnold Ehrhardt, "The Beginnings of Mon-Episcopacy," *The Church Quarterly Review,* no. CCLXXX (July-September 1945), p. 113.

35. *Ibid.,* p. 123

36. Justin Martyr, The First Apology, in *ANF,* vol. I, p. 186.

37. Eusebius, *Eccl. Hist.,* VI.xliii.11, in *Eusebius: Eccl. Hist.,* trans. Lake and Oulton, vol. II, p. 119.

38. Christopher Dawson, *The Making of Europe: An Introduction to the History of European Unity* (London: Sheed & Ward, 1953), pp. 27-28.

39. Williams, "The Ministry in the Later Patristic Period," in *Ministry in Historical Perspectives,* eds. Niebuhr and Williams, p. 63.

40. Quoted by Wilhelm Pauck, "The Ministry in the Time of the Continental Reformation," in *Ministry in Historical Perspectives,* eds. Niebuhr and Williams, pp. 112, 113-114.

41. Georgia Harkness, *The Church and Its Laity* (New York: Abingdon Press, 1962), p. 70.

42. *Ibid.,* p. 71.

43. *Ibid.*

44. *Ibid.,* p. 73.

45. *LW,* vol. 39, p. 155.

46. Quoted by Mueller, *Church and State in Luther and Calvin,* pp. 34, 166.

47. John Calvin, *Institutes of the Christian Religion,* trans. Henry Beveridge, 2 vols. (Grand Rapids, Michigan: Wm. B. Eerdmans Publishing Company, 1957). Hereafter referred to as *Inst.*

48. John Calvin, *Theological Treatises,* in *Calvin: Theological Treatises,* trans. J. K. S. Reid (Philadelphia: The Westminster Press, 1954), pp. 59, 63, 64.

49. Jay, *The Church,* p. 174.

50. George Huntston Williams, *The Radical Reformation* (London: Weidenfeld and Nicolson, 1962), p. 846.

51. Roland H. Bainton, *The Travail of Religious Liberty* (New York: Harper & Brothers, 1951), p. 55.

52. See Franklin H. Littell, "The Anabaptist Concept of the Church," in *The Recovery of the Anabaptist Vision,* ed. Guy F. Hershberger, (Scottdale, Pennsylvania: Herald Press, 1957), p. 119.

53. *Ibid.*

54. Franklin Hamlin Littell, *The Anabaptist View of the Church* (Boston: Starr King Press, 1958), p. 85.

55. Robert Friedmann, *The Theology of Anabaptism: An Interpretation* (Scottdale, Pennsylvania: Herald Press, 1973), p. 102.

56. Quoted in Littell, The Anabaptist View of the Church, p. 93.

57. *Ibid.,* pp. 92-93.

58. See N. Van Der Zijpp, "The Early Dutch Anabaptists," in *Recovery of Anabaptist Vision,* ed. Hershberger, pp. 69-82.

59. Quoted in Littell, *The Anabaptist View of the Church,* p. 42.

60. Williams, *The Radical Reformation*, p. 789.
61. *Ibid.*, p. 175.
62. *Ibid.*, pp. 255, 560, 563, 860.
63. *BEM,* pp. 20-32.

Part Five

1. Schaff, *Creeds of Christendom,*, vol. II, pp. 188-193.

2. See James A. Coriden, Thomas J. Green and Donald E. Heintschel, eds., *The Code of Canon Law: A Text and Commentary* (New York: Paulist Press, 1985), pp. 713, 717, 719, 720.

3. See "Ordain" in Robert Young, *Young's Analytical Concordance to the Bible* (New York: Funk & Wagnalls Company, n.d.) p. 722.

4. See "Ordain" in *New American Standard Exhaustive Concordance of the Bible: Hebrew-Aramaic and Greek Dictionaries,* ed. Robert L. Thomas (Nashville: Holman Bible Publishers, 1987).

5. *BEM,* p. 31.

6. *Ibid.*

7. See "Hand" and "Imposition of Hands" in John M'Clintock and James Strong, *Cyclopaedia of Biblical, Theological and Ecclesiastical Literature,* vol. IV (New York: Harper & Brothers Publishers, 1883), pp. 57-58, 521-523.

8. David Daube, *The New Testament and Rabbinic Judaism* (London: University of London, 1956), pp. 224-246.

9. *The Seventh-day Adventist Bible Commentary,* 7 vols. (Washington, D.C.: Review and Herald Publishing Association, 1953), vol. 1, pp. 653-654.

10. See "Semikhah" in Encyclopaedia Judaica; "Ordination" in *The Jewish Encyclopedia,* vol. IX (New York: Funk and Wagnalls Company, 1925); "Ordination (Jewish)" in *Encyclopedia of Religion and Ethics,* ed. James Hastings, vol. IX (New York: Charles Scribner's Sons, 1960).

11. See "Ordination (Jewish)" in *Enc. of Rel. and Ethics,* ed. Hastings, vol. IX, p. 553.

12. *The Mishnah,* trans. Danby, p. xiii.

13. Warkentin, *Ordination,* p. 17.

14. *Encyclopaedia Judaica,* vol. 14, pp. 1140, 1141.

15. *Ibid.*, p. 1141.

16. *The Jewish Encyclopedia,* vol. IX, p. 429.

17. Daube, *New Testament and Rabbinic Judaism,* p. 232.

18. *The Jewish Encyclopedia,* vol. IX, p. 429.

19. "The Sanhedrin," 4.3, in *The Mishnah,* trans. Danby, p. 387.

20. *Ibid.*, 4.4, in *Ibid.*

21. *Enc. of Rel. and Ethics,* ed. Hastings, vol. IX, p. 552.

22. See Hugo Mantel, "Ordination and Appointment in the Period of the Temple," *The Harvard Theological Review,* vol. 57 (1964), pp. 325-346.

23. *Ibid.*, p. 328.

24. *Ibid.*, pp. 336, 339, 340.

25. *Ibid.*, p. 342.

26. *Ibid.*, p. 344.

27. *Ibid.*, p. 341.

28. F. Gavin, *The Jewish Antecedents of the Christian Sacraments* (New York: KTAV Publishing House, Inc., 1969), pp. 101-103.

29. Daube, *New Testament and Rabbinic Judaism,* p. 245.

30. Easton, "Jewish and Early Christian Ordination," *Anglican Theological Review,* vol. 5, (1922), pp. 308-319; vol. 6 (1923), pp. 285-295.

31. *Ibid.*, vol. 6, p. 285.
32. *Ibid.*, vol. 5, p. 313.
33. *Ibid.*, p. 316.
34. Arnold Ehrhardt, "Jewish and Christian Ordination", *Journal of Ecclesiastical History*, vol V, (1954), pp. 125-138.
35. *Ibid.*, p. 131.
36. *Ibid.*
37. *Ibid.*, pp. 137-138.
38. Everett Ferguson, "Jewish and Christian Ordination: Some Observations," *Harvard Theological Review*, vol. 56, (1963), pp. 13-19.
39. Everett Ferguson, "Laying on of Hands: Its Significance in Ordination," *Journal of Theological Studies*, vol XXVI, (April 1975), p. 2.
40. *Ibid.*, pp. 1, 2.
41. Ferguson, "Jewish and Christian Ordination," Harvard Theological Review., vol. 56, p. 15.
42. *Ibid.*, p. 16.
43. *Ibid.*, p. 14.
44. Edward J. Kilmartin, "Ministry and Ordination in Early Christianity against a Jewish Background," *Studia liturgica*, vol. 13 (1979), p. 53.
45. Warkentin, Ordination, pp. 109-152.
46. Ira Maurice Price, *The Ancestry of Our English Bible* (New York: Harper & Brothers, 1949), p. 167.
47. Burn-Murdoch, *Development of the Papacy*, pp. 76-77.
48. Schweizer, *Church Order in the New Testament*, p. 208.
49. Daube, *New Testament and Rabbinic Judaism*, pp. 237-239.
50. Torrance, "Consecration and Ordination," *Scottish J. of Theology*, vol. II, pp. 235, 237.
51. Daube, *New Testament and Rabbinic Judaism*, p. 240; Torrance,"Consecration and Ordination," *Scottish J. of Theology*, vol. II, p. 237.
52. Kenneth S. Wuest, *The Pastoral Epistles in The Greek New Testament: For the English Reader* (Grand Rapids, Michigan: Wm. B. Eerdmans Publishing Company, 1953), pp. 87-88,
53. Birger A. Pearson, "Ministry and Ordination in the Early Church," in *Ecclesia Leiturgia Ministerium* (Helsinki, 1977), p. 133.
54. Kilmartin, "Ministry and Ordination," *Studia liturgica*, vol. 13, p. 45.
55. R. Newton Flew, *Jesus and His Church: A study of the Idea of the Ecclesia in the New Testament* (London: The Epworth Press, 1938), pp. 146, 147.
56. *Ibid.*, p. 38.
56. *The Apostolic Tradition of Hippolytus*, trans. Burton Scott Easton (Archon Books, 1962), pp. 33, 34, 37, 38.
57. *Ibid.*, p. 38.
58. Jay, *The Church*, p. 57.
59. Constitutions of the Holy Apostles, in *ANF*, vol. VII, pp. 391-505.
60. Williams, "Ministry in Late Patristic Period," in *Ministry in Historical Perspectives*, eds. Niebuhr and Williams, pp. 74, 75.
61. *Ibid.*, pp. 75-76.
62. Jay, *The Church*, p. 58.
63. Schaff, *History of The Christian Church*, vol. VIII, pp. 480-484.
64. Richard Walter Schoenleber, *The Sovereign Word: The Office of the Ministry and Ordination in the Theology of Martin Luther* (Ph.D. diss., University of Iowa, 1983), pp. 169-170.

65. *Ibid.*, pp. 182, 206.

66. *Ibid.*, pp. 194-195.

67. *Ibid.*, p. 198.

68. John Calvin, *Commentary Upon The Acts of the Apostles*, ed. Henry Beveridge, vol. I, (reprint, Grand Rapids, Michigan: Wm. B. Eerdmans Publishing Company, 1957), p. 238.

69. John Calvin, *Commentaries on The Epistles to Timothy, Titus, and Philemon*, trans. William Pringle (Grand Rapids, Michigan: Wm. B. Eerdmans Publishing Company, 1959), p. 190.

70. Calvin, *Commentary Upon Acts*, vol. I, p. 503.

71. Calvin, *Theological Treatises*, in *Calvin: Theological Treatises*, trans. Reid, vol. XXII, p. 59.

72 Schoenleber, *The Sovereign Word.*, pp. 240-241.

73. *Ibid.*, p. 241.

74. *Ibid.*, pp. 246-247.

75. *Ibid.*, p. 189.

76. Francois Wendel, *Calvin: The Origins and Development of His Religious Thought*, trans. Philip Mairet (London: Wm. Collins, Son & Co. Ltd., 1963), p. 71.

77. Robert G. Bolt, *The Conception of the Ministry and the Nature of Ordination in the Writings of John Calvin* (M.Th. thesis, Pittsburgh-Xenia Theological Seminary, Pittsburgh, Pa., 1961), p. 51.

78. *Melanchthon and Bucer,* ed. Wilhelm Pauck, The Library of Christian Classics, vol. XIX (Philadelphia: The Westminster Press, 1969), p. 239.

79. James L. Ainslie, *The Doctrines of Ministerial Order in the Reformed Churches of the 16th and 17th Centuries* (Edinburgh: T. & T. Clark, 1940), pp. 155-90.

80. *Ibid.*, p. 159.

81. *Ibid.*, p. 177.

82. *Ibid.*, p. 176.

83. *Ibid.*, p. 177.

84. *Ibid.*, p. 185.

85. *Ibid.*, pp. 163-164, 176.

86. Quoted in *ibid.*, p. 183.

87. Warkentin, *Odrdination*, p. 186.

Epilogue

1. F. Roy Coad, *A History of the Brethren Movement* (Exeter: The Paternoster Press Ltd., 1968), pp. 272-273.

2. Eastwood, *Priesthood of all Believers,* p. 241.

3. Eduard Schweizer, *Church Order in the New Testament* (London: SCM Press Ltd., 1961), pp. 188-189; also Karl Barth, "The Church—The Living Congregation of the Living Lord Jesus Christ," in *Man's Disorder and God's Design*, The Amsterday Assembly Series (New York: Harper & Brothers, 1949), pp. 68, 69, 72.

4. Schaff, *History of the Christian Church*, vol. VII, pp, 347-347.

5. Thurian, ed., *Churches Respond to BEM,* vol. II, pp. 347-348.

Title Pages

Introduction: Epistle to the Ephesians 1:18-23.

Part 1:   First Epistle to the Corinthians 3:11.
          Hymn "The Church Has One Foundation," Samuel J. Stone.

Part 2:   The Revelation 1:5-6.
           LW, vol. 36, p. 113; vol. 44, p. 127.
           BEM, p. 23.

Part 3:   First Epistle to the Corinthians 12:1, 4-7.
           Küng, *The Church,* pp. 466, 467.

Part 4:   Schaff, *History of the Christian Church,* vol. III, p. 95.

Part 5:   *LW,* vol. 36, p. 116.
           Canon 1008, in *Code of Canon Law,* eds. Coriden, Green, and Heint-
           schel, p. 717.

Epilogue: H. R. Mackintosh, *The Divine Initiative* (1921), p. 89, quoted by
           Flew, *Jesus and His Church,* p. 17.

           John Knox, *The Christian Answer* (N.Y.: Union Theol. Seminary,
           1946), p. 242, quoted in Schmidt, "The Church," p. v, book II of *Bi-
           ble Key Words* from Kittel's *Theologisches Worterbuch Zum Neuen
           Testament.*